Skills *in*
PSYCHODYNAMIC
Counselling & Psychotherapy

Skills in
● ● ● ●

Counselling &
Psychotherapy

Series Editor
Francesca Inskipp

Skills in Counselling & Psychotherapy is a series of practical guides for trainees and practitioners. Each book takes one of the main approaches to therapeutic work and describes the core skills and techniques used within that approach.

Topics covered include

♦ how to establish and develop the therapeutic relationship
♦ how to help the client change
♦ how to assess the suitability of the approach for the client.

This is the first series of books to look at skills specific to the different theoretical approaches, making it ideal for use on a range of courses which prepare the trainees to work directly with clients.

Books in the series:

Skills in Transactional Analysis Counselling & Psychotherapy
Christine Lister-Ford

Skills in Person-Centred Counselling & Psychotherapy
Janet Tolan

Skills in Cognitive-Behavioural Counselling & Psychotherapy
Frank Wills

Skills in Rational Emotive Behaviour Counselling & Psychotherapy
Windy Dryden

Skills in Gestalt Counselling & Psychotherapy, Second Edition
Phil Joyce & Charlotte Sills

Skills *in* PSYCHODYNAMIC
Counselling & Psychotherapy

Susan Howard

Los Angeles | London | New Delhi
Singapore | Washington DC

First published 2010

Reprinted 2012

SAGE Publications Ltd
1 Oliver's Yard
55 City Road
London EC1Y 1SP

SAGE Publications Inc.
2455 Teller Road
Thousand Oaks, California 91320

SAGE Publications India Pvt Ltd
B 1/I 1 Mohan Cooperative Industrial Area
Mathura Road
New Delhi 110 044

SAGE Publications Asia-Pacific Pte Ltd
3 Church Street
#10-04 Samsung Hub
Singapore 049483

Library of Congress Control Number: 2009924033

British Library Cataloguing in Publication data

A catalogue record for this book is available from
the British Library

ISBN 978-1-4129-4653-7
ISBN 978-1-4129-4654-4 (pbk)

Typeset by C&M Digitals (P) Ltd, Chennai, India
Printed by CPI Group (UK) Ltd, Croydon, CR0 4YY
Printed on paper from sustainable resources

CONTENTS

ACKNOWLEDGEMENTS

First and foremost I am very grateful to my husband, Peter, for his patience, support, and willingness to sacrifice some of his life while I wrote this. Secondly, I would like to thank Francesca Inskipp for her help and encouragement, especially when the book had to be delayed. I am also grateful for the work put in to reading the draft by Ralph Layland, Linda Morison, Mary John, Alesia Perkins and Katherine Choonucksing. Lastly, my thanks to those who have taught me so much, particularly my clients and supervisees and the trainees on the Surrey PsychD Clinical Psychology course.

1

THE PSYCHODYNAMIC APPROACH

The business of counselling and psychotherapy rests on a fundamental premise: that one person, through the process of being with and talking to another, can resolve his[1] psychological problems. Everything else flows from this: our theory about what brings about change as well as the technique or skills we use in doing so. All psychodynamic approaches agree that the more we are able to be honest with ourselves the better chance we have of living a satisfactory and productive life. Doing so is a huge challenge, and is difficult to accomplish without the help of a guide. With this in mind, Cox proposes that psychotherapy is 'a process in which the patient is enabled to do for himself what he cannot do on his own. The therapist[2] doesn't do it for him, but he cannot do it without the therapist' (1978: 45).

THE CORE OF THE PSYCHODYNAMIC APPROACH

So what distinguishes the psychodynamic approach and the skills we need to practise in this way? As someone who works closely with others, who use different therapeutic models, I am aware of how often we appear to be doing similar things but giving them a different name. This makes it all the more important to be clear about what differentiates the psychodynamic model, in order to determine which skills are needed to practise within it. I have grouped the areas I think define psychodynamic practice into four dimensions: theoretical; the aims of therapy; the particular skills and techniques we use; our understanding about the factors that lead to change.

Theory

Psychodynamic theory is a developmental theory which is based on the premise that early experience and phantasy[3] combine to create a person's internal world. The conflicts and deficits in that internal world then have a powerful effect on how he experiences and negotiates the external world, how he experiences himself and others, and his overall psychological adjustment. It is almost impossible for a psychodynamic practitioner to hear her client's story without thinking about its developmental origins, so rooted is our sense of the link between past and present.

The aims of therapy

The aims of dynamic therapy neither involve nor exclude measurable changes in symptoms or overt behaviour. Tyndale (1999: 54) proposes that the purpose of psychotherapy is to 'make sense of the past and to disentangle it from the present'. In this quest our role is to help our client repair the deficits in his developmental trajectory and face the hurts and conflicts he defends himself against. This allows him to become aware of and respect previously disavowed aspects of his personality. Dynamic approaches thus aim to make more of our client's mind available to consciousness so that he can live his life more aware of what motivates him, how he can care for his own needs, and a freedom and choice about how he acts. A further aim is to mobilise our client's own capacity for self-repair, and to help him achieve that in an ongoing way so that he no longer needs our physical presence to continue and maintain his emotional development.

Technique

A number of important areas distinguish psychodynamic technique from other models. The first is the use we make of ourselves. By developing our ability to work with our client's transference and our own countertransference we use ourselves as a finely tuned instrument to receive, track and interpret his inner world. This requires an ongoing evaluation of our own psychological functioning and responses as well as attention to his. Secondly, there is a difference in the way we inhabit the psychological space, which is manifest in the careful attention we pay to the setting, boundaries and containment in order to facilitate working with our client's unconscious. Other differences include the use of free association, the way we understand defensive processes and the use we make of interpretation. Lastly, psychodynamic practitioners are particularly attuned to the use of metaphor and symbolism in our client's communications and what they convey about his internal world. We take as our departure point that there is meaning both in how he relates to us as well as the material he brings to therapy. Decoding the meaning of our client's verbal and non-verbal communication is seen as a central technique in psychodynamic work.

Factors leading to change

Psychodynamic approaches consider that psychological change is brought about by a combination of three factors: insight, containment of distress and the experience of a new relationship. As you will see in Chapter 7 there is considerable disagreement between the different schools as to which of these is the most important. However, most therapies will include a mixture of all three, dependent on the length and intensity of therapy, the needs of the client and therapist factors such as therapeutic orientation.

MEMORY AND NEW LEARNING

Although our brains are at their most plastic[4] in the first few years of life, neural plasticity continues throughout life and we consequently continue to learn. Recent advances in neuroscience have shed a light on why insight, containment and the experience of a new object are implicated in the learning associated with psychological change. Hebb (1949) famously said 'cells that fire together wire together'; in other words when neural pathways are activated at the same time (fire together) they create new neural circuits in the brain (wire together) and with it new learning. Cozolino (2002) proposes that the simultaneous firing of previously dissociated neural circuits associated with feeling and understanding leads to psychological integration as they come together. The parts of the brain associated with feeling and thinking start to link up, which leads to a strengthening of the ego. It is likely that this is the basis for the finding that the quality of the therapeutic relationship is the most important factor in psychological change, since thinking takes place within a positive emotional context leading to neurological integration.

In my opinion the potential conditions for such growth and integration are both deliberately created and optimised in psychodynamic psychotherapy. Factors specific to psychodynamic technique, such as the creation of an analytic space, free association and the emotional impact of transference interpretations, may potentiate the kind of simultaneous firing and wiring that leads to new emotional learning, and with it an increased integration and strengthening of the ego.

Cozolino suggests, for example, that empathic attunement (which includes containment and the experience of a different way of relating) stimulates biochemical processes that increase brain plasticity and thus new emotional learning. Similarly one of our tasks as therapists is to regulate affect (containment) for our clients until they are able to self-regulate. Being able to tolerate and regulate affect is a core condition for growth in the brain, even in adulthood. The integration that accompanies working through, which involves insight, increases the ability to tolerate thoughts and emotions that previously had to be dissociated, defended against or inhibited. Lastly, the co-construction of narratives (for example about your client's history, or the story of the therapeutic relationship) supports the integration of multiple neural networks, which in turn supports affect regulation. Together these proposals give a new meaning to the concept of 'structural change' since recent understanding of how the brain works suggests some of the actual structures involved.

Schore (2003) has likened the psychotherapist to a neurosurgeon, suggesting that interpretation is the 'therapist's scalpel'. When we make an accurate, appropriate and well-timed interpretation, biochemical changes that enhance plasticity take place in the brain. Similarly, making a deep emotional connection with our client involves synchronous right brain to right brain activity, which stimulates opoid production and enhances pleasurable affect and emotional regulation. Cozolino proposes that, 'like breaking and resetting a bone that has healed badly, in this process memory systems are, in a sense, loosened so that they can be reformed in a more positive way' (2002: 306).

These memory systems are largely 'implicit' or 'procedural', meaning they are memories for being with others, rather than memories for events. Sandler and Sandler (1997) proposed that the past unconscious stores our earliest experiences of being with others, which then form the basis of how we experience ourselves, how we regulate our affect and how we conduct relationships across the lifespan. For example, the fact that we parent our children largely as we ourselves have been parented, is primarily a function of procedural memory. Because these experiences take place before we have language to encode them, they are not available as actual memories. Instead, they get enacted when we are with others, particularly when our attachment system is activated. Entering therapy is such a time, when our clients' way of being with others is activated in their relationship with us. The action of psychotherapy might then be thought of as involving changes in procedural memory which alter our client's relationships with others and himself.

A good working knowledge of how memory functions is a vital tool in your skills mix as a psychodynamic practitioner. For example, it is important to be aware that memory for events, or 'episodic' memory, cannot be laid down until the brain tissue involved is myelinated. Myelinisation is not complete until we are about three years old, which is why we have few autobiographical memories before that age. Memory is a reconstructive process; what we remember is rarely entirely correct (veridical), but is more commonly inaccurate to some degree and influenced by our own biases and ways of processing information. It is also important to understand how trauma affects memory, and to be aware of theories about how the brain functions during trauma.

There are some things we can be fairly sure of, for example that a person who has no memory before the age of eight or ten has probably used censorship to protect himself from psychological pain. A child whose mother dies in mid-childhood may not remember her because to know what he had lost would be unbearable. Other things we can be less sure of; for example, whether memories accessed during hypnosis are real or have been accidentally created in a state when the mind is less able to distinguish the real from the imagined. One of the strengths of the psychodynamic position is that we suspend judgement and tolerate the uncertainty of not knowing whether a memory is veridical. At the same time we are able to see that the narrative has a psychic relevance to our client, so that even if the actual truth of a memory might be debateable, we know that there is an underlying truth for him in his story.

HOW DO WE KNOW IT WORKS?

Because we live in a culture that increasingly asks us to justify what we do and establish criteria for its effectiveness, being able to demonstrate the efficacy of the psychodynamic approach is a vital skill for our profession. Most of us who practise are not engaged in outcome research, but we need to be aware of the evidence base that does exist and be able to discuss it. Saying we know psychodynamic therapy works is no longer enough. We need to be able to clarify how and why for the sake of our clients and our profession if referrers and potential clients are to maintain confidence in our approach.

The current 'gold standard' for psychotherapeutic research is the Randomised Controlled Trial (RCT). It has been used extensively in establishing an evidence base for cognitive-behaviour therapy (CBT), and psychodynamic psychotherapy has been criticised for not engaging in RCT research. However, neither the underlying methodological assumptions of the RCT, nor its capacity to ask relevant questions about the nature of therapy, make it an appropriate research method for determining effectiveness in any therapeutic model. It is important that you understand the limitations of the RCT and research based on it (see Vanheule, 2009). At the same time you also need to familiarise yourself with those approaches to outcome research that satisfactorily capture what we actually do and which address the complexity of clinical practice. It is important that we engage in critical scientific thinking about what happens in successful (and unsuccessful) therapies. Our slowness to recognise the necessity of undertaking the kind of research that demonstrates the effectiveness of dynamic psychotherapy has been to our detriment. There is a body of evidence that you can draw on, which has been summarised in books such as Leuzinger-Bohleber and Target (2002), Roth and Fonagy (2005) and Cooper (2008).

It is probable that advances in neuro-imaging and other techniques for measuring neurological change will soon permit a more accurate assessment of exactly what and how aspects of psychodynamic psychotherapy bring about change. As Cozolino (2002) and others have noted, the ingredients of psychodynamic practice map on to theories in neuroscience of how change is effected. Until now it has not been possible to demonstrate this, but in the future we may have a more accurate guide as to which, in the range of techniques we use, is the most effective with whom.

THE AIMS OF THIS BOOK

I have written this book in the full knowledge that, as Haynal (1993) has said, it is illusory to imagine that technique is something that can be learned and applied 'correctly'. Therapy is a subtle and multifaceted task, as well as one of the most private and complex of human interactions. As such, it cannot be reduced to a series of instructions. But, hand in hand with the experience of your own therapy or counselling and good supervision, a skills book can be invaluable in putting a framework around what you do, enabling a thoughtful appreciation of your work.

My first aim is to facilitate your understanding of 'how to' and enhance your practical skills. I hope that reading this book will give you confidence in using psychodynamic skills by taking the mystery out of psychodynamic practice. It is well documented that adults learn best through experience. I have therefore incorporated a number of case studies, including two that run throughout the book. I hope this will engage you in a form of analogous experiential learning by focussing on the experience of individual clients and the skills used by the practitioner. The people described are fictitious but, inevitably, some of the situations are rooted in actual events. I have also included practical suggestions for how you might approach particular technical issues. Again I emphasise that this is not a 'cookbook' that can tell you how to manage each situation that you meet as a therapist. Rather it is a guide to practice that you can use as a basis for your own thinking about your work. I consider our development as psychotherapists as being analogous to a tool that is crafted rather than a manual that is followed.

My second aim is to make links between theory and practice. It can be very confusing, especially at the beginning of one's career, if technique is taught and learned without clear reference to the body of theory that supports it. Since our theoretical position impacts directly on how we understand our clients' unconscious communication and the skills or technique that we use in our work, it is important to understand why we do what we do. An adequate conceptual framework also gives us some security in coping with the chaotic and disturbed, part of our client that propelled him into treatment in the first place. It also helps to maintain good practice and avoid 'wild' interpretations. During our training therapy or counselling we absorb our therapist's theoretical orientation through her use of technique. Because this experience is encoded into procedural memory it may not easily translate into conceptual understanding. Also, supervisors and trainers do not always make the links between their practice and their theoretical orientation clear to supervisees. Together these factors can make it difficult to detach ourselves from our therapeutic and supervisory experience and encode our understanding into words. It can then be hard to think objectively about how to adapt technique according to the needs of different clients, or understand the reasons for adopting one approach rather than another.

With this in mind I want to explain something about my clinical orientation, which has been shaped by my own experience and those aspects of theory that have made sense to me. My practice and approach to psychodynamic work has been influenced primarily by psychoanalytic writers, including Winnicott, Fairbairn and Balint in the UK, and Kohut in the USA. These writers have had their greatest influence on the Independent group within British psychoanalysis. My analysis and much of my supervision have been within the Independent tradition, though I have also been supervised across a range of psychodynamic orientations during my career. One of the features of the Independent group is that the client's internal world and his external reality are both considered important, and my stance throughout the book reflects that emphasis. I have also incorporated aspects of Bowlby's Attachment Theory into my work. Bowlby was a psychoanalyst, and Attachment Theory owes much to psychoanalysis, but it is founded in research. As a clinical psychologist I particularly value this link between research and practice.

THE CORE COMPETENCES OF PSYCHODYNAMIC PRACTICE

Lemma and her colleagues (Lemma et al., 2008) have identified the core competences, or skills, necessary to deliver effective psychodynamic therapy. These competences provide a framework for training and will become the basis for determining whether practitioners have the necessary skills to work independently in public-sector settings in the UK. This book is organised around systematically addressing the major core competences. Familiarity with the skills described will give you the basis for sound

TABLE 1.1 THE CORE COMPETENCES OF PSYCHODYNAMIC PRACTICE (ADAPTED FROM LEMMA ET AL., 2008)

Generic Therapeutic Competences	
Knowledge of, and ability to operate within, professional guidelines	Chapters 2, 13 & 14
Knowledge of a model of therapy and the ability to understand and employ in practice	Chapters 1 & 7
Ability to engage the client	Chapters 4 & 5
Ability to foster and maintain a good therapeutic alliance	Chapter 5
Ability to deal with emotional content of the sessions	Chapters 2, 9 & 13
Ability to manage endings	Chapter 12
Ability to undertake generic assessment	Chapter 11
Ability to make good use of supervision	Chapter 14
Basic dynamic competencies	
Knowledge of basic principles and rationale of dynamic approaches	Chapters 4 & 7
Ability to assess the likely suitability of a dynamic approach	Chapter 11
Ability to derive a dynamic formulation	Chapter 11
Ability to establish and manage the therapeutic frame and boundaries	Chapters 4 & 13
Ability to work with unconscious communication	Chapters 6, 9 & 10
Ability to maintain an analytic focus	Chapters 2 & 12
Ability to identify and respond to difficulties in the therapeutic relationship	Chapters 5 & 13
Ability to work with both the client's internal and external reality	Chapter 13
Specific dynamic techniques	
Ability to make dynamic interpretations	Chapters 8, 9 & 10
Ability to work in the transference	Chapter 9
Ability to work with the countertransference	Chapter 9
Ability to recognise and work with defences	Chapter 10
Ability to work through the termination phase of therapy	Chapter 12
Metacompetencies	
Ability to make use of the therapeutic relationship as a vehicle for change	Chapters 2, 5 & 13
Ability to apply the model flexibly in response to the client's individual needs and context	Chapter 9
Ability to establish an appropriate balance between interpretive and supportive work	Chapter 8
Ability to identify and skilfully apply the most appropriate dynamic approach	Chapters 7 & 11

© 1999–2005 UCL

practice within a competency framework. I have set out the competences and the chapters in which they are primarily addressed in Table 1.1.

Because the book is oriented toward skills I have anticipated that you already have a basic understanding of the concepts and theory underlying psychodynamic practice. I have consequently introduced some terms without defining them. For those of you who do not have that basic knowledge, Howard (2006) will give you a foundation.

NOTES

1 I will generically refer to the therapist as 'she' and the client as 'he' except in case studies.
2 For the sake of simplicity I have used the terms 'therapy' and 'therapist' to refer to both counselling and therapy practice.

3   I use the term 'fantasy' when referring to conscious processes, and 'phantasy' when referring to unconscious processes.

4   Plasticity refers to the brain's capacity to make new connections between neurones. Any new learning involves the creation of new connections. Although the brain is at its most plastic in infancy, our capacity to learn throughout life results from the brain's ongoing ability to make new connections.

FURTHER READING

Gerhardt, S. (2004) *Why Love Matters: How Affection Shapes a Baby's Brain.* Hove: Brunner-Routledge.

Hart, S. (2008) *Brain, Attachment, Personality: An Introduction to Neuroaffective Development.* London: Karnac.

Howard, S. (2006) *Psychodynamic Counselling in a Nutshell.* London: SAGE.

2

BECOMING A THERAPIST: The Personal Journey Towards Skilled Practice

Few of us begin our initial training with existing psychodynamic skills, but there are personal attributes that we need to possess which we can then build on to become skilled practitioners. Those attributes are honed through training and developed into the personal skills that make successful counsellors and therapists.

THE STARTING POINT

The capacity to understand that others have minds and therefore their own feelings, intentions and needs which may be at variance with her own is one of the first requirements for any nascent therapist. This involves being able to mentalize, which Bateman and Fonagy have defined as the mental process by which an individual 'interprets the actions of himself and others as meaningful on the basis of intentional mental states such as personal desires, needs, feelings, beliefs and reasons' (2004: 21). It requires a leap of imagination to be able to envision what other people might be thinking or feeling. Paradoxically, knowing that we cannot absolutely know all that someone else is thinking and feeling is an indication of an advanced state of mentalization. In other words, we need to know that other people have minds and be able to intuit their intentions, but at the same time be open to the possibility that we have misunderstood those intentions because of the way that we ourselves tend to interpret the world. The ability to mentalize is not something that is a fixed property of mind; rather, it is 'a process, a capacity or skill, which may be present or absent to a greater or lesser degree' (Holmes, 2006: 32). Being able to mentalize varies according to states of mind, for example people tend to lose something of their capacity to mentalize when under significant stress.

Fonagy and Target (2003) also draw our attention to the fact that an important part of mentalizing involves being able to look inwards and experience ourselves as mentalizing beings. Sometimes people who have been traumatised as children develop a partial form of mentalization in which they are sensitive, or even hypervigilant, to the needs and mental states of other people, but are only able to reflect on their own mental state in a restricted way. This, in part, is because of the fear of what they will see if they do look inwards. It is not unusual for those with this restricted form of mentalization to be attracted to working in the helping professions.

The capacity to mentalize is one of the core skills associated with our ability to relate to others and to reflect on our own contribution to the relationship with them. It is thus a basic requirement in anyone wishing to train as a therapist. An increase in the capacity to mentalize is associated with successful therapy and most therapists will find their capacity to do so increases during their therapy. For some it is a necessary area of growth during training.

Mentalization forms the foundation of empathy, which is one of the therapist qualities that researchers have identified as necessary for the successful establishment of the therapeutic relationship. Being empathic involves imagining what it is like to be the other person and to sympathetically see the world through his eyes. However, it is important to distinguish empathy from over-identification. In order to empathise we need to imagine what it is like to be the other person without becoming fused with him and imagining his experience as our own. If we over-identify with him we become confused between ourselves and him, and perhaps erroneously attribute to him feelings or intentions that are our own. If this happens our understanding of his situation becomes obscured by our experience or inner world rather than illuminated by it.

Establishment of a successful therapeutic relationship is also based on genuineness. Genuineness, in the therapeutic sense, refers to the therapist's capacity to relate to her client with a genuine emotional response which is authentic, rather than one that is contrived. This means being able to respond to her client from her True Self rather than a False Self position (Winnicott, 1965a). There are differences of opinion as to whether genuineness can be taught in a direct way and therefore whether it is a quality necessary in someone applying for training. My opinion is that it is necessary, as a therapist operating from a False Self position cannot spontaneously and authentically respond to the needs of her client. Someone with a False Self personality organisation usually needs a significant amount of therapy before being in touch with an authentic self, and Winnicott warned of the perils of such people undertaking psychodynamic work. However, where there is existing genuineness, it can be further augmented through training and therapy.

Being authentic as a therapist involves having a coherent and wide-ranging frame of reference which is large enough to enable your client to be able to free associate and disclose anything about anything. It also involves mutuality. By this I don't mean a sharing of information about yourself on a parity basis, but the creation of a shared therapeutic space in which you as a therapist respond with genuineness to what is happening between yourself and your client.

The putative therapist should also be able to stand back from herself and view her own state of mind, actions and thoughts with some objectivity, as though from outside herself. This is known as an 'observing ego'. Having an observing ego includes being able to see one's own intentions and actions as others may see them and recognising that one's behaviour and responses can be directed by inner, unconscious, needs as well as by conscious intention. One can only have an observing ego if one has a sufficiently well-developed sense of self. Someone who does not have sufficient ego strength will find it difficult to stand outside of herself or tolerate acknowledging the tension between her inner and outer world. Like mentalization, the ability to maintain an observing ego can vary, particularly under stress. Again, this is a function that might be expected to increase during training, particularly as a result of one's own therapy.

The last personal quality I wish to consider is integrity. Integrity includes character traits such as being honest, honourable, reliable, respectful and upright. It is another personal attribute that cannot be taught, although it can be enhanced through therapy and training. It is an important attribute as it forms the basis for practising in an ethical and professional manner, which is a required competency for therapeutic practice.

I now want to introduce you to Vicky, whose progress in becoming a therapist we will chart throughout the rest of the book.

Vicky is single and in her early thirties. She sought therapy because she was depressed. She felt her depression was caused by two things. The first was the break-up of a long-term relationship. The second was that she did not know where she was going in her career in marketing. She felt unsupported and unrecognised despite working hard. The breakdown of her relationship followed the pattern of other relationships in that her partner had found someone else. As on previous occasions her relationship had deteriorated once she and her partner had made a serious commitment to each other. She did not understand what had gone wrong.

Vicky had a complex and sometimes difficult relationship with her parents, in particular her father. She described her childhood until she was ten as 'normal and pretty uneventful'. Her family came from the north of England and she was the eldest of four children. Her brother James was born when she was a year old; he had a hole in his heart, which had required surgery when he was six months old. Her two other brothers, Edward and George, were respectively seven and nine years younger than her. When Vicky was ten James developed a rare cancer which he died from two years later. Her father was devastated by the death of his eldest and favourite son and turned away from the rest of the family in his grief. Her parents separated about a year later. After the divorce he moved to London and soon remarried and had a second family. Vicky saw little of him until she went to university in London. Her choice of university had been quite consciously influenced by a wish to be nearer to her father, who in fact encouraged her to move to London, and who was supportive of her during her studies. However, Vicky struggled with her feelings about the relationship her father had with his new family and was jealous of the attention that they had compared with what he had given her and her brothers after James's death.

(Continued)

(Continued)

Vicky's mother experienced undiagnosed depression following James's death and the subsequent break-up of the family. Her mother coped with her depression by being constantly busy; it was partly why she returned to work. This had the effect of her being less available for Vicky than she had been. Vicky became a carer and looked after her younger brothers after school and during the holidays. She also had significant responsibilities around the house. This meant that her opportunities to socialise with her friends were significantly curtailed and she often felt the odd one out at school.

Vicky did well academically, despite the pressures at home, and was determined to go to university. She chose psychology; she said she wanted to understand both herself and her family better. She had been disappointed that her degree had not given her the answers she had hoped for. She had considered a career in psychology, but vacation work in a marketing company led to a job offer. Flattered by being wanted, she had accepted. She worked hard and quickly rose to a senior post in a prestigious marketing firm. Although she spent a lot of her time mentoring and developing junior staff, she felt that her own career needs were not properly recognised by those senior to her.

Vicky's serious relationships had all ended after two or three years. She was aware that she was often attracted to men whom she nurtured and supported, both financially and emotionally. However, once successful, they left her for someone else. Her last relationship had initially appeared different. Ben was already professionally successful and appeared to be emotionally resilient. However, after a year he was made redundant and began drinking heavily. Vicky supported and helped him through these difficulties and eventually he found another job. Once his drinking was under control they began to talk about marriage. However, one evening he came home and told her he had been having a relationship with someone from his alcohol support group and was leaving her. Vicky was completely taken by surprise and utterly devastated.

Vicky presented as attractive, lively and competent; despite often feeling very low she was always well dressed and groomed. She had a number of long-standing female friends whom she valued; she worked hard at maintaining her friendships and was always on hand when needed, often at the expense of her own plans. Only one friend knew that she was depressed and in therapy; to most people she appeared in charge of her life. Even the friend who knew she came to therapy was surprised when Vicky told her she was depressed. Like nearly everyone else the friend had seen Vicky as strong and self-contained and coping well with the vicissitudes of her life.

Vicky was very careful of our relationship and tried to take care of me by working out what I wanted of her; she found it hard to accept that she had needs and that it was legitimate to ask for them to be met. She was terrified of breakdown and this made it difficult for her to really allow herself to be vulnerable. Nevertheless she worked hard in her therapy and was beginning to both understand the origins of her depression and make important changes in her life outside of the consulting room.

Vicky had been in therapy for just over a year when she told me that she wanted to train as a psychodynamic practitioner. Her search for a more fulfilling career had been a theme throughout our work and she had often commented that she wished she had used her psychology degree. Now she could see a way to do so.

THE IMPORTANCE OF PERSONAL THERAPY

Vicky's story of family disruption and personal struggle and her route via her own therapy to becoming a psychodynamic practitioner is not unusual. Although not everyone who decides to become a counsellor or therapist has been through these sorts of experiences, many have, and I agree with Mander (2007) that one of the most important things that we share with our clients is our vulnerability. Indeed, the notion of the 'wounded healer' is sufficiently familiar in psychotherapy's lexicon that there is a book that incorporates the term into its title (Rippere and Williams, 1985). It is our wish to repair the wounds both in ourselves and our families that so often leads us to choose this career. Like Vicky, some people will have already identified that they need help for themselves before choosing a therapeutic career and it is the experience of their own therapy that propels them in this direction. Others, however, will enter personal therapy once they have decided they want to train, in order to meet the requirements of a course, or because they recognise the importance of doing so before offering themselves as the vehicle through which to help others.

Whichever route the putative therapist takes, in starting her own therapy she is, in my opinion, embarking on the most important part of her journey towards becoming a skilled psychodynamic practitioner. As Bollas said in a slightly different context: 'In order to find the patient, we must first look for the patient in ourselves' (1987: 202). The process of therapy is that of two people coming together and entering a relationship with the stated purpose of helping one of them address his psychological and emotional needs. The main tool we have in this endeavour is ourselves and the most important way that we enhance the effectiveness of that tool is through our own therapy. Psychodynamic therapists need to have the skills of sensitive attunement, the capacity to contain the emotional needs of our clients while offering ourselves as a transferential object, and the ability to continue functioning under stress. If we don't know ourselves well enough we cannot succeed in this while simultaneously registering the experience of our clients in ways that are both profound and useful to them.

There are a number of further advantages that come from being in therapy. Firstly, the experience of being a client oneself is a lasting reminder of how it feels to be in the client's, rather than the therapist's, chair. Although it is now well over twenty years since I started my own therapy I can still vividly remember the anxiety I felt when I first drove to my therapist's rooms, wondering what she would be like, whether I would get on with her and whether she would want to help me. It is an experience I still draw on to remind me that, however routine it might be for me to meet a new client, it is not at all routine for that person, who may well have similar anxieties to those which I had. Furthermore, I know what it is like to be in need of help and concerned as to whether the person I am seeing will be able to give me what I need. I know what it is like to mind about my therapist taking a holiday or needing to cancel a session. I also know what it is like to struggle to say the things that need to be said, or give myself permission to feel what I know I feel and am reluctant to acknowledge. I know too what it is like to feel that I am inhabited by forces that are beyond my access and control, and the frustration of watching myself act these out in therapy. I also know of the frustrations when longed-for change is slow coming or there are reversals after an improvement.

I know as a client what it is like to be very distressed during, or at the end of a session and to leave that session feeling upset with my therapist for finishing it when I am not ready to do so and wondering how I will cope with my distress. I have discovered for myself that following such a session something can shift inside me and that I can feel much better as a result. I have also discovered that, however upset I was, I was not damaged by becoming distressed and I did recover from it. As a trainer of clinical psychologists (who aren't required to have therapy) I notice a real difference between those who choose to have therapy and those who don't. Those who don't are more likely to be anxious about their clients being damaged if they become very distressed in the session. As a result they can hold back from facilitating their clients to experience strong emotion because of their own anxiety and feelings of culpability. Those who have experienced their own therapy know for themselves that strong and distressing emotions can be survived, and indeed can lead to change. Consequently they are often less frightened about their clients experiencing strong emotions and feel more confident about containing them.

I'm not saying that I keep my experience of therapy at the forefront of my mind the whole time I am working – not only would it be self-obsessed it would also be counterproductive. Nor am I constantly telling my clients about my own experiences of therapy – that too would be counterproductive as well as an intrusion of things about me that they do not need to know. But at times it is helpful to remember what it was like for me, particularly if I am finding it difficult to empathise with my client. Like all other therapists there are times when I am less in touch with my clients than others, because of my own internal world or because of something happening in the therapeutic relationship. Putting myself in their place and remembering what it was like to be a client helps me to get back in touch with them. It can sometimes also be helpful to let clients know that you are aware from your own experience what it is like trying to face something difficult in therapy, particularly at those moments when they are feeling alone or shamed by their experience.

Those therapists who are profoundly helped by their own therapy can often have particularly well-developed skills of attunement and sensitivity. They can often also be very creative therapists. It is as if, by being deeply touched by another person themselves, such therapists can develop an ability to be in touch with the deepest needs and feelings of their clients that goes beyond normal levels of attunement.

My own need for therapy is a reminder that my client and I have a lot in common and is an antidote to any tendency I might develop to think otherwise. There is a lot of concern within the mental health professions about the process of 'othering' and the importance of recognising the ways in which we all do it and of taking steps to avoid it. By othering I mean seeing the person who has mental health or emotional difficulties as the other, and therefore as being different from oneself, the helper. Othering implies that the person doing the helping is, and always has been, untouched by difficulties in her own life and that she consequently derives her legitimacy as a helper from never having struggled herself. It contributes to the feeling that the therapist is powerful, all knowing and always right. This can result in the client being experienced by himself and the therapist as powerless, not knowing and in the wrong. We live in a culture where people can still be shamed by having emotional difficulties that they cannot manage on their own. Othering can sanction the therapist to look down on the client and the client to look up to the therapist purely on the basis that only one of them has identified emotional problems. The process of othering is seen as being at the root of much of the abuse of power both in the therapeutic relationship and the wider mental health community. Sometimes that abuse has been overt, such as in the physical, emotional and even sexual bullying of psychiatric patients. More often it is subtle, and imbued in our attitudes and the organisations in which we work. While we keep in our minds that we too have struggled to overcome our own emotional difficulties, and that we continue to do so, we are less likely to 'other' our clients.

Secondly, it is important to understand why we have chosen therapeutic work as a career. When asked, most putative therapists say 'I want to help others'. Although an important starting point, it is essential that we have a deeper understanding of why we need to help other people in this way. At that deeper level the motivation for becoming a therapist often has to do with an unconscious conflict or unmet need in our own developmental history. For example, it is not uncommon for people to want to help others in order to repair a damaged member of their own family through mending their clients. Likewise, some people seeking to become therapists find it difficult to make close relationships; relationships with their clients provide an opportunity for quasi-intimacy. Others become therapists in order to get their own needs for caring met vicariously by caring for the other. Such reasons for becoming a therapist are usually unconscious and rarely understood before the putative therapist begins her own therapy. They are not a bar to becoming a therapist, but they do need to be understood and worked with. Doing so is an important part of our personal and professional development.

If these issues are not worked with in personal therapy there is a danger that the therapist will use her clients to resolve her own developmental and emotional needs. There are a number of consequences that can flow from this, which are detrimental to the therapist, her client, or both. For example the therapist may have a difficulty in appropriately identifying with her clients, and consequently either over-identifies with them or is unable to identify with them enough and 'others' them. Alternatively, she may find it difficult to hold therapeutic boundaries because of her own needs. Or she may take on clients that she is not equipped to work with or who can't be helped and make 'heroic' and perhaps fruitless attempts to cure them, possibly damaging them further in the attempt. She may also be unable to identify when she herself is so disturbed that she is no longer fit to practise and needs to stop work either temporarily, or in some cases, permanently.

Psychodynamic therapy involves the interaction of two minds which influence each other both consciously and unconsciously. In each there is a pull towards repetition compulsion, the need to repeat developmental failures or traumas from the past in an attempt to successfully work through them. Normally the compulsion to repeat is tipped in favour of the client's inner world and developmental needs (Kumin, 1996). It is part of the skill of being a therapist that maintains the balance in this direction. However, therapists too can be caught up in a need to repeat the past and this can have damaging effects on the therapeutic work in hand, sometimes leading to dangerous acting out by the client or, occasionally, by the therapist. Those therapists who have insufficiently addressed their own needs are more likely to create situations in which their need to repeat traumas from their own past tips the balance of repetition away from the client's inner world towards that of the therapist. As Kumin has observed, this can sometimes lead to a repetition in therapy of traumas from the therapist's past.

Julia worked within a psychodynamic framework but had only undertaken a minimum amount of therapy herself from someone who never challenged her. Throughout her life Julia had experienced times when she was filled with a sense of dread and panic and a belief that she was about to die. She had not divulged this in her therapy as she was afraid her therapist would think her too damaged to continue her training. Julia found ways of coping with her feelings in adulthood, but she had never linked these feelings with the story of her own life other than in the most superficial kind of way. She had been brought up by her maternal grandmother from the age of eighteen months after she had been found filthy, locked in a room and tied to a cot, while her mother was in the pub. Her mother later admitted she had often wished Julia dead.

Some years into her career as a counsellor Julia began to see a teacher whose mother had abandoned her at a similar age and who was now incapacitated by anxiety. Julia developed a strong identification with her and began to experience increasingly powerful fears that she was about to die. As Julia became more distressed therapy became highly charged and felt uncontained. One day the client was very upset because she was convinced that she had poisoned one of the children in her class. Julia was so anxious about this that, without discussing it with her supervisor, she informed the client that she could not keep the information confidential, and reported her to the education authority. The result was that the teacher was suspended and, feeling betrayed by Julia, left therapy. She was later cleared of any allegations.

Realising that something had gone badly wrong, Julia sought help from her supervisor. It became clear that Julia had been unable to bear the thought that a child could have been damaged or at risk from her client and had therefore acted precipitously. She had not tried to assess whether the teacher's belief that she had poisoned the child was a symbolic communication or a concrete event. She had lost the capacity for symbolic thought herself and the ability to mentalize. In Kumin's terms the client, through 'poisoning' a child, had enacted the trauma of her therapist's past. Julia was unable to process and contain the client's paranoid anxiety because she had not previously metabolised her own experience of being at the mercy of a murderous mother.

While I do not for one moment believe that therapy can resolve all developmental failures, it should equip the therapist with the tools to recognise when she is in difficulty, for example that she is working with a client who pushes her to rework her own past. Whether she is in previously uncharted territory untouched by her own therapy, or her client has evoked developmental needs or conflicts in her that are insufficiently resolved, she should recognise her response as a signal that she needs to get help. This might be through supervision or, occasionally, through further therapy of her own. Julia was unable to recognise she was in difficulty because she had not done the work necessary to recognise her situation. Consequently, instead of being able to think about the material her client was bringing, she found herself compelled to act. The unresolved trauma in her own past became manifest when her client repeated important aspects of it. By contrast, Vicky was able to explore the trauma in her past.

I did not feel that Vicky was ready yet to pursue a career as a psychodynamic practitioner. I was therefore apprehensive about her wish to embark on a course immediately. I had a number of concerns: the first was I felt that she projected her own needs for caring into other people rather than acknowledging them and getting them met directly in any part of her life, including her therapy. She had found it hard to be looked after by me, and was often more concerned about my welfare than her own. I was concerned that if she began her training too soon she would care for her clients at the expense of her own needs. I had anxieties that, until she was able to receive care, she may not be able to properly care for her clients, and that additionally she could cause damage to herself, and perhaps them, by attempting to do so. For example, she may need to keep her clients dependent on her longer than necessary so that her needs for care could be met vicariously through caring for them.

When I expressed my concerns to her, Vicky was able to reflect much more than she had about how much of her life she devoted to caring for others and how angry she became when no-one cared for her. She realised how frustrated she was at work that while she mentored junior staff no-one mentored her in the same way. This put her in touch with a deep longing to be cared for, and she was able to acknowledge how much she longed for care from me and how scared she was of becoming that dependent on me. As a result of this work Vicky was able to address her own needs for mentoring with her line manager at her appraisal and was subsequently offered the support she needed.

Vicky was also able to tell me about how much she wanted to be like me and that becoming a therapist herself had elicited the hope that she could be like me in other ways. This led us to think about how she had twice lost her own mother and how painful this had been. The first time was when her brother was born so shortly after her own birth. The second was the unrecognised depression her mother experienced following James's death and the subsequent break-up of her marriage. Vicky realised that she had not wanted to be like her mother and in me had found someone she could want to identify with.

(Continued)

(Continued)

Paradoxically in exploring these issues I became less concerned about Vicky applying for training. Nevertheless, when she decided that she would wait another year before doing so I was relieved. In doing so she had allowed herself the opportunity to be cared for without the pressures to care for others that training would inevitably involve.

Not all of therapy is about working through developmental deficits or hurts from the past or present; therapy also creates the opportunity to widen and deepen self-knowledge, particularly about our blind spots, how we defend ourselves against psychic pain and the positive and negative factors in our early life that have contributed to who we are now. At the same time it can help us to recognise those times when we rationalise our behaviour, or practise the kinds of self-deceit that we can all be prey to in the service of seeing ourselves as a good person. Therapy can also further awareness that our world view is shaped by our experience and that it is unique to us, and not necessarily shared by others. It is this level of self-knowledge that helps us navigate our way through the vicissitudes of working with clients from a variety of backgrounds with a range of presenting difficulties and emotional needs. It also helps us to understand the relative contributions that we and our client make to the therapeutic relationship.

Many of the people who come to us for therapy feel themselves to be outsiders, either because of the emotional difficulties they are experiencing, which make them feel different from everyone else, or because they are, or feel, in some way displaced. Equally many of us who are attracted into this type of work are, or feel ourselves to be, outsiders. A crude way of illustrating this is the frequently observed fact that the composition of many UK psychotherapy organisations is disproportionately made up of people from other cultures and countries. Of course 'feeling an outsider' has many potential origins: it can be through something obvious, such as being from a foreign country; or it can be more subtle, such as moving from one socio-economic group into another. It can originate in the family, for example one client reported feeling an outsider all his life because he was excluded from the exclusive relationship (which included using their own language) between his identical twin brothers. Of course, we are all at some level outsiders in a profound way. The challenge of the oedipal situation lies in its requirement that we recognise that we are outsiders to the intimate relationship our parents have either with each other or with others close to them. Facing our own feelings of being on the outside during therapy can facilitate our empathy with our clients' feelings of exclusion. This of course is very alive in the transference relationship, when we have to face the reality of the fact that we are excluded from the greater part of our own therapist's life, just as our clients are excluded from ours.

At a more prosaic level, the therapist's own therapy offers her the opportunity to experience a senior member of the profession at work in a way that is not otherwise available in psychodynamic work. Unlike in other models of therapy psychodynamic practitioners do not routinely observe one-another either live or through video. This means there are limited opportunities for observing or modelling how someone else does therapy as a means of learning new skills. Her own therapy may be the trainee therapist's only opportunity to hear live how certain aspects of therapeutic work are undertaken, for example how very strong feelings are contained in a session. Of course she also has the experience of feeling the impact as the client. She not only has the opportunity to think what she would take from her therapist's way of working to use in her own practice, but also what she would not do with her own clients.

I am not advocating that you regard your own therapy solely as a means to find out 'how to do it'. Those who look on their own therapy primarily as an apprenticeship often don't get as much help from it as they could and, usually, need. Being in therapy as an apprentice can become a defence against being properly helped. Rather I am saying that it is an important contribution to the implicit learning about 'how to' that helps one develop as a therapist. I'm not the only therapist who has found herself structuring an interpretation and realising after she has said it that her words powerfully echoed what her own therapist would have said to her. And at times when I'm struggling with a difficult therapeutic dilemma that I had experienced as a client myself I think back on how my therapist managed it and this can be helpful in deciding what to do.

FURTHER READING

Cozolino, L. (2004) *The Making of a Therapist: A Practical Guide for the Inner Journey.* New York: Norton.

3

BECOMING A THERAPIST: Other Ways to Enhance Personal Growth

While therapy is undoubtedly the main vehicle through which personal growth takes place, there are other ways of enhancing our development which can complement it. In this chapter I wish to discuss some of these.

'JOURNALING'

Perhaps one of the most powerful of these is that of writing a journal which reflects on our experiences of training and, later, of individual practice. 'Journaling' is an established tool which has a proven track record in both therapy and training (Bolton et al., 2004). In training it is used as a means to develop reflective practice, and on some courses is compulsory and/or assessed. It can be used to reflect on all aspects of training including private reading, lectures, workshops and, importantly, your response to client work. McLeod (2004) makes a number of suggestions for keeping such a journal. These include dating each entry and giving it a title so you can track your development over time; writing quickly so that you don't censor what you write; deciding whether to keep a notebook with you so that thoughts can be jotted down while they are fresh or whether to write the journal up as part of your daily routine. McLeod also makes the point that there is a distinction between a learning journal and a private diary and that personal material should be confined to the latter. My own opinion is that the distinction should be based on whether the journal is to be assessed. If it is not to be assessed I would argue that the journal offers an important opportunity to examine the interface between the personal and the professional that so often causes us the most difficulty as we struggle to undertake this work. Our transference and countertransference to our clients is partly a function of our own internal world. Reflecting on that in relation to training or post-qualification is potentially a significant source of personal growth.

OBSERVATION

When people trained in other therapeutic models consult me about a client they are often surprised and intrigued that I pay attention to the small details in the work that often get overlooked. This is a trademark of psychodynamic work. The way a client enters a room, a fleeting look, a slip of the tongue, a hesitancy in his narrative – all these can point to something important that is either just below consciousness or something that the client cannot quite bring himself to say. As psychodynamic practitioners we pay attention to these things, and we are trained to become observers of such fragments of behaviour. This is not an easy thing to do, since in normal life we would quickly become overwhelmed if we took in all the detail around us. But it is an important skill in psychodynamic work because it does help alert us to the things the client is struggling to think or say. Both one's own therapy and supervision facilitate the development of this skill, but the opportunity to work with it directly in preparation for clinical work comes through undertaking an observation.

Some, but not all, psychodynamic trainings offer the opportunity to undertake a period of observation as a prelude to beginning clinical work. Some trainings include infant observation in the first year as part of pre-clinical training. This is before the first training client is seen and is an important part of the preparation for later therapeutic work. I found the infant observation I undertook to be one of the most informative parts of my training and I still draw on what I learned many years later.

Infant observation provides the opportunity to observe normal development in the first year of life. It exposes the trainee to the power of the affective relationship between mother and baby and how the baby impacts on a family. It gives the trainee practice in attending to the minute detail of what happens in transactions between people and how much information about the relationship is contained in those minute transactions. It provides an environment in which the trainee can observe the effect of relationships on relationships without having to manage a therapeutic session. Understanding the way in which infants and their carers communicate in the first year facilitates our understanding about the importance of pre-verbal processes; these are hard to describe – instead they are experienced by the observer. An observation creates an opportunity to develop attunement to transference and countertransference issues. It also enhances skills such as therapeutic abstinence and the capacity to contain strong feelings.

Not all trainings offer infant observation as part of the curriculum, and where this is the case you might consider organising your own observation. Observations can take place anywhere where you can observe the effect of relationships on relationships, for example a clinic, an educational establishment or a waiting room. The opportunities for observation are myriad, for example some years ago a colleague arranged for her trainees to undertake an observation in the waiting area of a magistrate's court. You need to gain permission to observe and should organise supervision in order to discuss it. When observing you should be unobtrusive, sit quietly noting what is happening and the effect on you of what you are observing. Observations usually last an hour and you do not make notes while observing. Instead you need to record it afterwards in as much detail as possible, with special reference to transference and countertransference issues. Infant observation should never be independently organised and should only be undertaken as part of a course.

EXPERIENTIAL GROUPS

Some training programmes offer the opportunity to participate in an experiential group as part of the course. This can be a powerful adjunct to personal therapy, though in my opinion not a replacement for it. Experiential groups bring us powerfully face-to-face with issues such as rivalry, jealousy and envy and the way in which we handle these strong emotions. The relative safety of a group can help us face them and acknowledge when these feelings can interfere with the relationship with our clients. This is important because unacknowledged jealousy or envy of our clients can be detrimental to therapeutic work. Being in a group also offers a first-hand experience of their power to elicit primitive emotions such as splitting and projective identification. First-hand exposure to the regressive powers of being in a group can be helpful when working with clients whose difficulties may be associated with conflicts in group situations, such as the working environment. Participating in such a group also forces us to examine how we function in a group setting and the role we take in it. This is often illuminating in relation to many of the assumptions we hold about ourselves and the positions we occupy in relation to others. It also provides feedback on how we are experienced by others in a way that we rarely get outside such a group.

Even if there are no formal opportunities to participate in an experiential group, being in a group of peers during or after training will inevitably bring some of the same issues to the fore and will provide opportunities to reflect on your response to them, both in personal therapy and in a learning journal. You may consider joining a therapeutic group outside of your training in order to expose yourself to this experience.

NEW ACTIVITIES AND CHALLENGES

Any endeavour can be grist to the mill if you are seeking to learn about yourself. Undertaking a psychodynamic training course is in itself a new activity and a significant challenge, but you might also decide to take yourself out of your normal comfort zone and try something else new.

You may choose to undertake a physical challenge, particularly one that requires physical courage, such as an outward bound course. Alternately you might take up a competency challenge, for example learning a musical instrument, a foreign language, or a new sport. We can learn a lot about ourselves when we undertake new ventures and it can be a significant growth point if approached in a way that privileges such learning. You might also consider other experiences that will put you in touch with people you would not normally meet in order to help you build the skills necessary to work in a diverse culture. It is easy to underestimate the extent to which most of us live lives that are untouched by other groups in society, so that we are unfamiliar with the psychological impact of being brought up in another class, culture, religion or gender. Recently I was invited to attend a cultural event with an ex-student who belongs to the Indian community. I am someone who has had friends and colleagues who are Indian; indeed parts of my extended family are Indian, so I understand a certain amount about Indian culture and about being Indian in our culture. However, through accompanying my ex-student to this event I realised how little I really understood about the competing demands on her of living as part of the Indian community while simultaneously being brought up within the British system. I was subsequently able to take this understanding, gained through experience, into my work with an Indian client. It is through finding and then reflecting on such opportunities to meet people from other groups in society that we can facilitate the growth of our skills in understanding diversity.

While obvious differences in race or religion can alert us to diversity, it can sometimes be quite surprising how people who have been brought up in what appears to be the same culture (for example are white, British and middle class) hold very different assumptions about the world based on the sub-group or the era in which they grew up. In the United Kingdom clinical psychologists in training are required to spend some of their time working with clients over seventy years of age. Listening to their clients' accounts of their lives they have the opportunity to understand what it was like being brought up in a different era, with the attendant mores and dominant belief systems. Furthermore, the fact that these clients' lives were dominated by the experience of war in a way that recent generations' were not brings to their lives a view of the world that subsequent generations can sometimes find difficult to understand.

In order to increase your diversity skills it can be helpful to undertake exercises with a group of colleagues in which you explore the differences between you based on your cultural experience. Questions such as 'What was the attitude to education in your family?' or 'What did your family feel were the most important items to spend money on?' can be enormously revealing about the subtle – or not so subtle – differences in your experiences and views of the world compared with that of your colleagues.

THE SUPERVISORY RELATIONSHIP

There are also significant opportunities for personal reflection and development in the supervisory relationship, particularly in those areas where one's personal style or areas of conflict have been influential to the course of a client's therapy. I will discuss this in more detail in Chapter 14.

READING: FICTION, BIOGRAPHY AND POETRY

Reading as a valuable source of understanding ourselves and others is a rather neglected area in therapeutic trainings. Reading fiction can help us broaden our awareness of how people from different backgrounds to us live their lives, what motivates them and why they hold certain opinions and beliefs different from ours. Writers of fiction often address those very areas that are the province of psychodynamic psychotherapy: loving, hating and the things that draw us together and push us apart. Like us they are concerned with relationships at all levels: as lovers, friends, within the family and in the organisations in which we spend our lives. Furthermore, writers of fiction often explore those areas of human experience that are often not discussed openly, such as the pain of bereavement or the destructiveness of envy. It is in these very areas that we, as psychodynamic practitioners, also work. If we read fiction in a reflective way, questioning our own assumptions and attitudes, it can deepen our awareness not only of our clients but of ourselves and what motivates us.

Reading biography or autobiography has in common with psychotherapy the privileged insight into the intimate details of another's life. Reading biography can help us see, through the eyes of a third person, how someone's early experiences can shape their later trajectory through life; how they overcome adversity and the personal resources they have drawn on in the achievement of their goals. Reading biographies of the great thinkers in our own tradition like Freud, Klein, Jung or Winnicott can help us to see them as people like us, who struggled with their own demons. It can assist us in reflecting on their contribution without either idealising or denigrating them. It can also help us understand how the development of theory was and still is powerfully influenced by the unconscious preoccupations of the thinkers who advance it. This can help us reflect on our own relationship to theory and why one aspect of psychodynamic theory speaks to us in a way that others don't.

Autobiographies have in common with psychotherapy the telling of his story from the writer's own perspective, with the inherent tendency to adopt favourable interpretations of one's own actions and preoccupations. It alerts us to the extent to which the lens through which we see our own lives can be distorted. As in psychotherapy, the reader is left to come to their own conclusions about the writer's conscious and unconscious motivation as well as the ways in which the author defends himself from knowing the truth about himself, as we all do.

Lastly, reading biography and autobiography can also prove something of an antidote to our work as psychotherapists. We can sometimes become myopic and believe that change can only come about through the therapeutic relationship. Becoming intimately aware of the life of another draws to our attention the fact that therapy and counselling are not the only routes to personal development and that in our bid for self-healing we draw on many resources and relationships.

Finally, I want to think a bit about the value of reading and writing poetry. For me writing poetry has a similar function to dreaming: it is the crystallisation of powerful conscious and unconscious preoccupations into a condensed form. As with dreams, in order to understand the full meaning of the poem one is required to look beyond its manifest or overt content to the layers of meaning beneath it – the latent content. As well as telling us something of the power of our feelings I believe that understanding poetry has a specific role in developing certain skills in psychotherapy. Unlike in other therapy traditions psychodynamic therapy is concerned with hermeneutics – that is with the meaning we attach to our lives and the actions, desires, feelings and thoughts that comprise them. We are concerned with the meaning of a symptom in a client's inner world, or the meaning of an event in his life. We are concerned with how those meanings influence the decisions our clients make and how they experience the world. Consequently we are concerned with symbols and how we symbolise.

Alice had a psychotic breakdown during her first visit to Spain, her mother's country of origin. Alice was six when her father forced her mother to leave the family because of an alleged affair. Following the separation her father had forbidden Alice and her siblings to talk about their mother, and he systematically destroyed all evidence that she had ever existed. Alice had no memory of her mother but had managed to keep hidden a photograph of herself with her mother that she had been given by an aunt. Her father was a very conscientious parent but a strict disciplinarian and was often harsh in his treatment of his children. As a result Alice sometimes wished her father would leave and her mother come back. However, she felt bad for having these thoughts about her father, who had given up so much in his own life to care for her.

When she was twenty Alice went on holiday to Spain for the first time, with friends. While there she became convinced that one of her friends had been recruited as an MI5 spy in order to follow her and report on her activities to the Home Office. She also believed that her camera was bugged so that the thoughts she had each time she took a photograph would be used as evidence of her spying activities. She became so distressed that her father had to collect her from Spain. Back in the UK she was briefly hospitalised and given anti-psychotic medication.

If we think about the symbolic nature of Alice's delusions we can see that they were a powerful unconscious communication about her predicament. Alice had no conscious memory of her mother. She had never been able to grieve her loss openly as her father had demanded total 'loyalty' by forbidding any acknowledgement of her mother's existence. Alice had complied with this to the extent that she had destroyed her own memory of her mother (we would expect that a six year old would remember her mother and can therefore hypothesise that her forgetting was purposeful). By secretly keeping a forbidden photograph she had 'betrayed' her father by clandestinely maintaining a relationship with her mother. With that betrayal there was a fear of the punishment she might receive should her father discover what she had done. Alice's journey to the land of her mother's birth could be understood as a symbolic attempt to find her mother; in doing so she further 'betrayed' her father. It was thus a dangerous endeavour, as she risked her father's wrath and possibly his expulsion of her from the family should he discover what she had done.

This makes sense of the symbolic communication contained in her paranoid anxiety. Her guilt about betraying her father became translated into a fear that her true reason for going to Spain (to 'find' her mother) would be reported back to the 'Home Office' (her father). In taking photographs of her mother's homeland we might say that symbolically she was photographing her mother and the camera contained (or 'knew') that information. Alice believed that her secret liaison with her mother would be captured in the bugged camera and reported back to the Home Office. She was unable to allow herself the conscious knowledge of why she was in Spain, and managed the stress of her visit beyond symbolic thought at the level of concrete thinking that is embodied in psychotic experience.

Developing the skill of understanding the symbolism in a client's story or symptoms comes to some more easily than others. Some people see symbolic or latent significance with very little difficulty. Others are more concrete in their thinking and have to work at developing the skill; often the experience of seeing the symbolism in one's own thoughts or actions during therapy can facilitate it. Another way we can enhance symbolic thought is through reading poetry. Some poets, such as Shakespeare, have critical analyses of their work available, and this can help in the process of understanding the latent meaning of a piece of work. It can also be helpful to discuss poetry with others to share ideas about the latent meaning and to contrast how different people see different meanings in the same piece of work. This is a good preparation for the experience of presenting clinical work which is understood differently by others according to their theoretical orientation and inner world.

FURTHER READING

Shriver, L. (2005) *We Need to Talk about Kevin*. London: Serpent's Tail.
Sternberg, J. (2005) *Infant Observation at the Heart of Training*. London: Karnac.

4

SETTING THE SCENE
FOR THERAPY: The
Therapeutic Frame

I will now introduce you to Tom, Vicky's first training client. We will track Vicky's work with Tom throughout the remainder of the book, as well as exploring aspects of her own therapy with me. Vicky has a training supervisor called Kate; it is the practice on her training course that potential training clients are assessed by a senior therapist for their suitability as training cases. We join Vicky and Kate as they begin to think about Tom together, prior to Vicky's first contact with him.

Tom, a dental student, was referred to the therapy service by a clinical psychologist because he had been experiencing high levels of anxiety in social situations which had not responded to a course of CBT. Because of his anxiety, Tom was having difficulty not only in social relationships but also on the dental course. He was afraid that he would not manage the clinical part of his training because he would not be able to cope with relationships with his patients. He had first become anxious five years ago following an incident when he was travelling abroad during a gap year between school and university. He was mistaken for another European man wanted by the police. He had been set on by a crowd and had to be rescued by the police. Apparently unscathed by his experience, Tom went to university but dropped out at the end of the first term. For some years he worked as a sales assistant in a bookshop. His anxiety problem worsened when his parents moved back to Canada a year before referral, soon after he started his dental studies.

Tom described an 'idyllic' early childhood, in which he was the adored only child until he was five. However, his first memory was of waking up at night when he was about three and crying for his mother and no-one came. Tom has a younger

(Continued)

(Continued)

brother and sister, with whom he reported a good relationship. When his parents moved to Canada, their country of origin, along with his sister, Tom and his brother decided to stay in the UK. They now share a flat purchased by their parents.

The assessing therapist had undertaken a risk assessment and reported that Tom's risk levels were sufficiently low to permit therapy with a trainee. He did not take either prescription or illicit drugs, although his alcohol intake averaged 35–40 units a week, which is almost double the safe level for a male. However, Tom did not report any other risky or self-harming behaviour. Although there were times when he did not want to go on living, Tom reported that he did not have an active wish to die, nor had he made plans to kill himself.

Although Tom said that he was highly motivated to change, the assessing therapist had some concerns that he would find maintaining a therapeutic relationship difficult. He had attended the university's student counselling service before asking for the referral to the psychologist. He had struggled to think of ways in which he had been helped by either the counsellor or the psychologist. Although she had recommended him for therapy, the assessor felt that Tom would experience a significant degree of ambivalence about therapy, and that he would find it difficult to address the negative transference.

Prior to offering Tom an appointment, Vicky and Kate had discussed whether Vicky wanted to take Tom on as a client. Kate pointed out that often therapists feel that they have to work with whoever is referred to them, but that in reality there is a choice. She underscored the importance of the decision to work together as a two-way process in which both therapist and client decide if they want to work with the other. Having established that she did want to see Tom, Vicky's tasks in her first session will be to establish the therapeutic frame and to begin to build the therapeutic alliance. Because Kate also felt that Tom was more than usually ambivalent about therapy she and Vicky discussed the possibility that he might drop out of treatment early. Vicky was quite anxious about the degree of his ambivalence and the fact he had apparently not made a strong therapeutic alliance with two previous therapists.

SETTING THE SCENE: THE FRAME

The term 'frame' refers to the basic rules or guidelines within which we conduct therapy. Psychodynamic therapists pay especial attention to creating the therapeutic frame in order to create a safe and predictable physical and psychological space in which therapy can take place. The reason for establishing this space is that it has been found to create the optimum conditions for the client to be in touch with his internal world and to enable the transference relationship to emerge. In establishing the frame with clients, we are essentially setting out a therapeutic contract. When either they or we deviate from the contract we need to be open to thinking about and interpreting that deviation.

The conventions psychodynamic therapists use to construct the frame are both very disciplined and incompatible with social relationships. Thus the frame acts as a clear demarcation, which sets the scene for therapy by separating the therapeutic relationship from other relationships in your client's life. This delineation implicitly gives him permission to express his fantasies, thoughts and feelings; some of these would be unacceptable in many other relationships and discouraged in other therapeutic models. In turn this facilitates your client in accessing unconscious material and provides a framework for clinical techniques including the exploration of the transference and countertransference.

The analytic frame comprises two components: the analytic setting and the analytic attitude. The analytic setting refers to the physical aspects of therapy, such as the management of time and place. The analytic attitude is the stance taken by the therapist towards her client. Lemma (2003) identifies five core features to the analytic frame which have been established over many years of clinical practice: consistency, reliability, neutrality, anonymity and abstinence. If the client feels safe within the therapeutic frame he is more able to 'use' the therapist to face the hurts, deprivations and anxieties that have brought him into therapy, as well as feeling safe in working within the transference relationship. Lemma's five features form the basic skills of psychodynamic therapy. The ability to deploy them comes largely from the work done in our own therapy and is further supported by reading, supervision and if we undertake an infant observation.

Vicky's first-hand experience of a psychodynamic frame in her own therapy, which she has internalised, will sustain her in establishing the frame with Tom. Vicky needs to be able to think, feel and observe rather than act, and be aware of those situations in which her own needs or those of her client may propel her into unthought action. She also needs to be able to reflect both on her wish to vary from the frame as well as reflect on any violations that actually occur. This is because violations are an important source of information about our client's difficulties and needs as well as alerting us to unresolved issues of our own which may lead to therapist acting out.

The setting

Winnicott (1965a) talks about the importance of the provision of a reliable, consistent and unobtrusive environment in both maternal and therapeutic care. The setting in which therapy takes place is the physical manifestation of the therapist's care for her client. This is why psychodynamic therapists pay such close attention to it. For a baby the environment *is* the mother; in therapy it symbolises her. In other words, the way we construct the environment in therapy is symbolic of the care we are offering our clients. If the physical setting is consistent, reliable and unobtrusive, it will allow your client to both internalise you as a 'good enough mother' (Winnicott, 1965a) and to take the setting for granted. It will thus facilitate him in establishing trust in you as his therapist and in the therapeutic process. Conversely, a setting that is inconsistent, unreliable or intrusive will come to represent a therapist who cannot be trusted. This may create conditions in which your client experiences a repetition of past inconsistent, unreliable or intrusive handling. He may then respond by becoming hypervigilant and unable to take the setting for granted, thus increasing his distress and preventing him from making proper use of therapy.

Time

It is important to be punctual about beginning and ending sessions. If a client arrives early he should generally be asked to wait until the appointed time; likewise even if he arrives late, the session should stop at the appointed time. As well as indicating that the frame is reliable and consistent, this careful attention to time signals to your client your general attitude towards boundaries. If you are meticulous about keeping one boundary, such as time, it will help give your client confidence that you will keep others, such as sexual or confidentiality boundaries.

It is very important that when you and your client agree a session time you can both commit yourselves to it. This is because it is important to see your client at the same time each week. The regularity of session times brings a rhythm and predictability to the work and can help anchor your client, which is particularly valuable when he brings disturbing material to therapy. It can also help to have something that is stable and reliable if your client's life is chaotic in other respects. Meeting at the same time represents a commitment that you are both undertaking to put aside a time each week in order to do the work of therapy. If a client requests a change of session time this is usually explored carefully. While sometimes a request to change a session may be about a real demand in your client's life, such as a hospital appointment that cannot be altered, other times such requests can be an expression of ambivalence about therapy, or may signify a wish to control the therapy. Frequent requests to change the time (perhaps because the client agreed to a time that was difficult for him to attend) might be considered as a way of undermining or challenging the therapeutic frame. Even when your client needs to change or cancel a session for a reason beyond his control it can be important to think with him about the meaning of doing so. He may be relieved not to have to come for his session; he may long for you to be with him; he may be furious with you that you won't see him at a time he can attend. A missed session will always have a meaning; that meaning will be idiosyncratic to your client at that point in his therapy – at another time the same thing may well have a different meaning.

Generally clients are discouraged from making contact between sessions unless for a specific reason. Again, this is to reinforce the sense of a therapeutic relationship that is contained within the frame and to maintain the integrity of the therapeutic space in which the work of therapy can be done. Generally speaking, if your client does make contact between sessions, it is important to keep the conversation brief and steer him to discussing the issue in the next session. There are times when it is appropriate to talk for longer, for example if a client has received some very bad news and needs your help to contain his distress and your next meeting is some days away. If there is contact between sessions it is important to refer to it at the next session, so that it becomes incorporated into the frame. Again, it is important to think with your client about the meaning of contacting you. Sometimes you will have a client who cannot hold on to a sense of you between sessions and needs to make some form of contact. Some years ago one of my clients regularly faxed me between sessions at one stage in our work together. Quite often between-session contact – especially in writing – is a way of telling the therapist something that cannot yet be said to her face. This needs to be gently explored to help your client get to the point where he can say these things in the session.

The physical space

Managing the physical space gives a powerful message to your client about your attitude towards him. If the space is reliable and consistent, we are experienced as reliable and consistent because clients understand that managing the space is within our control. If the therapeutic space is neutral and doesn't overexcite him, it will help your client to trust that you won't over-stimulate him or intrude into him. Managing the physical space indicates that we are providing a safe place in which he is protected as much as possible from external intrusion and in which his feelings can be contained. It can be difficult for a client to feel safe in being vulnerable and attending to a disturbing inner world if he does not feel protected from intrusion from the outside world by his therapist. The therapist who does not pay attention to discontinuities in the physical space may unintentionally give her client the message that she does not take his feelings of vulnerability seriously and that she is not a safe object.

> Like many therapists in private practice, Vicky was planning to use a room in her own home as a consulting room. The advantage of this was that it gave her more control over how she managed the physical environment, for example how the room was set up and furnished. The room was in the basement of her house and had a separate outside entrance for clients, as well as an entrance from the house for Vicky to gain access. Although there was no waiting room, there was a space for clients to wait in the lobby and a cloakroom with a lavatory and washbasin.

The provision of a waiting area and dedicated toilet facilities in private consulting rooms is part of providing a safe analytic space. Clients need to have use of a lavatory, but they should not have to access it through parts of the house that are private, and which might expose them to information about you and your life that they could find overwhelming. If clients have to access facilities that are also used by your family, all personal effects should be removed for the same reason.

It is important that, whenever possible, clients come to the same room for their therapy. It can be easy to underestimate how much attention we all pay to a new or changed physical environment, and how disturbing changes to the physical environment can feel at a deep level. Clients' confidence in the ability of their therapist to contain them can be undermined if the physical space in which we work constantly changes. If you are in a situation where you have to change rooms it is important that you acknowledge the potential significance for your client.

Often clients will talk about the importance of coming to the same therapy room in helping them feel safe, and some will openly discuss how even minor changes in the room are experienced as destabilising or intrusive. By using the same room each week your client is helped to relax into a physical space that becomes part of a 'secure base' (Bowlby, 1988) in which he can explore his inner world in safety. Clients sometimes experience the consulting room as a safe place before they experience the therapist as a secure person who they can hold in their mind. Clients will sometimes describe how, when distressed between sessions, they imagine themselves back in the safety of the consulting room as a physical environment, rather than necessarily with the person of the therapist. The therapy room is part of therapy in that it represents the therapist. If therapy takes place in different settings each session it can be difficult for your client to feel sufficiently safely held by the physical environment to have a sense of a secure base; that in turn will affect his capacity to symbolise and access his inner world. It is for this reason that, wherever possible, psychodynamic therapists working in the public sector should negotiate to have use of a room that is dedicated to therapy and is regularly available.

Likewise, changes within the room itself can feel destabilising. Recently, I changed the client's chair in my consulting room. All my clients needed to incorporate the change into their experience of the therapeutic frame. They also needed to mourn the loss of the previous chair which was part of their physical experience of the room. Some were very disturbed by it, fearing that a change in the physical frame heralded an unforeseen change in me. At that moment I became an unreliable object for them. The changes meant that my room, and by extension I, no longer felt safe.

In order to facilitate neutrality and anonymity most psychodynamic therapists avoid over-personalising their consulting rooms. The reason for this is to maximise the potential for fantasy and to avoid over-stimulating clients by revealing too much personal information. Certainly, in the years I have practised I have never seen family photographs on display in a psychodynamic consulting room. Some psychodynamic practitioners have no items of personal significance in their consulting rooms. The concern is that giving too much away about themselves will inhibit their client's capacity to fantasise or will impose their personality on him. Kate, Vicky's supervisor, felt that we cannot keep all knowledge about ourselves from our clients. They will draw their own conclusions from our clothes, jewellery and choice of furniture in the consulting room.

It is important that the setting in which we see clients should be private and as free from interruption as possible. There are intrusions that no therapist has control over, for example noise from outside such as aeroplanes or road works. But there are others that she can control, such as ensuring no-one enters the room during a session, that the telephone is in a different room, or, if that is not possible, that it is switched to a silent answering machine. It can be much more difficult to control privacy and interruptions in the public sector than when working in private practice.

> Vicky arrived for a session at the same time as a new window cleaner came to clean the windows. I asked her to wait in the waiting room and organised the window cleaner to start with the consulting room windows. I also paid him so that I did not have to interrupt the session later. Once Vicky and I were in the consulting room I drew the blinds so that the window cleaner could not see in. Vicky was angry with me that I had allowed the window cleaner to clean the consulting room windows. However, she was also cognisant of the fact that I had minimised the intrusion by paying him, by making the interruption predictable by asking him to clean the consulting room first, and by drawing the blinds until he had finished to maintain privacy. Later in the session she was able to acknowledge that she had felt looked after by me. It been important that I had realised how difficult she found the interruption and that I had responded to it without being asked.

As this vignette illustrates, it is not always possible to protect clients from all intrusions. However, the way we handle the intrusion can demonstrate that we are taking seriously our responsibility, as far as is possible, to maintain the integrity of the physical space.

Although less attention is paid in the literature to therapists' need for continuity, it is important for us also to have predictability in the physical space in which we work, so that we too are held by the physical setting. It is much easier for us to provide a holding or containing environment for clients if we feel comfortable and safe in the physical environment we inhabit. We are also much more able to be aware of our own internal processes, including our countertransference, if we feel held ourselves. Although part of our internal holding is our own therapy, supervision and theory base, the setting has an impact on our ability to access that internal holding.

The financial transaction

At some level all therapy has to be paid for, even if the client is not paying directly. Both client and therapist have to face the fact that, without some form of financial transaction, there would be no therapy and therefore no therapeutic relationship. In the public services therapists are paid a salary; voluntary organisations and charities have to find the funds to support the provision of a setting for therapy, even if the therapy itself is free. When therapy is free at the point of delivery, thinking about the implicit financial contract can be more easily avoided. References to money might therefore be more subtle and consequently you have to be more alert to these in the material of the session. For fee-paying clients the financial relationship is more explicit. Those practitioners who work privately will therefore be more directly exposed to the meaning of money for their clients, and the different ways in which they use it.

> At the beginning of her therapy Vicky was very careful about ensuring she had her cheque-book with her on the day I presented her with her account and always paid me immediately. When I gave her the account shortly after the first summer break, she was distressed because she did not have her cheque-book and so could not pay straight away. In exploring this Vicky told me that, if she did not pay me immediately, she would feel in my debt, whereas if she did pay me right away she could feel that the relationship was reciprocal and she was less dependent on me. Further exploration revealed that Vicky also feared that failing to pay me immediately would incur my anger and a subsequent withdrawal from her. In the transference I had come to represent a demanding mother whom she needed to appease as she had her mother when a child. In turn this led to us to thinking about the timing of the violation of this self-imposed demand to pay me as soon as I gave her an account – that it was after the long holiday – and that she herself was angry with me for going away and leaving her.

Forrester (1997) makes some interesting observations about the relationship between money and therapy. He points out that for some clients, and indeed therapists, money can create an illusion that there is a real reciprocity in the relationship. The payment of a fee can be perceived as cancelling out the client's indebtedness to his therapist, or reducing the power inequality between them, thus reducing the intensity of the transference. As Lemma (2003) notes, however, in therapy we are usually dealing with symbolic debt. The symbolic debt we owe our therapist (whether of a life that has been made worth living, or one that has been enriched by the relationship with her) can never be cancelled out by money.

Both clients and therapists can struggle with issues around payment, and it is part of the skill of being a psychodynamic practitioner that we manage the discussion around fees. In setting a fee at the outset of therapy, it is important to charge an amount that you feel comfortable with and that your client can sustain. Practitioners divide into those who operate a sliding scale for fees, charging according to ability to pay and/or number of sessions per week, and those who operate a fixed fee. My own preference is to operate a sliding scale that reflects my clients' financial position. I set an upper and lower limit and agree fees within those parameters. I have discovered over the years that fees too far either side of the upper and lower limits of my scale can interfere with the therapeutic process. If a young adult is being paid for by his parents, I always discuss whether he can contribute something towards his therapy. Even if it is a small amount, it can help him feel that the therapy is his own and reduce the acting out that often accompanies payment by a third party.

You also need to think about increasing your fees. There is considerable variety in how the topic is approached. Some therapists tell their clients at the commencement of therapy that fees will be increased and inform them of the time interval they can expect. Others do not do so until they feel it is necessary to increase the fee. Some therapists start at a relatively high fee and maintain it for a period of time, after which they negotiate an increase; others increase fees annually in line with inflation. In discussing the increase with their clients some therapists ask what they think the increase should be. Others will suggest a fee and then negotiate around it. I tend to address the subject about two months ahead of the proposed increase, to give my clients sufficient time to process it. Whenever possible I raise the subject at or near the beginning of the session, particularly if I am seeing someone once a week. This ensures there is time during the session to work with whatever the proposed increase means. However it is approached, it is important to give sufficient time for your client to know that his feelings about the increase are heard, and for the unconscious significance of this change in the frame to emerge and be worked with.

You also need to inform your client about the practical details of billing, such as how often you bill, how you will give them the account and when. Many psychodynamic practitioners bill their clients at the end of the month, though some give accounts at the end of each session. Practitioners also vary in how they present the account. Some bills are set out in a professional manner, others are more informal. Some therapists post them, others leave them somewhere to be picked up, while others give them directly to the client. Taylor (2002), in a thoughtful discussion of money in psychotherapy, notes that it is important to hand the bill personally to the client, since this underscores the monetary contract. She argues that doing so emphasises and protects the professional relationship and reminds both of the boundaries of therapy. She is one of a number of authors who have observed that formal guidance about the financial transaction is missing from most psychodynamic trainings. She comments that information has to be gleaned 'from private, piecemeal conversations with one's peers in an uncanny resemblance of how sexual knowledge is often acquired' (2002: 75).

Novice practitioners often find it difficult to discuss fees, since they can feel they are insufficiently experienced to warrant a proper fee. In some sections of society discussing money at all remains in questionable taste. If you have difficulties they need to be discussed in your own therapy, so you can think about the meaning for you of charging a fee (and of being charged one). However, sometimes quite experienced therapists can struggle with putting their fees up or chasing the late payment of accounts. If this is a continuing problem it needs to be discussed in supervision to understand the nature of the difficulty. From my own experience I know that, when I have a problem with fees, it is nearly always an expression of an unacknowledged difficulty in the therapeutic relationship. Once this is understood, addressing the issue of fees becomes more straightforward.

Holidays and breaks

Part of our attention to the analytic frame lies in the way we approach holidays or other breaks. Working psychodynamically involves making a long-term commitment to clients that we will not suddenly disappear for a period of time, unless for a very good reason. Taking holidays that are planned and discussed in advance contributes to clients' experience of you as reliable and consistent. For the most part therapists' holidays become part of the rhythm of therapy and are taken at more or less the same time each year. Changing the timings of our holidays can be distressing for clients, and needs to be discussed sensitively and well ahead. Likewise clients need to be given good advance warning of holidays, so that the significance of the break in therapy can be explored.

Breaks represent an interruption in the continuity of the therapeutic relationship and clients need to be able to prepare for that interruption and helped to face it. This is particularly important for those whose early life has been characterised by loss or unpredictable caring. If your client has not internalised you, a holiday or break can be experienced as the complete loss of you, with accompanying distress and disorientation. For this reason I sometimes let a client take something from the consulting room that symbolises me during a break. One colleague described how he had pocket handkerchiefs with his initials embroidered on them for those clients who needed something of him to help them manage breaks. I prefer my client to choose something for himself which has meaning for him, and which I am happy to let him borrow. As Winnicott observed, transitional objects need to be chosen to fulfil their function. I think it is important to add that I do not do this as a routine part of my practice, but only with those clients for whom I think it is developmentally appropriate and after careful consideration between us of the meaning of doing so.

ESTABLISHING THE FRAME:
THE ANALYTIC ATTITUDE

To establish an analytic attitude you need all the skills of consistency, reliability, neutrality, anonymity and abstinence that Lemma (2003) identifies. This in turn facilitates the development of the transference. In the following section Kate and Vicky think together about how Vicky will manage an analytic attitude in her first contact with Tom.

> Tom wanted to be contacted on his mobile phone. Kate highlighted the importance of maintaining a degree of formality on the telephone and that Vicky should not get drawn into any discussion other than the arrangements for meeting. This first contact was important because it set the tenor for the therapeutic relationship. Kate felt that it was important for Vicky to find a balance between remaining professional about what was discussed, while at the same time being approachable through her tone of voice. Being too informal might be experienced by Tom as seductive, or give the impression of a social, rather than a professional, relationship. Being too stiff or formal might be taken as a sign of unfriendliness in a society that is increasingly informal in the conduct of professional relationships.

Neutrality

Part of being neutral is to do with being non-judgemental. So, for example, if your client criticises you, you need to help him address the anxieties and distress that underlie his criticism, rather than defending yourself, however much you might wish to. At times significant effort needs to be deployed to manage one's feelings and the wish to act under pressure. When provoked you may wish to retaliate when criticised, or agree to an early termination of therapy. It is important to hold back from doing so. Neutrality involves holding on to and processing powerful, often uncomfortable, feelings or impulses and not acting on them.

Abstinence

Kate's emphasis on the importance of not engaging in social conversation when making the initial contact with Tom is part of maintaining therapeutic abstinence. This safeguards the therapeutic space through keeping it professional. There are a number of ways we do this, one of which is that we usually do not make social conversation (about the weather for example) or talk about ourselves and events in our own lives. Clients can initially experience this abstinence as coldness or a lack of caring, though in fact it can be done without being cold and the aim is to protect your client from the imposition of your needs or beliefs. Quite often, later in therapy, clients express relief that they don't have to make social conversation, with the implicit attention to their therapist's needs that this implies.

Therapeutic abstinence comes more easily to some than others. I can still be taken by surprise when clients comment on my restraint in the consulting room. My natural personal style is quite outgoing and over the years I have worked hard to find a way of being myself in the consulting room while remaining abstinent. Like other psychodynamic therapists I have learned to hold back from responding in ways that I might normally. I have learned not to automatically offer reassurance or advice to a client who is distressed; I have become aware of what my wish to make a joke might signify rather than making it. Therapeutic abstinence also helps the emergence of the negative transference, with accompanying feelings of anger, hostility or disappointment towards the therapist. Many clients come to therapy having difficulties with the experience or expression of negative affect, and one of the tasks of psychodynamic work is to help them to find a way of giving voice to thoughts and feelings that have often been out of conscious awareness. This can be hard to do. One of the reasons that new therapists find therapeutic abstinence difficult is that they are aware that it may well produce negative feelings in their client. Neutrality can therefore be quite a strain for both therapist and client.

Abstinence also involves not gratuitously giving away personal information to clients. Part of the skill in developing abstinence is to monitor the times when there is a strong urge to do so. In the absence of information clients come to their own conclusions about the type of person we are and the nature of our lives. The content of these conjectures and fantasies can give us important information about the inner world of our clients that would be less available if they had the information as a matter of course. As already noted, we all give away information about ourselves through our general presentation and demeanour. If we have private consulting rooms, particularly if they are in our home, the house we live in, how we furnish it and the car standing on the drive are all sources of further information. Beyond that the amount a psychodynamic practitioner reveals varies according to theoretical orientation and individual style. My personal stance is that what I reveal will be determined by my assessment of whether telling my client something about me would progress or hinder the work we are doing. It is also influenced by what I personally feel happy about revealing. I believe that it is important for clients to explore their fantasies first, but then it can also be important to explore reality and how that fits with fantasy.

Like many new therapists, Vicky was anxious about managing abstinence without falling into the trap of being cold and unresponsive. Perhaps one of the most difficult things to accept as a beginning therapist is that during and just after training the novice therapist's analytic superego is likely to be more rigid. As a result she may go too far in the direction of neutrality or abstinence. However, this is generally considered preferable in a new therapist, as it is important to understand the value of the frame and how to work within it. It is only when the importance and significance of the frame is really understood and internalised that an informed decision can be made about when it is safe or desirable to challenge the frame in a given situation.

Clients often find therapeutic abstinence difficult since they will probably never have had another relationship as an adult that is so one-sided. Part of the skill we develop as therapists is being able to address their feelings about our abstinence.

Clients can become angry, hurt, dismissive and compliant in the face of neutrality and abstinence. Helping them to talk about these feelings, while remaining abstinent, is a highly developed skill, particularly if the subject of their interest has a high personal valence for their therapist at that moment.

William and his wife had recently separated. One of William's clients, a widower, was worried because William's wife's car was no longer in the drive. He was frightened that William's wife had also died. William neither wished, nor felt it appropriate, to tell his client about the separation. Discussing the session in supervision, William described his struggle to remain abstinent while being overwhelmed with his own distress about his wife's departure, and the realisation that he wished that the separation had been caused by death.

The last area I wish to discuss is touch. This is a very sensitive area within psychodynamic work and, in reviewing what you are about to read, I notice that this is one of the most heavily referenced parts of the book. I see this as testament to my own anxiety in writing about it. Many clients have needs that are expressed through either the wish to be touched and/or the fear of it. However, it is generally considered taboo to routinely touch clients in psychodynamic work. If we do so it may be considered as a form of therapist acting out which has therapeutic, ethical and legal implications.

The early psychoanalysts eschewed touching because of anxiety about the potential for sexualising the therapeutic relationship. Although partly determined by the fact that psychoanalytic theory was psycho-sexual, the anxiety about touch also stemmed from early psychoanalytic scandals when prominent psychoanalysts had sexual relationships with clients. Freud's concern about the potential for this bringing psychoanalysis into disrepute meant that it was only a few prominent analysts (including Ferenczi, Winnicott, Balint and Little) who subsequently deliberated the value of touch: 'The spectre of this ultimate excess has made almost impossible a dispassionate assessment of the technical implications of lesser forms of physical contact' (McLaughlin, 1995: 434). Although our understanding of the centrality of sexuality in human development has changed in the intervening years, most psychoanalytic practitioners still advocate restraint from touching clients (Brafman, 2006). There is anxiety that to do so might stir up longings and phantasies that could overwhelm them and us, and that this will lead to therapist acting out and the abuse of clients.

There is now a more open debate amongst psychodynamic practitioners about the value of touch and its place in therapy, which is to do with the recognition that touching 'is a basic behavioural need' (Montagu, 1986: 46). Indeed, a survey of 30 American psychoanalysts by Fosshage (2000) revealed that every one of them had hugged or been hugged by their clients. However, touching in therapy remains something of a closet phenomenon, which is discussed between colleagues, but rarely written about (Breckenridge 2000).

My opinion is that the skill involved in deciding whether touch is appropriate lies in making an assessment as to whether the client's wish to be touched is an expression of a developmental need, or the wish for gratification that is not developmentally driven. There is an argument that meeting a developmental need to be touched can be therapeutic. However, as Patrick Casement (2000) has pointed out, it is difficult to prescribe when touch is appropriate. He argues that it has to be assessed within the context of a particular client with a particular therapist. I would add 'at a particular moment in therapy', since a hug at one point in therapy may have a completely different meaning than at another.

There are three guiding principles that should steer you in this area. Firstly you should not initiate touch; you should only do so reactively, rather than responding to your own wishes. Secondly, whenever touch occurs in your work you should be prepared to discuss it in supervision; if you are not prepared to do so you need to think about what you are trying to avoid. Thirdly, as in all other areas in psychodynamic work, the wish to touch or the experience of touching needs to be understood between you and your client at some stage in your work together. However, it is preferable that your client initiates this discussion if possible, since it can be very shaming if you initiate it.

Confidentiality

Clients must be able to trust their therapist to respect their confidentiality. We are not at liberty to gossip about our clients and need to take precautions to ensure their privacy is maintained; some of these precautions are covered under legislation. Confidentiality helps to mark the therapeutic relationship as different from other relationships in that information stays within the consulting room. However, complete confidentiality is rare, and indeed may be to the detriment of the client. Quite frequently information is shared, for a variety of reasons, particularly in the public services when clients may be in the care of a number of different professionals. Private practitioners vary as to how much information they share with other health professionals. While not all therapists do so, I generally feel it is important to have my client's GP details and an agreement that I can contact him/her. I make it clear that the limits to confidentiality are determined by whether I have concerns around risk issues. This may be to the client, or someone else. In the UK we have a legal duty to report risk if a child is involved. It is always important to ensure that we only share information on a 'need to know' basis with other professionals, and that sensitive clinical material is kept confidential wherever possible. In the UK clinical governance requires that therapists in both the public health service and private practice discuss their work in supervision and this inevitably involves a breach of absolute confidentiality, even if the client's personal details are anonymised. Similarly when a therapist is in training she will be discussing her work in supervision.

THE OVERT THERAPEUTIC CONTRACT

There is both an overt and covert contract in any therapeutic work; the covert contract that your client makes with you will be both conscious and unconscious and will become the subject of exploration in your sessions as the work unfolds. Similarly the unconscious contract you make with your client is the subject of exploration in your supervision and/or your own therapy. It is important to set out the conscious contract in the early sessions as part of establishing the framework for therapy which in turn will support the therapeutic alliance (see Chapter 5).

The overt contract includes:

- Making explicit the length of each session; usually psychodynamic sessions are 50 minutes.
- Agreeing the length of the intervention (whether it is time-limited or open-ended). If time-limited this includes whether there are arrangements for extra sessions and under what conditions those sessions are negotiated.
- Agreeing the timing and frequency of sessions and explaining how you approach requests to change sessions.
- Explaining when you take holiday breaks and the amount of notice you generally give.
- Agreeing a fee if your client is paying himself. You need to indicate how and when the fee will be reviewed in the future, when you will present your account, and your policy regarding payment for missed sessions.
- Discussing the limits of confidentiality, particularly in relation to risk, whether to self or others. Your training supervisor or organisation may require you to explain that you are being supervised.
- Explaining any irregularities in the way you work; for example my consulting room is situated directly off the waiting room and, in order to maintain privacy, I cannot let clients in until the previous client has left.

THE INTERNAL FRAME

It is a major developmental milestone in a therapist's professional growth when she can be authentically herself with her clients. 'There is a skill in maintaining relative anonymity and at the same time being a person' (Cooper, 2002: 18). Cooper calls this 'naturalness' and sees it as 'a necessary and important analytic attitude' (ibid.: 19). An authentic practitioner is one who can respond to her clients by taking account of their needs rather than adhering to a set of tightly prescribed rules. By working in this way she is both the same and different with every client. To be able to achieve this you must first have a coherent sense of the frame which you have internalised. This will guide you and ensure that you work ethically. Secondly, your sense of the frame must be stable, so that you are consistent within it. Parsons (2007) calls this 'the internal setting'; it is the space in the therapist's mind in which she can receive her client. A secure internal setting can allow flexibility in the external setting without sacrificing analytic rigour and is the mark of a mature and boundaried therapist. Parsons, a senior psychoanalyst, gives an example of this, describing how one client asked to bring her dog to her analysis. The dog slept on her stomach and facilitated bringing into awareness aspects of the therapeutic relationship that had previously been unconscious. Parsons was able to use his internal setting to give him confidence that 'whatever having the dog in the room might lead to it could still be part of the analysis' (2007: 1445).

One reason psychodynamic therapists become anxious about naturalness is the fear that it will lead to unethical practice whereby deviations from the frame are rationalised in the service of the therapist's own needs. When this happens almost inevitably it is to the detriment of the client and can be abusive. Winnicott sums up the challenge when he writes 'In doing psychoanalysis … I aim at being myself and behaving myself' (1965b: 166). In writing about his experience Parsons indicates the importance of being able to discuss deviations from the frame. If we cannot do so with our peers or in supervision, and use any feedback to reflect on our own unconscious motivation, we are almost certainly deviating from the internal setting that Parsons describes.

FURTHER READING

Lemma, A. (2003) *Introduction to the Practice of Psychoanalytic Psychotherapy.* Chichester: Wiley.

5

THE FIRST SESSIONS: The Therapeutic Alliance

The therapeutic alliance is that part of the therapeutic relationship in which we and our client agree to work together to help him achieve the changes he needs to make. The other two aspects of the therapeutic relationship are the unconscious relationship, which is largely manifest through the transference, and the 'real' relationship, which is to do with the reality judgement our clients make about us. In reality these three aspects of the relationship overlap, but for the purpose of clarity in this chapter I will be focussing on the therapeutic alliance. Establishing a therapeutic alliance is a priority in the early sessions, though it cannot be ignored at any stage of the work.

WHAT IS A THERAPEUTIC ALLIANCE?

The therapeutic alliance involves the notion that there can be a split in the way your client relates to you. While one part of his ego is caught up in the transference relationship, the other part is available to think with you about what is going on and collaborate in the therapeutic endeavour. The therapeutic alliance addresses the aspect of the relationship that is in touch with external reality. By contrast the transference relationship is concerned with internal reality. If your client experiences a powerful transference (particularly a negative transference) he can be assisted in managing it, and continuing with the work, if a strong therapeutic alliance has been established.

As Etchegoyen (1999) notes, the transference relationship is asymmetrical. In other words, it is an unequal relationship because we speak to the child in our client. By contrast the therapeutic alliance should be an equal relationship between two adults – in other words, symmetrical. Meltzer (1967) also proposed that the therapeutic alliance should be approached through the client's adult self, arguing that one does not interpret to the adult part, but rather speaks to it.

Psychodynamic practitioners sometimes treat the alliance as though it is an asymmetrical relationship, which can lead to inappropriate and unhelpful interpretations. For example, someone who came to me for a second therapy expected me to interpret her resistance to therapy when, soon after starting, she cancelled some sessions because she had to attend mandatory training at work. Her previous therapist had always interpreted such reality-based difficulties solely within the transference relationship, and she expected me to do the same. I usually treat such situations as a symmetrical issue first; once we have resolved the practicalities I explore the meaning for my client, which will almost certainly include an exploration of the transference implications and the asymmetrical relationship. It is very important for clients to know that we respect and acknowledge the adult part of them; it is this that helps them when the transference relationship becomes more powerful, particularly if they act out.

Etchegoyen argues that treating the therapeutic alliance as an asymmetrical relationship can interfere with our client's capacity for perception and critical reasoning. Recognising that practitioners can feel much more comfortable in an asymmetrical relationship which maintains a power imbalance, he cautions that 'We should take care not to utilize the asymmetry of the transference relation to ease the symmetry of the therapeutic alliance' (1999: 257). This is particularly the case when we have done something that our client pulls us up on. Etchegoyen cites the example of an analytic colleague who cancelled a client's session the day before it was due when he could have done so sooner. The client was angry that, with more notice, he could have done something else with the time. The analyst responded by interpreting the client's separation anxiety. While at some later stage it might have been appropriate to make such an interpretation, Etchegoyen argues that this should have happened only after the analyst acknowledged the client's very real anger with the analyst's very real lack of consideration for him.

Research has consistently found that the quality of the alliance predicts the outcome of treatment. Crits-Christoph and Connolly Gibbons (2003) propose that the therapeutic alliance is particularly important to the outcome of psychodynamic therapy and counselling. The quality of the therapeutic alliance is partially based on your client's ability to work with another person. When a new client tells me he has not stayed in a job very long, and that his relationships are short-lived, I know it will be difficult for him to build a solid alliance. However, if your client does have the basic capacity to work with you, it is your job as a skilled practitioner to facilitate the development of the therapeutic alliance.

THE ROAD TO THERAPY

The therapeutic relationship starts at the moment that a referral becomes possible in your client's mind and there are a number of factors that can influence the establishment of the therapeutic alliance before he arrives for the first session.

The referral route

Clients find us via many different routes, including referral from a colleague, self-referral to an organisation, a register of qualified practitioners, a personal recommendation or advertising.

The route your client takes can have a significant impact on the early therapeutic alliance, since it may determine how long he has had to wait for therapy. Being on a waiting list for a long time can diminish the impetus to do something about problems. Your client may be reluctant to open up painful areas that have begun to heal over, even though the root cause of his difficulties remains the same. This can increase the initial resistance to therapy and if so it needs skilled management to ease him into the work. At some level your client may already feel that you have neglected him because you were unavailable at the time he really needed you (Howard, 2006). Unless you acknowledge that he has waited a long time to be seen your client may feel that you don't know or care that he has been kept waiting. This may increase the possibility of a negative transference before the therapeutic alliance is strong enough to cope with it. The acknowledgement does not need to be complex; the example below is often enough and could be one of the first things said to a new client who has waited a long time:

Therapist: 'You've waited a long time for this; I wonder how it feels to be here now.'

The route taken into therapy can also indicate how comfortable your client is with other people knowing he is seeking help. He may have chosen to find a therapist through an advertisement or a register because he doesn't want anyone else, including his GP, to know he is in therapy. This could indicate a greater than usual degree of shame about being in therapy, which might undermine the early therapeutic alliance.

Whose decision is it?

Who decides that your client should enter therapy can also influence the early therapeutic alliance. There are a number of possibilities: he could decide himself; he could come as a result of seeking advice; he could be coerced into it, for example by his spouse; he might be sent for compulsory therapy, for example by a court. Those who have come via the former two routes are more likely to be motivated to use the opportunity and therefore ready to build a therapeutic alliance. However, there is a sharp decrease in motivation for the latter two routes, and your client might be looking quite consciously for reasons that either you or the approach is not right for him. Again, it is important to acknowledge early on how difficult it is for the client if he has been 'sent'.

Therapist: 'Perhaps it is difficult to imagine that you can get anything from a process that you haven't [don't feel you have] chosen'.

Your client may be robust in agreeing that that is indeed the case, and the honesty about his position may in itself be facilitative of a positive relationship and may prevent the development of an early negative transference.

Who is paying?

Whether your client is paying for his own therapy is also an important factor in the establishment of the early therapeutic alliance. Clients who pay for therapy themselves know they have more scope for choosing a therapist. Having a choice can facilitate an early positive alliance for some clients, though others may hold back knowing they could go elsewhere. Those who are paid for by a third party will bring particular complications into therapy. If an insurance company is paying there is usually uncertainty about how long funding will last; if a parent or relative is doing so there may be aspects of your client's relationship that get played out in therapy, for example by missing sessions that still have to be paid for. Sometimes the strings attached to being funded can have an impact on the therapeutic relationship. It is important to acknowledge the implications for therapy of third party funding.

> *Therapist*: 'I wonder whether you might find it difficult to feel these sessions are just for you given your parents are paying for them'.

Previous therapy

The road to therapy may be one your client has taken before, and this can have an impact on how he anticipates engaging with you even before you meet. Clients who have been caught in the 'revolving door' of the health system, will, inevitably, carry with them expectations of therapy based on their previous experience. Clients who have seen a number of previous mental health practitioners often complain at having to tell their story again and may come to therapy resentful at having to do so. Others may be reluctant to engage with a new therapist after previously making a meaningful therapeutic relationship and having to say goodbye, perhaps before they were ready to do so. They may then treat us with the lack of consideration they feel they experienced themselves. These sorts of factors can have a significant impact on the therapeutic relationship before we meet them. As with the examples given above it is often best to acknowledge an issue at the outset.

> *Therapist*: 'I wonder if it's difficult coming to see yet another person and having to tell your story all over again'.

Barriers along the way

It is more difficult to establish a therapeutic alliance when clients fail to come to the first appointment, both from the therapist's and from the client's perspective. The client might be embarrassed or guilty about not attending and then feel angry towards the person who has made him feel uncomfortable. You may be irritated at a wasted session when you have a waiting list and pressure on you to reduce it, or at the loss of income if you are in private practice. Both of you have to get past your negative feelings in order to begin the process of building a therapeutic alliance. Again it is important to address this issue at the outset:

> *Therapist*: 'It might have been quite difficult to come today after missing the first session'. If the evidence is there, you may continue 'I wonder if you were concerned I might be upset with you for not coming last time?'.

Even today many people regard the need for counselling or therapy as a sign of weakness and can be contemptuous of those who need it. How the people around the client view therapy can have a significant impact on the therapeutic alliance. If your client has gone against the values and beliefs of his own family, friends or culture, he may be so ambivalent about therapy that it is difficult for him to establish a therapeutic alliance. If he signals that this is the situation, you need to acknowledge the difficulty for him as soon as you are aware of it in the same way as in the other examples given.

With all the above examples a number of things are happening simultaneously. Firstly, a source of potential difficulty is being attended to near the beginning of the relationship so that any work around the issue can be addressed early on. Secondly, the therapist is giving an early message that difficulties in the therapeutic relationship can be discussed, thus providing an experience the client can model. Lastly, the therapist brings herself into the picture, indicating from the start that the relationship between her and her client can be thought about. This is the precursor to working more overtly with the transference relationship. Your client may find this helpful if he has not had previous experience of working dynamically. You might be concerned that, by inviting your client to tell you how he feels, you are unnecessarily encouraging negativity about therapy. However, being able to express anxiety or concerns about therapy can facilitate the therapeutic alliance as it indicates that we can tolerate our client's negative affect. It also demonstrates that we are in tune with the fact that he might both want help and not want help and that he is ambivalent about the process of therapy.

BASIC SKILLS IN BUILDING A THERAPEUTIC ALLIANCE

Maintaining an open mind is an important skill in psychodynamic work, and is manifest in an underlying attitude of not knowing. It is therefore essential that we remain curious throughout our client's therapy to help us maintain an open mind. Curiosity is conveyed by not making assumptions, or allowing yourself to be rushed into preemptive conclusions. It also conveys a non-judgemental stance, which is important in helping clients cope when they discuss difficult material.

Listening

Clients often comment on how I listen to them, which is different from their everyday experience and a central skill in psychodynamic work. We can prepare ourselves to listen by creating an atmosphere in the consulting room which is calm and unhurried, and by a therapeutic stance that is a mixture of quiet calm and alert attentiveness. This will facilitate your client in feeling that he can both tell his story, and that he can listen to it and know he is being listened to by you.

Psychodynamic practitioners' work is much more about listening than talking. As McWilliams observes, when we listen well, clients can discover a sense of agency and become increasingly confident in their own judgements. She makes the wry observation that 'The therapist is deprived of the illusion that it is his or her clever formulation that has created that change, a frustration that it takes a good deal of training to be able to give up' (2004: 133). Listening is a central competence in building a therapeutic alliance. It involves allowing your client to tell his story without being distracted by external events; not interrupting him unless necessary; communicating interest through your facial expression and body language; hearing the subtext to a story and the emotions behind the words. In Chapter 4, I talked about the importance of the analytic internal frame. It is from within this frame that we *hear* our clients, which is why how we listen is different from everyday listening.

Analytic listening requires discipline; we do not engage in the normal social conventions of back and forth discussion. It requires holding in check our own need for self-expression in the service of our client's psychological needs. At the same time we need to maintain high levels of attention and concentration. The quality of our listening is also emotionally receptive, which facilitates our client in being able to explore more deeply those issues that are painful for him or previously unacknowledged. We are thoughtful about what he says and convey that we take it seriously. Casement (1985) is among a number of writers who have likened this kind of receptiveness to hypnosis. It may look as though not much is happening, but in order to listen properly we have to 'work with our full self-expression throttled back to near-minimum' (Coltart, 1993: 43). Doing so is very demanding and can be exhausting.

Silence

Listening happens when we ourselves are silent, but there are times in the session when both participants are quiet. The silent therapist of popular culture is mostly a caricature, but there is a reality that part of listening involves allowing silence. For many clients it is the first time they have experienced thinking or feeling in the presence of another without the pressure to fill the space with words. However, it is important early on in therapy not to allow silences to extend for too long until you know your client well enough to understand what silence means to him. At the beginning of my career I learned a valuable lesson with a very vulnerable client who experienced any silence on my part as a punishment and a challenge. In a therapy characterised by a powerful negative transference she sat in furious silence challenging me to be the first to speak. Needless to say my mind went blank! Looking back I am aware that, as a novice psychotherapist, I would have struggled with this client however I managed silences and may have been unable to prevent the early termination that inevitably followed. However, I do wonder whether the outcome might have been different had I been better able to understand and help her cope with her distress about any lapse in our discourse. Although she attributed any silence on my part to my adherence to technique, it was also a reflection of her experience of silence being used as a weapon in her own family.

It is not unusual for a client to come for his first and perhaps second session and pour out the distress that propelled him into therapy, then return for a subsequent session and not know what to say next, potentially resulting in painful silence at a time when the therapeutic alliance is not yet established. In this situation I do not allow the silence to continue for too long, but will address it. I usually start by commenting on how difficult it seems for my client to know how to start/what to say, then to ask if he has any thoughts about why it might be difficult today. Often this is enough to begin the session or unblock it. But sometimes more is needed and an exploration of what my silence signifies to the client usually moves us both forward, not least because by doing so we are ending that silence.

While some clients perceive their therapist's silence as a provocation, others become terrified of halts in the conversation because the analytic space does not represent a place in which they can explore, but rather one in which they will get lost. As a profession we are good at allowing silence, but I think we are sometimes less good at identifying when clients become lost in the space we have created for them. For these clients our silence often traumatises them.

These feelings are both more difficult to tolerate and more difficult to talk about at the start of therapy. Sometimes I will explain to my client that in the silence I am thinking about what he has said, and that I don't want to intrude on what he is thinking. This is part of helping him to understand the reasoning behind why I haven't spoken, and important in helping him to begin to reflect on his own relationship to silence. However, being silent is not something I 'do' to my clients. Some years ago a supervisee told me that she had 'used' silence with her client as a deliberate technique. She explained that her own therapist had 'used' it with her, so she felt this was the right thing to do. She needed to be helped to understand that to 'use' silence in this way goes against the idea of an analytic space in which therapist and client can explore. 'Using' silence implies something much more active than 'being' silent, and might mean that we have lost sight of the client as a person.

We need to continue to pay attention to how our clients experience silence throughout therapy. There are times when we are silent because we don't know what to say that would feel useful. At those times it is important to acknowledge that is why we are silent as the vignette below demonstrates.

Vicky had my account in her hand and sat down looking furious. 'You might have told me you were increasing my fees' she said, angrily. I asked her to explain what had happened. I had given her an account that charged her an extra £5 a session. This was clearly an error on my part and I said so. She said 'I know you think I don't pay you enough, but I can't afford any more'. I was processing a lot of feelings and thoughts: I was pleased that she had been angry with me in such a straightforward way. I was curious about the unconscious determinants of my mistake. I was wondering when to apologise for my error – I did not want to spike her anger, but at the same time I needed to apologise and in such a way that felt real to her. I was aware that she had taken an enormous risk in being so angry with me and would be dealing with the emotional consequences of that. Possibly at this moment she experienced me as a greedy therapist, who would take what little she had from her.

I suddenly became aware that I had been silent for a couple of minutes, and that she may well think that I was angry and had withdrawn from her; she had often described the distress she felt when her mother withdrew when depressed or angry. I said 'I'm not quite sure what to say to you right now, but I feel I need to say something. I've been silent because I was thinking about what you told me, but I want you to know I am still here with you and have not gone away'. Vicky immediately calmed down, and we began to talk about how frightened her anger had made her, and how furious she was with me for doing something that made her angry. Yet at the same time she was relieved that she had felt confident enough in our relationship to be angry. I apologised to her for the mistake in her account, and said that it was something that I would take away and think about.

Talking

If listening can be a challenge for a new therapist, talking can be even more of a challenge. Especially at the beginning of your career you may well find that you feel you have to talk to demonstrate that you have something to offer your client, perhaps an interpretation or a formulation of his difficulties. Since this is the time when you probably fear that you don't have much to offer, the temptation is to over-compensate by saying too much. You don't need to sit in stony silence, however; like most therapists I make 'hmms' and other kinds of noises that indicate I'm interested, I understand, etcetera – which helps my client to know that I am fully engaged with what he is saying.

Your job at the beginning of therapy is to communicate to your client that he is safe with you, that you are interested in what he says and that you want to understand. It is important to use ordinary language and not to create a pseudo-professionalism through the use of technical jargon, which only serves to underscore the power differential between you. Finding a common language that you and your client have developed together is an important part of the therapeutic alliance.

There are a number of basic counselling skills that facilitate responding to your client's material. While these are necessary throughout the work, they are particularly important in the first sessions (see Jacobs, 2004). These include reflecting responses, which help move your client's story along; exploratory responses, which attempt to draw from him something beyond what he has already said; and linking responses, which set the scene for interpretation by bringing together different elements in your client's story in an attempt to help him make sense of something he had not previously understood in that way.

Cozolino (2004) makes the distinction between therapist-centred and client–centred interactions. Therapist-centred interactions are those that are to do with meeting the therapist's needs. Trainee therapists are more prone to making therapist–centred interventions, in part because of the anxiety of trying to manage all the elements of a new skill. Other times they can be driven by the therapist's personal internal needs, for example to reduce her own anxiety or by voyeurism. Cozolino cites the example of a trainee therapist who 'interrogated' a 'client' in a role-play about the details of a road accident because of his need to control his own unbearable anxiety. The 'therapist' had had a similar accident in the recent past and had still not processed it. This left the 'client' feeling unheard and distressed and forced to acquiesce to the therapist's needs. Sometimes therapist-centred interactions are driven by the need to get information from the client, for example to assess risk with someone who is known to be suicidal.

By contrast client-centred interactions are those that facilitate your client in feeling heard and being able to express his feelings. Such interactions are characterised by 'coming alongside' him. It is quite a good discipline to check every now and then how often you make therapist-centred interventions in a session, and whether there are clients you do it with more than others. I have found that such an audit of my work can be quite revealing about my relationship with certain clients.

The last thing I want to think about in this section is to do with how we respond differently to clients according to their individual needs. Although each of us develops a recognisable and fairly consistent style as we mature as therapists, at the same time we need to adapt our response according to our clients' needs. However, there is no formula for doing so, and usually we are guided by trial and error as we work out what is needed at a given moment. Bollas (1987) distinguishes between maternal and paternal styles of relating to clients. A maternal style involves a more holding and receptive therapeutic stance; a paternal style involves a more active, interpretive stance. The extent to which you choose one stance over the other is partly a function of your own style and theoretical orientation. It is also a function of the client's needs at a particular juncture in therapy.

Vicky and Tom: building a therapeutic alliance

Vicky's task is to begin the process of building a relationship. She does not have to undertake a further assessment or make an initial assessment of risk, although she will be mindful of ongoing risk assessment. Vicky needs her basic therapy skills of being empathic, being authentic and listening to what her client is saying to her with an 'analytic ear'. She also needs to be sensitive to Tom's responses to her and to observe his behaviour in the consulting room, for example his body language and any hesitations that might indicate a difficulty in saying what is on his mind. At the same time she needs to be able to contain Tom's anxieties sufficiently for him to feel safe with her.

Tom is a good-looking young man of average height and weight, who is casually, but neatly dressed. He arrived late for his first session, and was disoriented by the realisation that he had a different time in his diary and thought he was early. At a loss to understand how the mistake had arisen, Tom was reluctant to attribute any responsibility for the confusion to Vicky. She decided against interpreting that he might be ambivalent about coming to therapy. Although potentially an accurate understanding of his lateness, she felt it was unlikely that he could use it so early, and may experience it as an attack. Instead, she first acknowledged his feelings of discomfort about being late, and possible anxiety that she might think badly of him.

Vicky asked Tom to tell her in his own words about what had brought him to therapy. She explained how much time they had and that this was an opportunity for Tom to decide if he wanted to take up the offer of therapy with her. She also explained that she would leave time later in the session for them to agree a fee and session times. Tom outlined the story much as he had told Dr Smith. However, as he told his story he had difficulty in making eye contact with Vicky and was soft-spoken, sometimes mumbling. She felt she needed to pay close attention to hear what he was saying. When she made a trial interpretation in which she suggested to him that he might both want to tell his story, but be sure she was listening to him, he thought her interpretation worth considering.

Later in the session Vicky took up his possible ambivalence about therapy when she commented on his previous therapeutic experiences. Noting that he had told the assessor that he hadn't found his previous experiences of therapy helpful, Vicky wondered aloud to him about whether he may also be concerned that she too would have nothing to offer him. When he reluctantly agreed that this was the case, Vicky added that it might have been difficult to come if he feared being disappointed again.

In the last part of the session Vicky negotiated a fee and time. Tom found this quite difficult; he was caught between wanting to demonstrate that he was able to afford the top end of the fee scale, while in reality he was struggling with money. Vicky decided to treat this as a symmetrical issue, and had an adult-to-adult discussion with him about what he could afford, since therapy would continue over a fairly long period of time. Negotiating session times was more straightforward. Vicky had been able to offer him the time that he had indicated he could attend during his assessment.

Vicky had a lot of work to do in this first session. By arriving late Tom had immediately created a situation that was difficult for them both. Vicky could not know what being late signified, what it meant to him or what reaction he expected from her. So she needed to be sensitive about how she managed it while still being mindful of the possible implications of the lateness. By keeping interpretation to a minimum Vicky tried to maintain symmetry in the relationship in order to establish aspects of the frame, such as time and fees, that needed to be negotiated in the first session. At the same time, appropriate interpretation indicated that things could be thought about together. The interpretations Vicky made were client focussed and were to do with the beginning of therapy; they addressed the kinds of concerns that are often present in the first sessions.

Managing shame

Therapy is an inherently shaming experience and, unless we help our clients with these feelings, they can undermine the therapeutic alliance. Shame can be heightened at the beginning of therapy because there is a problem in your client's life that he cannot resolve on his own. Starting therapy involves a client allowing a stranger access to the damaged and needy part of himself, which is something most people want to keep private. The admission that he needs help can result in a narcissistic injury, which is the source of shame feelings. People who pride themselves on being self-sufficient are particularly vulnerable to feeling shamed, seeing starting therapy as an admission of failure.

Shame can also be elicited because attachment needs are heightened at the beginning of therapy as your client seeks someone who is stronger than he, and able to care for him. This can result in quite powerful longings for and fantasies about being cared for, which can be sexualised. Adults, who are used to caring for themselves, often hate having such powerful longings, and feel that there is something wrong with them. In addition the asymmetry, or power differential, in therapy lends itself to feelings of shame. Although power is difficult to manage in all therapeutic models, it is difficult to manage in psychodynamic work because of the regressive pull inherent in this model.

One of the reasons it is important to be non-judgemental in the way you explore issues with your client is that being judged elicits shame. While we cannot anticipate every trigger for shame, there are some words or phrases that are particularly shame-inducing and we must seek to avoid them, particularly 'should' and 'ought'. The use of humour can also be risky, since there is usually an implied aggression and/or denigration in the things we find funny. While laughing with your client at something outside of the two of you is generally safer, laughing at your client, no matter how well-intentioned and affectionate, is a highly risky endeavour and likely to elicit shame.

There are a number of ways to help clients with shame. The most important is to always remember that your client may well experience asking for help as shameful. If you keep this in mind, you will find it easier to think of ways to phrase interactions that are potentially shame-inducing in such a way as to minimise shame. It is also helpful to review what you are going to say before you say it and think how you would feel if your therapist said it to you. Some clients are more shame-prone, and these are the clients with whom empathic attunement can be particularly helpful. You might say something like 'I sense that you might really hate having to ask for help with this' or 'I'm aware that you're a very private person, so letting me see the parts of you that you normally keep hidden might be very hard.' These interventions indicate to the client that you are able to empathise with his difficulties and may help him in talking more openly about feelings of shame.

EDUCATING YOUR CLIENT TO THE PROCESS

When staring work with a new client, especially one who has never had psychodynamic therapy before, it is important to remember that things we take for granted as part of establishing a therapeutic frame and attitude are likely to feel very odd to him. He may experience your formality and neutrality as unfriendliness, or your unwillingness to answer personal questions or engage in social conversation as a rejection. He may be frustrated by the fact that you don't engage in problem-solving. Paradoxically, those with experience of therapy in other models can find adapting to the psychodynamic approach more difficult than people who are new to therapy. They can find it difficult to adjust to the exploratory nature of the work and that we do not set homework.

Some practitioners make few concessions to their client's unfamiliarity with the way in which the work is conducted. I feel this can tilt the interaction towards an early negative transference before the alliance is strong enough to sustain it. Giving your client a period of time when he can gradually acclimatise to the way you work can facilitate the therapeutic alliance. 'Socialisation to the model' is a CBT term which refers to explicit teaching about the model of therapy. While explicit teaching about the model would not be congruent with the psychodynamic approach, a number of clients benefit from the opportunity to ease their way in to a relationship that so markedly differs from all others in their experience.

There has not been much written about how to educate clients regarding what to expect and do in the client role. Therapists generally find different ways that concord with their personality and background. Like many therapists I find using metaphors helpful. A common metaphor when starting therapy is that of a journey. Many clients begin dynamic therapy believing that there is a set way of doing therapy and that, as practitioners, we will know exactly what is about to unfold. I explain that I am like a guide on a journey who has successfully undertaken similar journeys before and can recognise the landmarks, but the map I am using doesn't identify the precise journey that we will take. Like other stories, a metaphor can often make emotional sense of something that is difficult to explain in other ways.

With regard to explaining the frame, I usually do this in a fairly straightforward manner, making clear that the therapeutic process is enhanced by the sessions being regular – coming at the same time each week. I also explain that one of the ways that we can understand some of the difficulties he has identified is through what happens in the relationship between us. That we all have templates of relationships, which become manifest in the ways we relate to people, including therapists. One of the most difficult things to explain is how important the therapeutic relationship can become, and after much trial and error I now leave it to emerge as therapy progresses.

Often clients need educating about the potential therapeutic significance of discussing fees or breaks. In psychodynamic therapy such discussion should constitute part of the session because it is intrinsic to therapeutic work. I therefore give such information during the session, and not at the end. However, sometimes simply because he is unaware of the potential significance of changes in the frame, a new client will regard informing me about a forthcoming cancelled session, a holiday, or a request to change a session as something separate from the work of therapy. Consequently, the issue is raised after the session has ended. Unless he is cancelling the next session, I say something like 'You might not think this makes sense at the moment, but there is often quite a lot to think about when a session has to be cancelled. It can have a meaning that is not immediately obvious, but which becomes more so when there is the time to discuss it together. Can you let me know the dates next time we meet, and then we will have an opportunity to do that thinking.' This kind of approach incorporates symmetry into educating your client about a process which is inherently asymmetrical.

Whatever your own approach to easing your clients into psychodynamic working, there is one area in which I am clear that we should always answer his query rather than immediately seeking to elicit an understanding about the nature of the question. This is when clients ask about our qualifications. Of course such a question has transference implications, requiring elaboration and interpretation in due course. But it is first and foremost an entirely reasonable adult question about who your client is entrusting himself to and should be responded to as such. Asking about your qualifications and experience can be an indication of a functioning adult self. To impose asymmetry on the question by early interpretation unnecessarily reinforces the power imbalance.

It is more difficult to feel confident in answering this question when you are training however, since you will have less experience to report, and might be fearful of a reversal in the power balance if your client feels undermined by your trainee status. However, in my view, the client is still entitled to know, and his response will be grist to the therapeutic mill. It is important to remember that you will already have experience of therapeutic work through your own therapy and will have done significant preparatory work before seeing any clients. You could say 'I am currently at an advanced level in my training. I will be talking about our sessions in supervision, which means that there will be two of us thinking about the work we are doing.' I have found that the notion of a parental couple (therapist and supervisor) can be quite containing for clients who are seen by a trainee.

Informed consent

Informed consent implies that your client has sufficient relevant information about psychodynamic therapy to understand what he is agreeing to in starting therapy. It means that he understands how psychodynamic therapy works and the potential risks and benefits associated with it. It also means that he has been given sufficient information about other therapeutic models that he has made an informed choice to undertake psychodynamic therapy. Informed consent is one of those areas of practice that sits in the area between litigation and good practice. The increasing requirement that we gain informed consent from clients in all forms of therapy is largely driven by the need to protect ourselves in an increasingly litigious culture. This is particularly the case in the USA, where the level of litigation against therapists led Hedges (2000) to produce template documents for clients to sign which indicates an agreement to proceed with psychodynamic treatment.

Although the move to informed consent is largely driven by defensive practice, there are nevertheless good ethical reasons for helping our clients to understand the implications of what they are entering into. Beginning psychodynamic therapy can be quite traumatic; not uncommonly clients feel worse before they feel better, which can be distressing for them and the people around them. Sometimes therapy can uncover a previously disguised underlying depression, which if serious may necessitate time off work. Family members, friends or colleagues may need to provide greater levels of support than they usually do. At the same time it is not uncommon for major relationships in clients' lives to change as a result of therapy. Changes in relationships can be positive, but there are also losses involved. Relationships with parents may worsen for a period of time, and sometimes other important relationships will deteriorate; this can include marital/partnership breakdown where the relationship has contributed to or maintained a client's distress.

There is a difficulty in the whole notion of informed consent for psychological therapies, and in particular for psychodynamic therapy. How informed can consent be until a client has had experience of therapy? I think this applies to CBT as well as psychodynamic approaches, despite the fact that CBT overtly works with conscious processes. Psychodynamic therapy is not like surgery where there are limited outcome options and a fairly predictable recovery cycle. We do not know what we are going to find as we get to know a client and work with the unconscious manifestations of his distress. Even if we explain this to him it is unlikely to mean very much at the beginning of therapy. I feel that there is a real danger that the formal obtaining of informed consent may actually have a negative effect on therapy if it inhibits ongoing negotiation between client and therapist about what they are doing in therapy.

There is also the question of timing regarding consent. Clinical governance requires that clients in the public health system are given so much information in the first session that this can negatively impact on the amount of time they have to talk about why they have come. My own view is that my first task is to facilitate the development of the therapeutic relationship. If a client is in distress he is unlikely to want to hear about the advantages and disadvantages of a particular approach; he wants his distress to be heard and taken seriously, and to be reassured that I am more concerned with his needs than my own. Having said that, should a client ask about the nature, risks and benefits of therapy or other approaches in the first session, this should be discussed.

Elsewhere I have advocated that consent should be obtained following a period of assessment (Howard, 2006); this gives your client the opportunity to experience what psychodynamic therapy involves. Obtaining consent in this way occurs after several sessions and requires you to think about what you consider as an 'assessment period'. Since psychodynamic practitioners hold that assessment is an ongoing process throughout therapy and that therapy begins in the first session, the assessment phase in psychodynamic work is generally much less clear-cut than it is in other therapeutic modalities. In addition there is an inevitable tension between giving your client sufficient information to make an informed choice, while at the same not doing anything that will disrupt the nascent therapeutic relationship between you.

When discussing the risks associated with psychotherapy, I again find it helpful to use metaphor. These metaphors tend to be based in physical medicine, since it often makes more sense to clients, despite the problems inherent in using the language of physical medicine, which is often more definitive than we can be in psychological therapy. One metaphor concerns the need to re-set a bone which can't properly weight-bear, which requires a splint for a period of time while it is mending, after which it will hopefully work properly. I do also give a 'health warning' around relationships, that there may be unpredictable changes as therapy progresses. Clients have often said to me later that they have appreciated the warning when relationships changed, particularly when they became more difficult.

Lastly, it is important to be realistic in what you tell your client he can expect to achieve in therapy. While hope is an important non-specific curative factor, we cannot make absolute promises about therapeutic outcome. You will only begin to understand the real nature of the task ahead of you once you have been working with him for a while. The course of therapy is inherently unpredictable and its outcome does not necessarily reflect the severity of your client's difficulties. Sometimes a person with apparently less severe difficulties may find the work of change more difficult than someone who has more severe problems, but is prepared to take greater risks in the service of getting better. If a new client asks me if he will be better at the end of therapy, I generally give a variation on the following reply: 'I can understand that you would like a precise answer to this question, but I'm afraid that I can't give you one. As yet I can't know what difficulties we will face as we work together, and I am only just beginning to find out about you and the kind of help you need. What I can tell you is that I have successfully undertaken similar journeys before; that I have confidence in this approach and that your own willingness to embark on it is very important.'

FURTHER READING

Jacobs, M. (2004) *Psychodynamic Counselling in Action* (3rd edition). London: SAGE.

6

WORKING WITH UNCONSCIOUS COMMUNICATION

In the previous two chapters I have looked at how we create the conditions that allow your client to bring his unconscious preoccupations into the consulting room through the establishment of the frame and the therapeutic alliance.

HOW THE UNCONSCIOUS COMMUNICATES

Freud, in his Structural Model, divided the mind horizontally into three systems – the conscious, the preconscious and the unconscious. Ideas that are deeply unconscious are usually inaccessible, while those in the preconscious are more easy to access. The process of therapy is designed to help clients gain access to previously unconscious material that has been repressed once it becomes part of the preconscious. Unconscious processes are dominated by primary process thinking, so there is no 'as if'. It is important to remember this when working with clients whose functioning is dominated by their inner world. Such clients can hear 'I wonder whether you might fear I'm angry with you' as 'I'm angry with you.'

More recently there has been an increasing interest in vertical divisions of the mind. Vertical divisions lead to dissociative states; a client in one state is unable to feel, or perhaps even know, about how he experiences other states. These kinds of dissociative states can be experienced by people who have suffered significant childhood trauma. The task for therapists working with these clients is not so much to make unconscious material conscious, but to heal the vertical splits so that the client's conscious experience is more continuous. Mollon states 'to understand the dynamics of the mind we need both a concept of repression ... and also that of dissociation in order to take account of the interplay between inner psychodynamic conflict and trauma resulting from external impingement' (2000: 66).

Our work as practitioners often involves decoding our clients' unconscious to help them make sense of behaviour or feelings that are otherwise beyond their comprehension. As there is no direct access to the contents of the dynamic unconscious, we have to infer it through indirect means such as how people behave, the things they say, or the dreams they have. This is why we are trained to observe the minutiae of interactions and non-verbal behaviour, and how to understand the latent meaning behind our clients' stories and dreams.

The lack of access to the dynamic unconscious may be because of repression. Freud argued that the function of repression is to keep beliefs, wishes and phantasies that are unacceptable unconscious or disguised because they are a threat to our conscious equilibrium. The concept of repression remains significant as a mechanism for protecting the conscious mind from unpalatable knowledge about oneself or others. However, there is an inherent tendency for repressed wishes to return to consciousness.

Claudia was in her mid twenties when, on an unexpected visit to Edinburgh, she saw her recently-married best friend's husband with another woman in a hotel. Not only was she distressed by what she saw, but she was afraid that somehow she would unintentionally tell her friend. She knew that sometimes she said things she later regretted. Many years later Claudia suddenly remembered the incident, and realised that she had not thought about it since it had happened.

In this example Claudia was experiencing a conflict that resulted in unbearable anxiety. On the one hand she wanted to tell her friend, since she hated to think that she did not know her husband was betraying her. At the same time she did not want to cause her friend distress and was afraid that telling her could irrevocably damage their relationship. By repressing the memory she solved the problem. What she did not 'know' she could not tell.

Channels of communication

Kernberg (2004) proposes that there are three channels through which we listen to our clients:

- Channel one is the client's verbal communication – the manifest and latent content of what he says, the sequence of free associations, and the things those associations refer to. It also includes the affective aspects of what he says.
- Channel two is the non-verbal parts of the communication – how his behaviour conveys affect or motive; how he structures his language and talks.
- Channel three is the countertransference.

Kernberg makes two important observations. Firstly, that that the three channels operate with differing levels of intensity at different times with the same client. Secondly, that the more severe the client's pathology, the more he will communicate non-verbally, including through the countertransference, rather than verbally.

For example, your client may reveal his true, but unconscious, wishes or conflicts through jokes, or slips of the tongue. Mollon notes 'the unconscious speaks – often embarrassingly, as if in humiliating mockery of our illusions of conscious awareness and control over our desires and intentions' (2000: 4). Mollon is pointing to one of the difficulties in working with the unconscious aspects of our clients' communications – it can be humiliating to have something that you are unaware of pointed out to you. One reason that you need to frame your interpretations of unconscious material carefully is that it can be very shaming for clients if a therapist sees things he has not yet become aware of. It is also good practice to interpret your understanding of your client's unconscious only as it reaches near-consciousness. If something is too deeply unconscious your client is unlikely to be able to make use of what you are saying because he does not feel the interpretation 'belongs' to him.

Dreams

Dreams are still seen as important in indicating our unconscious preoccupations. Sometimes clients report a series of linked dreams across their therapy; one client's dreams were a variation on the theme of us being in my house together. Her dream evolved over time, so that in her early dreams I was on the doorstep of the house; as therapy progressed I was first allowed into the 'public' rooms, like the sitting room. Later she talked of me being in her bedroom, the most private room in the house. Her dreams reflected the changes in both her internal world and her relationship to me. They became a useful vehicle for us to think about the changing relationship between us as well as their significance for the progress she was making.

Like all other activities in therapy, the relating of dreams can be used defensively. For example a new client might spend most of each session describing his dreams in detail, while avoiding talking about the distress and anxiety that originally brought him into treatment. If this happens, it is important to gently take up with him the things that are not being talked about, since if you don't do so your client might fear that you also do not wish to face them. I might say 'I've been thinking that we have talked a lot about dreams, and that they have been very helpful in understanding certain difficulties that you have. However, I'm aware that when we talk about one thing inevitably something else doesn't get talked about. I wonder whether there are things that we need to look at together that are getting squeezed out as we concentrate on your dreams.'

SKILLS IN WORKING WITH THE UNCONSCIOUS

The way that you work with your client's unconscious material is a function of a number of factors that will come together in a unique pattern. They are your own individual idiom; the defences your client uses; the stage of therapy the client is at; his and your level of engagement at any one time.

Helping your client to free associate

Free association is a way of gaining access to the unconscious through talking about whatever comes to mind, trying not to censor it. Known as 'the fundamental rule', free association is a central part of psychodynamic technique. Your task is to create the conditions in which your client can free associate and thus gain access to thoughts and feelings currently outside his conscious awareness. The tools that assist you are the frame, the analytic space, and your analytic attitude as you respond to what your client says. Free association is actually quite difficult, and I regard it as an achievement rather than a given. Being able to free associate is a sign that, at that moment, your client's resistance to the therapeutic process has decreased. It is also a sign of trust, since quite often what comes to mind is difficult or embarrassing to speak about.

There is no fixed method for facilitating free association. Some therapists overtly suggest that clients say whatever comes to mind, but others only do so if necessary. If you give instructions at the outset it is helpful to say something like 'Try and say whatever comes into your mind, even if it doesn't seem particularly relevant or is perhaps difficult to say.' My own stance is not to say anything initially, since most clients quite naturally say what is on their minds. By responding to what they say in an analytic way, we reinforce the process of exploring their own thoughts. However, at any stage in therapy, clients can struggle and at such times I may say 'I wonder if you are able to capture what's going through your mind at the moment?' Sometimes a client begins the session by saying 'It's your turn today, I've got nothing to say.' I usually reply 'Although it might get us started, I'm not sure how helpful it would be, since it might divert us away from discovering what's important for you at the moment.'

Sometimes clients need help to realise that everything is grist to the psychodynamic mill, however fleeting or apparently irrelevant the thought.

Mandy repeatedly said that she was not thinking about anything. She discarded as irrelevant any thought or feeling unless it specifically linked with the 'problem' she came into therapy for. One day she was very quiet; she had nothing to talk about. After some prompting, she eventually said that she was wondering if the pot plants outside my consulting room had been watered recently. She was initially resistant to exploring this thought further, saying it was irrelevant to why she was coming to see me. I said 'Sometimes thoughts or feelings that don't seem to have an immediate relevance can still be worth exploring. At the very least if you are thinking about the pot plants it prevents you from thinking about anything else. So I wonder if we could see where it takes us.'

Although initially reluctant, Mandy gradually made a rich series of associations concerning her anxiety about whether I could care for things that could not care for themselves. This included her. When we discussed her reluctance to tell me what she was thinking she said that she only wanted to tell me about things she could identify as a problem. She hated me seeing things that she had not yet worked out for herself. This led us to examining how much she hated the power differential between us; she did not want to 'give' me anything that would make me even more powerful.

Clients' relationship to the process of free association can be influenced by the material under discussion, who you are in the transference at that moment, or the stage of therapy they are in. For example a client may suddenly be unable to free associate if he is upset by something he cannot speak about, or he might report that his mind has gone blank just as he had begun to explore an area of difficulty. Like any other activity in psychotherapy it can also be used defensively. For example, a client demanded of herself absolute obedience to the fundamental rule of free association, and would not allow herself any thought in her session without expressing it. It was only after some time that she came to question this, and consequently realised that she experienced her therapist as an intrusive father from whom she could keep nothing private. Paradoxically, by saying everything in her mind, she kept him out, because it prevented true free association which would have allowed her therapist access to her inner world.

Listening with an 'analytic ear'

Freud's adjunct for the therapist to 'surrender himself to his own unconscious mental activity, in a state of evenly suspended attention' (1923: 239) is still relevant today. It requires being open to, and moving freely back and forth between, your client's communication and your own state of mind. To do this you need to be able to tolerate the uncertainty of not knowing quite what is going on in the session, or what your client means at any one moment. You therefore have to be able to resist the need to be certain and provide answers, which can be difficult, especially if your client is very upset or you are feeling inadequate and want to show you have something to offer. Paradoxically, the more we try to think in a session, or the more we try to remember what went on in the last session, the more difficult it is to 'catch the drift of the patient's unconscious' (Freud 1923: 239). Bion put it succinctly when he said 'In order to exercise his intuition, the psychotherapist has to let go of memory, desire and understanding' (1970: 315). While he didn't literally mean forgetting everything we know about a client (which would be impossible), Bion also reminds us that starting a session with a conscious agenda interferes with the capacity to hear what our client is trying to tell us.

While we strive to listen freely and objectively, there is an inherent paradox: in order to do so we need to acknowledge that our own preoccupations shape what we attend to. We inevitably listen within a theoretical frame which may distort or restrict what we hear. Furthermore, our own unconscious will influence how and what we listen to. Kernberg (2004) stresses that those practitioners who acknowledge these limits to their capacity to listen freely and objectively are less likely to impose their theoretical frame on their clients. However, those practitioners who believe that their listening is not affected by their theory base are more likely to impose their theoretical frame on their clients.

It is safe to assume that almost everything your client says and does between greeting you at the door and leaving the premises is meaningful. You may not immediately understand in what way something is significant. It may become apparent further into the session or even in a later session. It is important to bear in mind that your client has a very short time with you in his week. Since most clients see their therapist once a week this usually involves an hour or less, so how he chooses to use the time is an indicator of what is most important to him at that moment. Paradoxically, the most important thing for him might be to keep you at a safe distance, so he may appear to 'waste' the session by not doing anything very much in it. However, just surviving being with you may be an achievement. The most important issue may not be immediately apparent in what he discusses. The latent communication may not be in the story, but in how he uses or behaves in the session. The following vignette illustrates this.

A month into therapy Vicky noticed that, as she opened the door to Tom, he was lent against the outside wall in a languid and rather insouciant fashion. She felt Tom was being seductive and she was uncomfortable. Her fear that she was taking his behaviour personally prevented her from thinking about it further and she did not include her observation in her session notes. However, after a few weeks, Kate noted that there seemed to be an element of contempt in some of what Tom said to Vicky. Vicky suddenly made the connection with her discomfort when she answered the door; she had felt contempt in the way that Tom looked at her. She then told Kate about her experience at the beginning of the sessions and together they thought about how Tom conveyed his contempt in a sexualised manner and what this might signify about his internal object relationships.

In listening to your client's communication you need to balance two opposite requirements. Firstly, you need to ensure that you are sufficiently separate from him that you don't over-identify with him. Secondly, you need to remain sufficiently identified with him that you are empathic. If you over-identify with him you may allow yourself not to take up any inconsistencies in what he says; or you may assume that you both have a shared understanding of the meaning of what he has said. But if you are too separate from him you can become insensitive to him, or undermine him.

Listening to both the manifest and latent content of your client's story or dream involves a number of separate tasks. The first task is to engage sensitively with the actual story and help him tell it through the use of basic counselling skills such as reflecting, using prompts or summarising. In doing this you are also facilitating your client in hearing himself, which may help him begin to make his own links. Constructing an understanding of latent material is only meaningful to the client if he has been part of it. If you feel pressured to comment on the latent content too soon he may well (and rightly) feel you have not really heard him. We can all be seduced into demonstrating how clever we are by pronouncing on what a client is really thinking or saying. But we need to resist the temptation, because to do so gives the message that this is not a collaborative endeavour. It can increase resistance and can ultimately lead to overt and/or unconscious hostility disguised as passivity or compliance.

You also need to be aware of how he tells his story including any silences, gaps and inconsistencies, as well as his body language. You may then begin the process of trying to understand the latent or 'unconscious' story. At this juncture you need to ask yourself questions such as 'Does this story link with other material in this or a previous session?'; 'How does this story fit with everything else I know about my client?'; 'What impact is this story having on me – what am I feeling and thinking at the moment?'. The story's transference implications may seem obvious, or you may need to consciously ask yourself to consider them, while also monitoring your countertransference.

Listening to our clients is not a passive activity – it is both active and hard work. Being able to listen with an analytic ear is an advanced skill that develops over time. Lemma cautions us to take nothing for granted when listening in this way: 'It is about a kind of listening that is attuned to the human tendency towards self-deceit and the resistances that are operating to shield the patient from painful affect' (2003: 176). Similarly, you cannot expect to understand everything that is going on in a session during that session. It is inevitable that, as you get drawn into your client's world, you will miss things, and monitoring your own responses in parallel is very difficult. The practice of writing process notes during training (a detailed description of what is said and felt during the session) often helps one to realise what has been missed. This includes possible meanings or resistances that were missed in the session, or links that were not previously obvious. I no longer routinely write process notes, but find it useful to do so when I see a new client, when I am struggling with my countertransference, or following a major event in therapy, such as client or therapist acting out. Doing so will often reveal aspects of the transference and countertransference that I had been unaware of and also helps me listen in a different way the next time I see my client.

Interpreting latent content

In interpreting the latent content in our client's behaviour or stories we are helping him to make links between an event, feeling, thought, wish or phantasy that he is not consciously aware of, and something in his conscious mind that he is aware of. In this section I will be mainly focussing on extra-transference interpretations – these interpretations are aimed at helping your client make sense of something that is not directly linked to his relationship to you.

Decoding the latent content in your clients' stories and dreams requires the skills of being able to symbolise and to understand metaphor. We all use metaphor much of the time – indeed, when people can't symbolise or understand metaphor we describe them as being concrete in their thinking. Concrete thinking is associated with autistic disorders and psychotic experience. Some metaphors seem to have a fairly consistent meaning, for example when a client talks or dreams about a house, it can often be a reference to himself; similarly a roof or an attic can symbolise a person's mind. Descriptions of being underground or under the sea can indicate a concern about the unconscious mind. However, it is a mistake to be too deterministic about what things symbolise. A reference to a house may imply concern about the self, but it may not. Being too deterministic can interfere with the client reaching an understanding of what that particular metaphor means for him at that moment.

The first three months of Tom's therapy were difficult for him, and he continued to manifest his ambivalence through sporadic lateness. He often dismissed Vicky's interventions as predictable and inferred she had nothing to give him. Vicky was concerned that he may drop out of therapy, and was mindful that he had not valued his previous therapy.

Shortly after the first break Tom arrived at his session on time, but clearly agitated. He explained that he was thinking of taking up a new hobby. A television programme about pot-holing had caught his interest, so he had gone on the internet to find out more. He was excited by the physical challenge, but also the idea of underground exploration and going where few other people venture. As he spoke he became increasingly animated. Vicky began to wonder if he was about to quit therapy in favour of his new interest. 'There's just one thing' he said. 'When you go down into a cave you're on the end of a rope. I don't know whether I'd feel ok about someone else holding the rope. They might drop me.'

As Vicky listened she began to hypothesise that Tom was talking about his anxieties about therapy. Was he telling her that he now wanted to explore what was underground – in his unconscious – but that he was frightened that she would not be able to hold him safely, that she might drop him? She was aware that to offer this hypothesis too soon would probably shut off further exploration, so she pursued further discussion of the manifest content of Tom's story – what it might mean for him to take up this new interest. When he repeated his concerns about being dropped Vicky said, 'I wonder if you're caught between your excitement at the idea of going underground, and your fear of being dropped. Are you worried your fear might prevent you from trying?' He agreed, but added that he really wanted to do so. Vicky continued 'It's clearly a dilemma for you, and I wonder if it's made all the more difficult because it might echo another situation in which you're not sure if underground exploration is safe – that is, here in therapy?'

In this extract Vicky first takes up the conflict in the manifest aspect of Tom's story – that he wants to explore and take up the challenge of his new interest, but his fear that he will be dropped as he descends into a cave may prevent him from attempting it at all. Only once she is satisfied that he feels heard about the manifest story does she take up its latent aspects. She has taken a gradual approach to the unconscious communication that she has hypothesised, and she offers it tentatively with the implicit acknowledgement that she may not be correct. She also makes an explicit link between the manifest and latent aspects of the story to help Tom make the connection, so that he does not feel her interpretation has come out of the blue.

There is no formula that tells you the right moment to offer a hypothesis about the latent content in a client's story. It will vary with each client and at different stages in the same client's therapy. Vicky's use of a graded approach is appropriate for new clients who are still learning about therapy; with someone who is going through a period of resistance to therapy; when the client is very distressed or caught up in a story; when you are talking about a new area with a client you have known for a while; or you think that your interpretation of the latent content might be difficult to hear.

However, at other times it is appropriate to interpret the latent content much sooner and more directly, but you need to be confident that you and your client are working well together to do so. For a moment let's imagine that Tom has come to understand that stories and dreams are communications from his unconscious mind and is able to hear a direct interpretation. In this case Vicky might have said 'I wonder if you are frightened that if you allow me to hold you while you explore the underground areas of your mind, I will drop you.' Here Vicky is not making explicit the link between manifest and latent content because she has confidence that her client can see the link. She also takes it up much more directly in relation to herself, rather than generally about therapy as she did in the vignette, because her client is more able to think about the relationship between them.

When a client brings a dream to therapy we need to assume it is significant and that an important communication is being attempted through telling it. Most dreams are forgotten, so the fact that a dream has been remembered and then brought to the session is of itself meaningful. Like other communications we need to listen not only to the content, but also to how he relates it, particularly if he has difficulties in doing so. Paradoxically, once clients understand that their dreams have meaning, telling them can become more difficult. Since dreams are often the vehicle through which wishes or phantasies are expressed, clients can feel significant embarrassment in relating their content, particularly if the material is sexual or involves evidence of longing for their therapist.

Once the story of the dream has been told you have a number of options. You might decide to ask the client to tell you what he makes of the dream, you might see what associations he makes to it, or you might make an initial observation yourself. Understanding dreams is no different than working with any other material in a session; both the manifest and latent content need to be addressed. Some practitioners argue that everything else that the client says or does in the session is an association to the dream because the dream is unconsciously preoccupying him throughout the session and he works on it throughout.

Positive and negative interpretations

One of the strengths of the dynamic position is that we are prepared to thoroughly engage with the negative aspects of our clients' inner worlds and experience and help them face this. However, I think we can focus on the negatives in our clients' communications at the expense of acknowledging the positives. Symington (2008) argues that, in over-interpreting the negative in our client's communication (for example his destructiveness), there is a risk that we reinforce the negative aspect of him and a pessimistic outlook. By contrast he argues that making a positive interpretation (for example that the client is becoming more constructive) can help access the positive, or generous part of him, which reinforces a more benign outlook. Clearly there needs to be a balance between the two, but I agree with Symington that we need, as a profession, to reflect on whether the over-use of negative interpretation might inadvertently lengthen therapy by reinforcing a pessimistic outlook. I think we also need to consider why we sometimes choose a negative interpretation over a positive one, and whether we sometimes do it to punish our client, or assert power over him.

The limitations of insight

There is a distinction between having an intellectual understanding of one's difficulties or inner world and emotional understanding. Intellectual insight involves being able to see the links, but the understanding is at a cognitive or thinking level. Emotional insight, on the other hand, occurs when your client becomes aware of a fact or link which is accompanied by an emotional response. Something shifts inside and your client's relationship to his inner world changes. Psychodynamic practitioners hold that therapeutic change only takes place when emotional insight is linked to cognitive awareness. This is one of the reasons why we need to work at the client's pace, so that we don't offer him intellectual insight before he is ready to use emotional understanding. Indeed, intellectual insight on its own can actually be used defensively, to protect clients from emotional understanding, and thus slow the pace of change.

Lorraine had been in various therapies for many years for help with Obsessive Compulsive Disorder. Although insightful about why she had the difficulty, what precipitated acute episodes, and how this impacted on her relationships with others, nothing changed inside her. In desperation she 'watched' herself undertaking rituals, 'knowing' why, but unable to stop herself.

However, sometimes intellectual insight in the absence of emotional insight can be useful, for example if it provides a 'scaffolding' for a client who is very disturbed or distressed. Occasionally, helping a client have an intellectual awareness of what is happening can facilitate the process of therapy when he is finding it difficult to tolerate or make sense of how he is feeling. This may seem to go against much of what we often do – we more usually try to help people access their feelings and discourage too much intellectual understanding. However, it is as important to help those people who feel too much to think as it is to help those who think too much to feel.

Working with vertical splits

Clients who experience significant vertical splits are those for whom there is a discontinuity in their experience. This means that they might be in touch with powerful feelings in one session or at one point in the session, and then cut off from them. Mostly such clients remember that they had the experience as a fact, but are no longer able to be in touch with the part of the self that experienced it, so it does not feel as though it belongs to them. As noted earlier, this experience is particularly associated with people who have had a significant level of trauma in their early lives.

After about six months of therapy Vicky had to change or cancel some of Tom's sessions at short notice because her mother was admitted to hospital. Tom became disoriented by the sudden lack of continuity in his sessions, and for the first time began to talk about times when he was little and his mother left home, sometimes for two or three days, following a row with his father. Each time he was convinced his mother would not return and his father made no attempt to reassure him. Eventually Tom distanced himself from his feelings. He described watching himself beg his mother not to go, as though he was an observer rather than a participant in the unfolding drama.

During some sessions he was very distressed. During others he could just about remember the events of his mother's leaving, but was completely out of touch with any feelings about it. Vicky became quite frustrated, since when she made links about his distress he would sometimes be quite dismissive, as though what she said had nothing to do with him. In supervision she gradually came to realise that Tom had needed to separate himself from the trauma of his mother's departures because it was overwhelmingly painful. This had created a vertical split in which his traumatised self was cut off from the part of him that continued to exist as though nothing had happened.

Schore (2003) has made a number of recommendations as to how to work with clients to heal these splits. Vicky needs to bear the strength of Tom's feelings, both about past events and in the transference. She also needs to focus on being attuned to his emotional states and being able to track those states and to help him identify and regulate strong emotions through being empathic. She needs to be consistent with him and continue herself to reflect on what is happening between them. Lastly she needs to help him to move beyond the experiencing of strong feelings into being able to reflect on them and on himself experiencing them.

RESISTANCE

One of the most frustrating things for you and your client is when, despite an expressed wish for change, he seems to undermine the help he seeks. This might be quite overt, for example by regularly arriving late for his session, so that he never gets the opportunity to fully engage. Or it might be much more subtle, such as when a client agrees with everything his therapist says so that his hostility is hidden and cannot be explored. The more overt forms of resistance are 'in the room' and offer more of an opportunity to be worked with. However, the hidden forms usually only become apparent because the client is not changing, sometimes despite the fact that therapy appears to be going well. Either way resistance provides a potentially rich source of information about your client that can be used therapeutically to help understand him better.

While there is a close link between resistance and defence, many writers have emphasised that these are not the same thing. While defences are a part of the client's psychological structure, resistance is his way of protecting himself from the threats to his psychological equilibrium that therapy represents. As Greenson (1967) notes, not only does this resistance oppose the therapist but it also opposes the client's own wish to change, thus maintaining the status quo. Very often we assume that resistance is the consequence of conflict within the client between the part of him that seeks change and the part that resists it, perhaps out of fear of the consequences of change. Experiencing conflict assumes that there are mental structures in place that can be in conflict with one another. However, an apparent resistance might in fact represent a developmental deficit; in other words, the client does not have the psychological structure in place to resist with. As Lemma (2003) reminds us, it's not that the client 'won't' – he 'can't'.

We ourselves can contribute to resistance in our clients at any stage of therapy, particularly through faulty technique. Some clients find reference to the infantile parts of themselves shame-inducing, and this needs to be handled sensitively in order to decrease resistance. Identifying something as resistance when it is not can increase resistance, for example if we wrongly interpret his disagreement with something we have said as resistance. In extreme instances this can lead to a therapeutic impasse. It is important to underscore that disagreement is not necessarily the outward manifestation of resistance. It might be a sign of trust that your client feels able to disagree with you, or an indication of a growing maturity that he can think for himself about the value of what you have said. We have to be able to manage the injury to our own narcissism when a client disagrees – we may just be wrong! On the other hand it is important to also remember that, when trying to help a client recognise resistance, he will use both justification and rationalisation to ward off any attempt to explore what he is doing.

Sandler and his colleagues (Sandler et al., 1973) point out that there is an infinite range of forms that resistance can take, and that trying to list them all is a meaningless task. However, I think it is helpful to look at some of the most common forms.

Resistance at the start of therapy

Although resistance can arise at any time, it is often most evident at the beginning of therapy. However, it is important not to automatically assume that uncertainty at the beginning of therapy is solely due to resistance. There can be other reasons, which are to do with not knowing how to use a psychodynamic approach. For example, as they begin therapy, many clients do not have a concept in their minds of what a mutual therapeutic relationship looks like, and so don't know what interactions are possible or permitted. It can be difficult to untangle a lack of awareness from resistance, and my inclination is to keep an open mind while at the same time educating my client to the process. For example, there may need to be some direct education about the kinds of interactions that are possible in psychodynamic work.

At other times clients are ambivalent and their resistance can be manifest in the first contact, for example through being unable to agree a time for an initial meeting. Tom demonstrated his resistance by getting the time wrong for his initial session with Vicky. Resistance can also be manifest through inviting you into a more social relationship by asking personal questions or making comments about where you work.

Ruby, a new client, worked in an allied field. As she entered my waiting room she looked around then commented: 'This is a nice set-up you have for yourself here. I've always wanted somewhere like this to work from.' Her comment had a number of effects on me. Firstly, I felt rather intruded into, as though she had stamped around in the analytic space I was about to invite her into. Secondly, I thought that she might find it particularly difficult to be a client and engage in an asymmetrical relationship. This was later proved correct and she had significant difficulties in coping with being vulnerable in my presence. Her anxiety about, and resistance to, being vulnerable were manifest immediately by beginning with a comment that reminded us both that she could be a colleague. Once in the consulting room I said 'It might be quite difficult coming here as a client when you and I could so easily have been colleagues.' By saying this I was opening up a space in which she was being invited to reflect.

Asking personal questions can indicate resistance since it is a way of attempting to balance the relationship through challenging the frame. Many people find it hard that, as their therapist, I know so much more about them than they do me. With more directly personal questions, like 'Do you have children?' I respond by saying something like 'I wonder what it would signify to you if I told you whether or not I have children?'. If the client asks again I might say 'It might be really hard that I am getting to know so much about you, when you know so little about me.'

Advice-seeking is another area that can indicate resistance, though it is important to also remember that your client may ask for advice out of ignorance of how psychodynamic practice functions. However, it can feel as though a new client is throwing down the gauntlet if he says 'I know as a psychotherapist you don't give advice, but this time I want you to tell me what I should do.' In this instance I would start by making an empathic response such as 'I think it is really hard for you that I'm not the kind of therapist who tells you what to do.' I might then add 'I'm wondering if you might feel that if I wanted to I *could* help you by telling you what to do.' Or I might say 'Perhaps it feels like I'm deliberately withholding my help if I don't tell you what to do.' If the client continues to ask me to give them direction I might add 'It seems to me that you find it quite hard to feel helped by what I can give you.' Such an interpretation of the client's resistance begins to tackle the negative transference that may accompany ambivalence about change.

Questions about my qualifications and experience can be a manifestation of resistance, but when they are asked at the beginning of therapy I always answer in a direct way, for the reasons I discussed in Chapter 5. Having done so, it is also useful to discuss the significance of the question, since it will vary from client to client. Clients who ask the question well into therapy may do so because they are discontented, so giving a straightforward answer to the question might sidestep a negative transference. I would probably say something like 'I would be happy to tell you; indeed I'm glad you've asked, but before I do perhaps we could think about what it would mean to you to know.'

It is not uncommon for clients at the beginning of therapy to say the thing that is most important at the point of leaving. This can be to do with difficulty in discussing something that is painful or conflictual, or it may be because they are finding it difficult to leave, or are attempting to take control of when the session ends. It is important to take this up, and I generally say 'This sounds important, but we have to stop now. I wonder if you could come back to it next time.' If a client continues to do it I will look for an opportunity in the material of the next session to address the issue raised at the end of the previous one. I will then start the process of exploring what bringing the most important issue at the end of the session signifies.

I am always careful about interpreting resistance too early. While at times it is essential to do so, it can also lead to further resistance if it is experienced as persecutory. This is particularly the case with lateness at the beginning of therapy. Often clients come a long way and, especially when travelling in the rush-hour, can find it hard to predict how long the journey will take. My response is an indication of my own particular therapeutic stance, which attends to the importance of external reality as well as internal reality.

Not free associating can also be a form of resistance, since your client is not engaging in an activity that is central to the therapeutic endeavour. At the beginning of therapy this can be a function not only of resistance, but also of a lack of conviction that saying whatever is on one's mind is actually going to be useful. Sometimes clients need time to see that free association is of value.

Resistance in the later stages of therapy

Sometimes after making good progress a client can begin to resist the process of change because of the meaning of that change. For example, changes in his feelings and ways of relating may have serious consequences for an intimate relationship outside therapy. Resisting further insight might be a way of protecting that relationship from breakdown. Quite often resistance increases as the client gets close to the core of his difficulties, particularly if they are to do with how his character is structured and if change represents a threat to who he is. As he gets better the client also has to face the loss of the relationship with you as the possibility of discharge looms. If he does not have many other intimate relationships in his life he may find the loss of his therapist unbearable, and may get worse as a termination date gets closer.

In working with resistance in the middle and later stages of therapy, it is important to keep in mind that clients both wish for and fear the consequences of change. Quite often clients can become frustrated with their resistance, and we can respond to that with our own frustration and impatience. This can make it difficult to stay empathic and to be in touch with the fear associated with the resistance. If we can remain empathic we have a much better chance of helping that part of the client that does want to change.

FURTHER READING

Mollon, P. (2000) *Ideas in Psychoanalysis: The Unconscious.* Cambridge: Icon.

7

THE THEORY UNDERLYING TECHNIQUE:
Transference and Countertransference

More has been written about how we understand and use the transference and countertransference than almost any other area of psychodynamic endeavour. It is central to psychodynamic theory and fundamental to what defines our technique. However, as Tonnesmann (2005) points out, there is little agreement as to an exact definition of these terms amongst the different psychodynamic schools. This is because each practitioner has a different view determined by her own model of the mind and preferred way of working. The aim of this chapter is to guide you through some of the complexities of the area, so that you understand the basis on which you make use of the transference and countertransference in working with your clients.

At the heart of our theory there are two fairly straightforward central tenets which apply inside and outside the consulting room, but which are fostered and brought into focus by the analytic frame and technique.

- Firstly, we all have a template in our minds about how the world and relationships work. This is based on our actual early experiences with the important people in our lives plus what we made of those experiences in phantasy. Without realising it, we then perceive others, and actively attempt to construct new relationships and situations to fit our template.
- Secondly, minds affect one another. When two people come together they have an impact on each other, which creates a unique relationship configuration. This means that both you and your client contribute your conscious and unconscious minds and expectations about relationships to the mix. The discussion in a therapy session will address understanding your client's transferential experience of you. Your transference and countertransference feelings will be discussed in your own therapy or supervision.

Although transference is manifest in our everyday lives, the process is intensified as a client enters therapy. This is because the very act of seeking help for something we cannot manage ourselves results in the activation of our attachment system. This makes us prone to feeling vulnerable, particularly towards the person we are seeking help from, and fuels transferential longings and anxieties towards that person. The establishment and specific use we make of the therapeutic frame (see Chapter 4) is intended to create an environment in which the client's internal reality comes to the fore, creating a situation in which the transference can flourish, so that dynamic work can be done.

While transference is a universal phenomenon, the extent to which our relationships are dominated by our transference expectations rather than by reality will vary according to the strength of our ego. People whose egos are fragmented or vulnerable tend to find their relationships are more dominated by the reality of their internal world, including their transference to others. They are less likely to see others as fully rounded people, and instead see them as all good or all bad. Those with more robust egos are able to take into account the reality of the external world, including others' actual attributes or behaviour. This enables them to see others as being more rounded, with both strengths and vulnerabilities.

Our clients communicate their inner worlds and transference relationships in many different ways, including the stories they tell us. Luborsky and Crits-Cristoph (1998) found evidence that the stories clients tell about their relationships reveal the core conflict that they are struggling with. They developed the Core Conflictual Relationship Theme (CCRT) as a way of understanding the meaning underlying clients' stories. Their research found a link between the stories that clients tell about significant others in their lives, and the way in which they interact with their therapist. This research supported the notion of transference, and the legitimacy of accessing it through clients' stories. They also found that accurate interpretation of clients' CCRT patterns is linked to successful therapeutic outcome.

Countertransference has been described as an advanced form of empathy. Like transference it has its everyday manifestation, as well as a specific role in dynamic work. People's capacity for being sensitive to others' projections and transferences varies, and part of psychodynamic training involves fostering that capacity. What we do with those sensitivities in psychodynamic work is different from in social situations. While it is legitimate to aid someone in distress by doing something to actively help in a social situation, in therapy there is generally an injunction against acting on our feelings. When we do so it is understood as an enactment and can be viewed as a failure of our capacity to contain what is projected into us. Sometimes therapist enactment can have a positive outcome, for example if it shifts something that is stuck in the therapy. However, it always needs to be carefully and honestly explored with both your internal and external supervisor. Enactments can be a valuable source of information about aspects of the work that you have unconsciously struggled with, but unexamined they can also lead to unethical practice.

There is still controversy over exactly what we mean by countertransference. There are two possibilities: the first involves the therapist's transference to the client – in other words who the client represents in the therapist's inner world. The second takes as its starting point the client's transference and represents the therapist's unconscious response to it. Both of these happen, and both are important. The question is whether it is useful to think of them both as countertransference, or whether we should just consider the latter as true countertransference. Conventionally most therapists still hold to the position that the concept should be limited to the reaction of the therapist to the client's unconscious. However, a number of writers have argued that it is limiting to think of the countertransference as taking the client's transference as its starting point, since from the first moment of contact there are two minds participating in the interaction, each of them acting on the other, each of them bringing their own transference fantasies (see Berman, 2000).

There remains considerable debate about whether the concept and use of countertransference has become too ubiquitous and, in the process, has become a cover for poor practice. Segal argues that 'Rationalisations are found for acting under pressure of countertransference, rather than using it as a guide to understanding' (1993: 20). How to understand and use the countertransference is one of the areas that separates the different schools of dynamic theory and continues to be the subject of sometimes heated controversy. This is because how we understand the relationship with our clients touches both the heart of who we are as practitioners, and the theoretical system that sustains our work. It is one of the reasons why, during training, therapists are often advised to chose supervision from someone whose theoretical stance is concordant with that of their training therapist. Not to do so can lead not only to confusion, but to feeling inadequately held if there are problems in the countertransference which are understood differently by training therapist and training supervisor.

A BRIEF HISTORY OF THE CONCEPTS AND ACCOMPANYING TECHNIQUE

Differences between how psychodynamic schools understand and use the transference and countertransference are the result of divergent theories about the developmental origins of mental distress and how the mind is structured and develops. The central debate is about whether psychological difficulties are primarily the result of internal, dynamic, conflict or caused by developmental deficit. Both Freud and Klein developed conflict theories, while Winnicott and Kohut developed deficit theories. This is a crude delineation of their respective positions, but it helps us to make sense of the technical differences that have developed in the different schools. In addition there is a debate about when different schools date the emergence of the ego, the role they assign to innate factors, and the importance that is given to the role of phantasy in constructing a person's relational world.

FREUD

The transference

Freud first conceptualised transference at the end of the nineteenth century, when he reflected on an incident involving Anna O, a young woman who was in analysis with his collaborator, Breuer. As a result of Breuer's, and then his own experiences he initially regarded transference as an embarrassing and potentially dangerous phenomenon. Later, he also came to understand it as a form of resistance to the work of analysis and therefore a source of valuable information about his client's repressed unconscious. He initially thought that it was enough to identify its existence and it would then disappear, but he later came to recognise that it needed to be repeatedly understood and 'worked through'.

Freud thought that working therapeutically with the transference was only possible with people whose psychological development had progressed sufficiently that they had an ego, or sense of self, which could be differentiated from the other person. This required the client to function at the oedipal stage of development, which he dated at around three years old, when the child incorporates the notion of a third person (his father) into his mental functioning. He maintained that people dominated by pre-oedipal, or psychotic, modes of functioning were unanalysable and should therefore not be taken into psychoanalysis.

Freud's theory of development had an inevitable impact on how he understood the transference and the types of interpretation that he made. Because he thought that an analytic cure was achieved through insight, his interpretations were quite cognitive and oriented towards conflict and defence. He paid much less attention to affect-laden exchanges or the non-verbal aspects of therapy that contribute to change.

The countertransference

Freud initially understood the therapist's role as being like a mirror that reflects the client back to himself. This implied that the therapist maintained the function of uninvolved observer, rather than participating in the transference relationship. Perhaps I should underline that this is no longer how it is understood or used, though it remains a caricatured representation of psychodynamic work amongst practitioners from non-psychodynamic orientations. Just as Freud initially conceptualised transference as interfering with analytic work, his first reaction to evidence of the psychoanalyst's countertransference was to see it as an impediment to the progress of psychoanalysis. He understood countertransference as the psychoanalyst's unanalysed resistance to the client's material, and especially to the client's transference. Freud felt that counter-transference feelings needed to be mastered and advocated psychoanalysts seek further psychoanalysis if they were unable to do so. Although our conceptualisation of the countertransference has changed profoundly in the intervening years, I think that Freud's concerns about unanalysed aspects of the therapist are applicable now. I'm not advocating mastery as Freud did. However we all need to be aware of the potential for unanalysed resistances in us to contribute to our countertransference.

KLEIN AND THE ENGLISH SCHOOL

The transference

Klein's work on the importance of early object relationships had a profound influence on our understanding of the transference. She saw the infant as object related from birth, which requires a rudimentary ego that functions from birth. Klein consequently had a very different understanding of the transference from Freud. She asserted that the early stages of development (manifest in the paranoid–schizoid position) appear in the transference, and therefore can be grasped and reconstructed by the therapist. This widened concept of transference had an impact on who she considered analysable. It opened the way for the treatment both of people with psychosis, and those who functioned on the cusp between neurotic and psychotic functioning. Klein believed that unconscious phantasy is always active in every interaction between the client and his therapist, even when the client is at his most coherent. This had a significant impact on how she approached interpretation, in that she felt all communication was available for interpretation in the transference. She also took the concept of transference beyond a repetition of the past. She proposed that the client understood his therapist as the object of his unconscious phantasies. This changed the focus of interpretation from the past to the 'here and now' relationship with the therapist, based on phantasy.

Klein's view was that the client transferred his whole experience of life as well as his inner world into the therapeutic situation, so that his therapist would come to experience, and then understand, the world from his perspective. She called this the 'total situation', which included 'all the emotions, defences and object relations which exist between objects and between self and objects in the internal world' (Steiner, 2008: 41). In this way Klein gave the client's internal world a significance as real as his external world. These understandings of the transferential relationship have led Kleinians to feel much freer to interpret the transference and do so much more often than practitioners from other models. This can lead to accusations that Kleinians are insufficiently attuned to non-transferential aspects of clients' material.

In another important contribution to theory, Klein maintained that there is a inherent tension for all of us between the wish to grow and develop and the wish not to grow and develop. She emphasised the inherent conflict between these two positions. To put it in her terms, there is both an impulse towards integration (growth) and one towards disintegration (falling apart). Her concept of an instinctual impulse towards disintegration has had a number of implications for the way in which Kleinians have interpreted the transference. The primary impact is on how the negative transference is both understood and interpreted. Unconscious aggression, in the form of the death instinct or the impulse to disintegration, is interpreted much more than it is in other dynamic models. Practitioners influenced by Klein are likely to interpret the negative transference to a greater extent, and much earlier in the therapeutic relationship, than those working in other models. They argue that in doing so the client experiences relief that his hostile and destructive feelings can be recognised and worked with, and that the therapist can be trusted to contain that part of him. This facilitates the therapeutic alliance. However, it has led to technical disagreements between Kleinians and therapists from other dynamic schools, who have been more inclined to interpret the negative transference once a positive transference and robust therapeutic alliance have been established.

The countertransference

Kleinians were also the first to make a distinction between transference as communication and transference that is an attempt to get rid of an unbearable internal state into another person. Transference as communication refers to the therapist experiencing in herself those inner states that her client cannot consciously communicate to her. Getting rid of unbearable inner states refers to the process of projective identification, which I describe in more detail in Chapter 10. Bion (1962) elaborated the concept of projective identification into a more interpersonal direction and it became the cornerstone of the Kleinian approach to countertransference. Bion (1963) conceptualised the mother/therapist as having a 'containing' function for her baby/client. This involved the mother taking in the baby's painful and hostile feelings and metabolising or detoxifying them. She then hands the feelings back in a form that the baby can manage according to his current stage of development. Bion proposed that when projective identification operates in the depressive position it becomes the basis for empathy. However, like Segal after her, Klein was sceptical about the value of the countertransference. She was concerned that it could be used both to hide from oneself and to justify poor practice.

WINNICOTT AND THE INDEPENDENTS

The transference

Winnicott also had a profound influence on how we conceptualise and work with the transference in clients who present with problems originating in the first months of life. Winnicott describes such clients as being in the state of 'primitive emotional development' as a result of early environmental failure. By early environmental failure Winnicott means that they have not had adequate maternal attunement in the early months of life. Etchegoyen puts it succinctly when he says that 'According to Winnicott, it is not the past that comes into the present (or is reproduced in the present) but the present has become transformed plainly and simply into the past' (1999: 218). This points to one of the important differences between Winnicott and Klein. Winnicott understands the client's present relationship with his therapist being experienced as if it had already happened. In other words the therapist becomes the object who was not there for the client in his childhood. Klein sees the past as if it were the present, so that past difficulties and phantasies are experienced as though they are happening now.

Winnicott disagreed with Klein over a number of other theoretical issues:

- He held that the baby does not have an ego at birth.
- He did not accept the idea of innate aggression or innate envy.
- He did not accept that conflict exists at the beginning of life.

Winnicott's theory, like that of his contemporaries Fairbairn and Balint, emphasised the role of the baby's actual experience of his caregivers in both healthy psychological development and in the development of psychopathology. He termed this the 'environment', which is another term for maternal holding, and which needs to be attuned to the growing baby's developmental needs. Winnicott argued that in the context of an appropriately facilitating environment, the baby's 'inherited potential' will find expression and he will develop his True Self. He emphasises that the True Self is only a potential, and that it will only come into being through the right kinds of experience. In the face of very early deficit, that is an environment which is not facilitative, the baby develops a False Self which protects his True Self from impingement. This inevitably has an impact on how the transference is both understood and interpreted. In particular Winnicott understood resistance to either interpretation or the process of therapy as being the result of deficit. He proposed that the client does not have the developmental tools to react differently, and therefore holds on to maladaptive ways of coping or defending himself.

Winnicott's optimistic view of childhood development is reflected in his view of the aims of therapy, which is one of facilitating the client to develop his potential. He proposed that every child has the impulse to grow and develop. His optimistic view of development was at variance with Klein's notion of a conflict between the wish to grow and the wish not to grow. Winnicott also proposed that conflict and aggression are environmentally determined, meaning they develop because of the mother's lack of attunement to her baby's developmental needs. Again this differentiates him from Klein, whose position was that aggression is innate.

This has implications for the way in which Winnicott interpreted the negative transference with clients functioning in early stages of development. He sees both the client's anger and his resistance at this stage as being in response to environmental failure in his therapy – in other words that the therapist has, in some real way, failed the client. The client uses the therapist's current mistake to protest about an error which occurred in the past. According to Etchegoyen this gives the client 'the opportunity of becoming angry for the first time about the issues and failures in adaptation that produced the disturbance in his development' (1999: 222). The failure should be understood both in terms of the past and the present and it is important that the therapist takes responsibility for his error. The client's expression of the negative transference in this state represents his hope that the therapist can respond to his needs.

Winnicott was a technical innovator. He developed ways of working that addressed the needs of clients who have disturbances in their primitive emotional development through providing a concrete experience, permitting them to regress and repair those deficiencies. He proposed that, in the unique setting of the therapeutic relationship, the client can regress so that healing of the True Self can take place and the False Self can be relinquished. He called this regression in the service of the ego, and understood it as providing a corrective emotional experience. It involves the client returning to a state of early dependence, and the therapist's role is to allow the regressive process to take its natural course and to take care of her client. The therapist meets the client's developmental needs through non-verbal means, using ways of being with the client that are similar to maternal care. Verbal interpretation has a place, but it is less central. Various writers after Winnicott have talked about the importance of transference interpretations that are 'beyond words' and that involve either the therapist doing or being in a way that itself becomes an interpretation and thus healing. Baker (1993), for example, describes how he survived his client's verbal attacks and continued as a functioning object. His client experienced this as mutative and it became central to his recovery.

The countertransference

Winnicott became one of the major thinkers in what became known as the Independent school of psychoanalysis. Theoreticians in this school, including Balint (1968) and Little (1986), have made some of the most important contributions to our understanding of the countertransference. In her landmark paper, Heimann (1950) defined the countertransference as the emotional response of the analyst to the patient's communications. This gave the therapist a way of understanding her client's unconscious communication. However, it did not sanction acting on those responses, instead the therapist is required to experience her feelings and use them to understand her client better. Heimann (1956) later went on to say that the main question for the therapist was 'who is speaking to whom, about what and why now?'

All these writers worked with clients who experienced early trauma which they re-experienced in their therapy. During sessions they regressed and experienced pre-verbal states of being. At such times the therapists felt that the countertransference became the main guide to recognising their clients' vulnerability. For example, Little (1986) describes suddenly feeling the urge to cover a regressed client with a blanket. Although she did not act on this powerful feeling, she used her understanding of her wish to do so. Later in the session she made an interpretation about the client's need to be held by her, which the client received with relief.

Winnicott's concept of countertransference was wide and included the therapist's own unresolved conflicts, her personality and experiences, and her rational, objective reactions. One of his most original contributions lies in his understanding that, just as at times normal mothers hate their babies, therapists hate the psychotic parts of their clients. In 'Hate in the countertransference' (1975) he argued that the client can only tolerate his hatred for his therapist if the therapist objectively hates him. Interestingly, as Etchegoyen notes 'an analysis will always be incomplete if the analyst has never been able to tell the patient he felt hate for him when he was ill. Only after this interpretation has been formulated can the patient cease to be a child' (1999: 301).

KOHUT

I am going to include a brief overview here of the work of the American psychoanalyst, Heinz Kohut, whose thinking came out of the self-psychology tradition in American psychotherapy. His theories have much in common with those of Winnicott and Fairbairn. Like Winnicott, Kohut's theory is a deficit rather than a conflict theory and he too emphasised the value of regression for clients who have an undeveloped sense of self (see Mollon, 2001).

Kohut believed that in order to flourish the baby needed an empathic and responsive human milieu and that relating to others was vital to his psychological survival. He understood the infant ego as weak, without structure, so that it could not function in isolation from its objects, who provided the structure necessary for survival. Kohut called these others 'self-objects' and saw them initially as being undifferentiated from the self. If development goes well, the person's own psychic structure gradually takes over the functions of the self-object and he becomes increasingly independent. However, a lack of sufficient empathic attunement leads to a continued reliance on external self-objects to provide the structure necessary to survive. This results in a massive dependency on his objects and can result in a transference that is imbued with terror at the prospect of abandonment by his therapist.

Kohut made a number of contributions to technique. Firstly, he held that the transference is spontaneously constructed and that the therapist must neither encourage nor interfere with it. This differentiates him from both the classical Freudian and Kleinian approaches which both actively encourage the development of the transference. He has also contributed to a shift in emphasis from verbal interpretation per se to providing crucial developmental experiences that have been missing from the client's early relationships. This he did through empathic attunement. He also accentuated the need for practice to be non-authoritarian and non-objectifying, arguing that behaving in an objectifying manner towards clients is traumatising.

INTERSUBJECTIVITY AND RELATIONAL APPROACHES

In the latter part of the twentieth century the winds of post-modernism and social construction swept across the psychodynamic world as they did with all other philosophical and academic disciplines. One impact on psychodynamic theory was an increasing interest in the notion of intersubjectivity, the way in which minds influence one another. Developmental researchers contributed to the theory base with elegant research paradigms that demonstrated the impact of parental states of mind on the developing infant. Theories that took account of how the minds of therapist and client come together and impact on one-another impacted on the existing theory base as well as leading to new developments.

One of these was to do with ideas about the co-construction of the therapeutic space. The notion of a transference-countertransference matrix, which is contributed to by each member of the therapeutic couple as well as specific to them, was not in itself new. However, the particular emphasis that relational theorists placed on the matrix involved a paradigm shift. Because it is a space occupied jointly by both client and therapist as they bring their conscious and unconscious minds to the endeavour, relational theorists argue that trying to tease the transference and countertransference apart can feel artificial. Relational therapists such as Berman (2000) propose that both transference and countertransference not only mould each other, but are also actually parts of one total cyclical process. The idea of a co-constructed space goes some way to helping us understand why clients who have a second or third therapy report having very different experiences and attending to different issues in therapy. We can understand this as the space being opened up in the client's mind with one therapist is different from that opened with another.

The relational therapist is taken out of her role as 'expert'. Instead, like her client, she becomes constructed as a flawed interpretive instrument whose personal psychology plays its part in shaping how therapy unfolds. The task of the therapist is to function as a participant-observer, who is both aware of how her client 'pulls' on her interpersonally, while at the same time developing awareness of her own participation in the process. This emphasis on the therapist's contribution to the unconscious interactions between herself and her client goes further than in other models and has an impact on technique. Relational psychotherapists are more likely to use self-disclosure as a tool of therapy, for example by acknowledging both sets of unconscious experience. They also place somewhat greater emphasis on the 'real' relationship. It is therefore important for the client not only to know that he exists in the mind of this therapist (as in Winnicottian theory) but also that he knows and understands the mind of his therapist.

Relational therapists use a technique they call evocative interpretation, involving comments and behaviours that are designed to build trust and create affective experiences. The exploration of these new experiences is considered to be an important active ingredient in bringing about change. The approach also places emphasis on the value of reconstruction of the client's early history, which helps the client place himself in the context of his own life. Like the developmental approaches of Winnicott and Fairbairn, relational therapists are less concerned with the interpretation of aggression, and see it as a result of relational breakdown rather than being innate.

For many therapists the idea of a co-constructed relationship is challenging. Arguably it faces us with the limitations of our objectivity and asks us to tolerate an even greater degree of ambiguity than in other approaches. It also asks us to confront the impact of our own unconscious processes not only *on* our client but *with* him in the room. This is not a comfortable position for many therapists.

MOVING TOWARDS PRACTICE

Such a richness of models can feel confusing, especially since they rest on some fundamentally different premises which are irreconcilable. For this reason I think it is timely to remember that an important competency as therapists is to be able to use theory to guide and reflect on our practice rather than being straight-jacketed by it. We need to work out how our theory fits our client rather than trying to squeeze him into a theoretical Procrustean bed, chopping bits off him in order to fit. As Safran and Muran point out, 'Theory can provide the therapist with leads, but the therapist's real task is to engage in a dialogue with the ever-changing clinical situation, through which theory is tested, fleshed out, and modified on an ongoing basis' (2000: 72–73). I find myself drawing on the whole range of theory within attachment theory and the psychoanalytic stream of psychodynamic theory, and sometimes beyond, in order to understand my client. Not to do so, and to behave in a partisan way, may deny him an understanding that would be helpful to him. So, for example, ignoring a new client's hostility in the first session, because to interpret aggression early in therapy is viewed as 'Kleinian', may deny him the necessary early reassurance that I would be prepared to see and work with his hostility.

Nevertheless, I find certain explanations about what brings about psychological change more compelling than others and am more likely to understand my client through the lens of one set of theories rather than another. I think that it is important to acknowledge the subjective elements in our choice of theory and how that impacts on our relationship to it. We also need to be aware that, because when we evaluate psychodynamic theories we are influenced by highly personal factors, disagreement can feel as though it attacks the core of who we are. This can make communication between the proponents of different positions very difficult. It can reinforce the tendency in psychodynamic practitioners from the different traditions to question the validity of other approaches and to 'point their pens at one-another and say in effect "What *we* do is psychoanalysis, and what you do is not"' (Luepnitz, 2002: 16, emphasis in the original).

Communication between schools is particularly vulnerable to breaking down around the issue of interpretation. Part of the reason for this is that interpretation is seen as the active ingredient in our work, and like any 'medicine' it has the power to damage as well as repair. We all have anxieties about our capacity to damage our clients, as well as a tendency to project those anxieties onto others, who hold different opinions as to what is curative. Currently tension is partly expressed in the different values we ascribe to maternal and paternal modes of therapist functioning. Maternal modes are highlighted in developmental approaches, which emphasise the environmental milieu in which therapy takes place. Paternal modes are more associated with conflict, and approaches which lay greater emphasis on verbal interpretation and the value of insight. One defence against the accompanying discomfort is to retreat into a certain and rigid position, espousing one 'correct' way of understanding how the mind works and the accompanying understanding and interpretation of the transference and countertransference. However, I think that to do this we deny our clients the opportunity to be thought about using the full range of our discipline's understanding.

In recent years there have been attempts to find the commonalities and areas of shared interest between schools, in recognition of the importance of acknowledging the core underlying beliefs about the human condition that unite the different theories. As Wallerstein (1992) observes, although there are significant theoretical differences between schools, there is a lot of common ground in the way that practitioners work clinically. He suggests that, while practitioners from different orientations vary in how they interpret, the fact that they all *do* interpret is important. He gives the example of how three clinicians differently interpret a client's dissatisfaction with an analyst's unscheduled break and proposes that what unites them is that they all take the client's objection to the break seriously. He proposes that it is the act of taking the client seriously that brings about change – or, to use the technical term, is mutative.

FURTHER READING

Casement, A. (2001) *Jung and Analytical Psychology*. London: SAGE.
Symington, N. (1986) *The Analytic Experience: Lectures from the Tavistock*. London: Free Association.

8
TYPES OF
INTERPRETATION

Making interpretations is *the* primary intervention in psychodynamic work and the ability to interpret correctly, in a timely manner and in a way that our clients can use, is a core competency in our discipline. The main function of an interpretation is to create links. These can be between thoughts, feelings and actions, past and present, one event and another. Their purpose is to deepen the therapeutic relationship, to help your client to place himself in his world, to understand his past, and to know himself. As in other therapeutic models, psychodynamic practitioners use interpretation to link conscious aspects of the material of the session. Unlike other models we also use them to make links with the dynamic unconscious and make it available to conscious processing.

I want to emphasise that an interpretation is a hypothesis. It is not a truth, but a way of understanding something from a different perspective. Your client can accept or reject your hypothesis. An interpretation is an invitation to your client to think about something differently from the way he currently perceives it. Therefore it is more or less helpful to him, rather than objectively right or wrong. Of course the fact that you have made the interpretation sets off a chain of events between you and your client, whether he accepts or rejects it. It is like dropping a pebble in a pond – once you have dropped it the ripples are inevitable.

It is important that we don't become too invested in the interpretations we make and that we maintain an open-minded stance towards their correctness or usefulness. If you ever find yourself insisting to your client that your interpretation is correct, you need to regard this as a warning that you may have become too attached to your own ideas, or rigid in your stance. It may also mean that a problem in the relationship between you is being enacted through your interpretative work.

Before going further, I want to add a caveat. Much has been written about the art and science of interpretation. This chapter aims at giving you an overview of what we do when we interpret. However, interpretation is a subtle and complex process and this chapter can only scratch the surface of it. My aim is to give you a structure within which you can begin to understand what we do when we interpret and why we do it.

REASONS FOR INTERPRETING

Psychodynamic interpretation is an action aimed at trying to produce a particular effect in your client that will lead to change. You will need to make a choice about whether, when, what and how to interpret. In making this decision it is helpful to think about why you are interpreting.

- *Interpretation as a demonstration of interest in your client* is a highly validating experience for him. This may sound prosaic, but many clients cannot take it as a given, and struggle to believe that anyone has a real interest in them. This kind of interpretation is particularly important in the early stages of therapy as you work to deepen rapport and establish a therapeutic alliance. However, with some clients it can be a significant reason for interpreting throughout the work.

- *Interpretation as an experience of being thought about* is important throughout therapy. Many clients have had insufficient experience of being thought about by a benign other in a way that demonstrates an awareness that that client has a mind. Being treated as someone who has thoughts, feelings and needs that can be made sense of is a powerful stimulus to emotional growth. Being treated as though he has a mind also facilitates your client's own capacity for self-reflection.

- *Interpretation as making sense of your client's communications in order to reach a shared understanding* is particularly important in the early stages of therapy. Some clients need prolonged experience of being understood before they can bear to engage in the process of coming to understand themselves (Steiner, 1993). They need an extended period of being understood by the other before they can think about their impact on others, or reflect on the workings of their own mind.

- *Interpretation as an extension of your client's understanding* should take him just beyond his current level of awareness to somewhere that is new. It is important that the increment between where he currently is and where the interpretation takes him is bridgeable. If it is too big it will not make sense to him. As you get to know your client better you will have an increasing sense of the increments that he can manage at different times in the work. It is generally good practice to offer the interpretation in two or more 'chunks'. If you do this it will give your client the opportunity to make the final link himself, which will increase his capacity and confidence in his own ability to make links. If you always do this for him you are likely to leave him feeling that he cannot think for himself, and reduce his belief in his own capacity to open his mind to new thinking.

- *Interpretation as an aid to integration* facilitates ego development. By linking up feelings, thoughts and behaviours within your client and adding meaning to his communications, interpretations expand the knowledge your client has about himself and the world he inhabits. When you make these links with your client's history you enable him to create a narrative around his life, which can help him have a sense of where he came from and his place in the world. An interpretation can also be used to deepen the affective relationship between you and your client. The neuropsychoanalysts describe this kind of connectedness as the result of right brain to right brain activity, which is similar to what happens between mother and baby when they are synchronous. Schore (1994) and Siegel (1999) have proposed that right brain to right brain activity produces hormones which stimulate new neuronal growth in the brain, which is the physiological basis of psychological change.

- *Interpretation as a way of working with feelings* can be a powerful experience for clients who have not previously had access to their feelings. An interpretation can help the client access cut-off feelings as well as validate those he is aware of. At the same time interpretation can help your client put a membrane of understanding around powerful feelings that are threatening to overwhelm him. An appropriate interpretation can act as a container when your client is very distressed, and enable him to manage a situation that might otherwise feel unbearable.

- *Interpretation to make a breach in the closed system of the client's inner world* enables him to make contact with the external world and reality. Fairbairn (1958) described how very damaged clients maintain their internal world as a closed system, which they guard against access by the external world. Interpretation is one of the ways in which we can gradually facilitate a breach in this closed system.

RELATING INTERPRETATIONS TO THE STRUCTURE OF THE MIND

It is important to decide which area of your client's functioning you are directing your interpretation to. You might direct it to:

- the transference relationship, linking material in the session to his relationship with you;
- his defensive system, and the way in which he protects himself from psychic pain, including his resistance to the process of therapy;
- your client's psychological structure.

I discuss the interpretation of the transference in Chapter 9, and working with defences in Chapter 10.

Conflict interpretations

Interpretations which address conflict assume the existence of a functioning ego that can mediate between external reality and your client's superego or his id. Conflict-oriented interpretations are linked to more active, paternal modes of functioning in the therapist.

William began to feel depressed about a year before his referral to me. He tried to see the best in everyone and, if he was critical about anyone, he felt terrible and punished himself. He did this by telling himself he was cruel and uncaring and just like his hated father.

Soon after beginning therapy William began a relationship with Judy and over the next three months they spent an increasing amount of time together. However, as their relationship developed, he became increasingly demoralised by the way she criticised him. No matter how hard he tried, he found himself blamed for some or other misdemeanour. One day William described how he

> had been late picking Judy up for a date because he had a flat tyre. She had greeted him saying 'I've been waiting an hour; you don't care about me waiting here for you.' He had apologised profusely and tried to make it up to her. During the session he accused himself of not taking sufficient care; he should have made it on time. He should have foreseen that something could go wrong.

The first part of my interpretation could be directed towards his superego by commenting that William was being very hard on himself for being late, as though he should have known that he would have a flat tyre. My aim would have been to challenge his omnipotence and open his mind to another possibility (whether he should feel to blame for the flat tyre) and to ameliorate the harshness of his superego. I might then make an interpretation aimed at recognising his ego, which was in touch with the reality of the situation. I might say that I wondered if he might find it difficult to be upset or angry with Judy for not realising that he would not have been late on purpose. This interpretation would have signalled that I was aware of his actual qualities, as was he. I might then have addressed the conflict between his superego, which blamed himself for being late and would punish himself for any criticism of Judy, and his ego which was aware that he was someone who would not be late without a good reason. I might then have said that he seemed to be caught between seeing himself as someone who respected others and tried to arrive on time and someone who didn't care enough to make appropriate contingency plans and was bad because he felt critical towards Judy for her attack on him.

The purpose of a conflict interpretation is firstly to help the client through uncovering an internal conflict. The second purpose is resolution of the conflict through exploration of the affects, thoughts and behaviours associated with it. Conflict-oriented hypotheses are more often openly shared with the client in the form of verbal interpretations, which take the form of interpreting the past, present and transference manifestations of the conflict.

Deficit interpretations

Deficit-oriented interpretations are linked to more passive, maternal modes of functioning. If your client's difficulties originate in deficit, you will take as your starting point that the prime purpose of interpretation is to strengthen his ego or sense of self. Interpretations designed to strengthen a weakened ego are different from those which assume the existence of a functioning ego. The purpose of a deficit-oriented interpretation is less about the attainment of insight and more about giving your client an affective experience that will facilitate growth and integration. The focus is therefore much more on empathic attunement and the management of any regression, and with it a deepening of connectedness between both of you. You are seeking to heighten the affective resonance between you rather than providing understanding per se. Understanding is seen as the result of ego growth, rather than a requirement for it.

Returning to William, in making a deficit-oriented interpretation I would have been empathic about how misunderstood he felt; or how he had felt helpless about trying to get it right for Judy, and not being able to, or how frightening it was to feel angry towards her for her lack of understanding. The aim of my intervention would have been oriented towards holding and containing his distress rather than at that moment trying to make sense of it.

In reality most practitioners incorporate both modes into their work, but will privilege one over the other with different clients and at different stages in therapy.

VERBAL INTERPRETATIONS

The purpose of a verbal interpretation is to:

- Bring into conscious awareness material that is in the unconscious – usually just below the surface in the preconscious. Ideally the material has come closer to consciousness as resistance to knowing about it has decreased. Often your client will already have made the link just below his conscious awareness, so when he becomes aware of it through interpretation he recognises it. Generally speaking, making interpretations that are addressed to your client's deep unconscious is not helpful. They are unlikely to resonate with him, and he may find them incomprehensible; indeed, they might lead to either compliance or hostility.
- Help your client to recognise and overcome a particular resistance to the work, for example when Vicky helped Tom to understand that his lateness was linked to his ambivalence about being in therapy. Significant therapeutic tact is required in making this kind of interpretation, since an exploration of the issues may produce shame.
- Facilitate your client in working with the affects that are most salient at that moment. For example, if your client is both despairing and angry and you ascertain that the stronger of the emotions is anger, you will focus your interpretations towards his anger.

There are various ways of categorising interpretations, but conventionally they are thought about along two dimensions. The first dimension involves the distinction between those which are extra-transference and those which are transference-based. The second dimension distinguishes between those interpretations which address the past and those which address the present. However, when we interpret in one dimension we should always be aware of the existence of the other, and the links with it. For example, if you are making an extra-transference interpretation you should always be aware of how the issue you have identified is played out in your client's relationship to you. When you make an interpretation about the present, you also need to hold in mind the past. What, when, and how you interpret will be determined by your client's needs and what he can work with at that moment as well as your theoretical orientation. While for the purpose of thinking about the different types of interpretation I am going to treat them as separate entities, it is with the caveat that they can never be truly separated.

Extra-Transference Interpretations

At one time extra-transference interpretations were seen as no more than preparation for 'the real thing' – the transference interpretation. Today all interpretive work is understood as important in internalising the therapist as a new object for her client. An extra-transference interpretation refers to making links for the client that are outside of the transference relationship. This is usually making links with the client's previous history or his external relationships in the past or present.

With some clients extra-transference interpretations are a way of being able to explore issues that are present in the transference, but which may be too threatening to him to approach directly. You are particularly likely to use extra-transference interpretations as a proxy for addressing transference issues with clients whose difficulties are the result of having experienced massive trauma perpetrated by their carers when they were young. This is because the client may not be able to tolerate the emotional impact of a transference interpretation that could be experienced as a concrete repetition of the trauma in the present with the therapist.

Very traumatised clients are likely to experience transference interpretations in a literal way and may not be able to hold on to the 'as if' aspect of them. Although it might eventually be possible for such clients to undertake transference work, they need to be able to tolerate the intense feelings that accompany it, which requires an enlargement of their ego capacities. Sometimes this is not possible, and most of the work is done outside the transference. Nevertheless, as Stewart (1992) noted, useful work can be done when the transference regarding someone else brings about insight and significant change. Therapists influenced by developmental theories and the notion of deficit particularly value the opportunity made possible by extra-transference interpretations, not least to demonstrate the therapist's ongoing interest in, and concern for, her client.

Historical interpretations

Also called genetic or reconstructive interpretations, historical interpretations are concerned with helping your client make sense of his previous history. The purpose of such interpretations is to facilitate your client in placing himself within his history in a more realistic and helpful way, and to see himself in the context of his own life. There is a link between narrative competence in telling one's own story and ego strength. By making reconstructive interpretations you join with your client in the process of thinking about himself, which can act as an integrating force and which helps to strengthen his ego. Such interpretations can be particularly valuable when working non-intensively with clients who have a weakened ego, and who may not be able to cope with the intensity of the transference.

When clients tell us the story of their history we need to be aware that there are two forces at work which militate against them being able to tell us an entirely truthful story. The first is that memory itself is not an entirely accurate representation of what has happened; it is reconstructed. This does not mean your client is consciously lying. Rather it means that, over time, memory traces degenerate, so that when we access memories they tend to be incomplete. Without realising it, we fill in the incomplete parts with what we expect to be there. While there is an essential truth in what we remember, and indeed it is largely accurate, it is not completely so.

Childhood memories are particularly prone to distortion. In early childhood the line between phantasy and reality is much more indistinct than in adult life and therefore inner reality can dominate. This means that early memories are particularly prone to distortion and coloured by the nature of our internal object relationships.

> Harriet frequently told me that her mother never cuddled her as a child and cited this as proof that her mother did not love her. During her therapy an aunt, who had lived with the family when Harriet was young but who had subsequently moved to South Africa, made a visit. Harriet used the opportunity to find out about her childhood and was surprised when the aunt told her that her mother had often tried to cuddle her, but that Harriet had pushed her away. The aunt said Harriet's mother was devastated by this. She recalled that Harriet changed from being a cuddly and responsive baby to rejecting her mother after her sister was born when Harriet was a year old.

So, Harriet was both right and wrong. Her memory told an essential truth about the relationship with her mother – that her mother had not had the capacity to cuddle her in the same way at around the time of her sister's birth. However, Harriet had projected her rejection of her mother into her mother, which in turn coloured her memory of the cause of the ongoing inability to be intimate with her.

Current interpretations

There are a number of reasons for paying proper attention to your client's pain in its own right. Firstly, helping him to manage his present concerns is part of being attuned to his state of mind, which in itself is therapeutic. Secondly, help in making sense of what is happening in his present life can facilitate integration and an accompanying strengthening of his ego. You may correctly assess that the pain in his present situation is a current manifestation of a past hurt, or that it has obvious transference links. However, if he is very distressed about a current situation an attempt to switch focus may constitute a failure of attunement. The therapeutic alliance could be undermined if current concerns are ignored in favour of what your client might consider as therapist, rather than client-centred, interpretations.

Cautions and caveats

The extent to which you use one type of interpretation in favour of others will depend on factors such as your theoretical orientation, your client's current anxieties, his current level of functioning and the stage of therapy. For example, if the transference is emotionally very intense, to the extent that it threatens to overwhelm your client's ego, it can be helpful to make extra-transference interpretations. An appropriate genetic interpretation, that is one which links present events to your client's history, can de-escalate the intensity of the transference so that the work can continue.

We need also be aware that we can use interpretation defensively. If we become uncomfortable with an intensified transference we may use extra-transference interpretations to take the heat off the transference relationship. This might be done to alleviate our own discomfort, rather than because the client needs us to. Equally, we may interpret in the transference because the client's distress about earlier trauma or a current painful situation is unbearable for us if it has touched on something unresolved in our own life or history. Bion (1963) was of the opinion that therapists often make interpretations in order to deny the anxiety about the fact that they are working in a situation that is unknown and uncertain, and which can therefore feel dangerous. While this is particularly true of inexperienced therapists, even with experience there are times when we make interpretations to manage our own anxiety in relation to the work. In doing so we can fool ourselves into thinking we have brought certainty into a situation which is inherently uncertain.

Klauber (1986) draws our attention to the fact that we can be so caught up in the content of an interpretation, that we miss how important the meaning of the interpretation is in the complex relationship of mutual transference between client and therapist. When we interpret in a way that takes our client just beyond where he is at the moment we convey to him that we have paid close attention which in itself is both healing and integrating. This brings me to the other category of interpretation that I want to address, which is the interpretation that is beyond words.

NON-VERBAL INTERPRETATIONS

Traditionally interpretation has been thought of as a verbal activity, but for some years attention has been paid to the non-verbal aspects of therapeutic work (Hurry, 1998; Tyndale, 1999). This involves creating a milieu in which what we do can be experienced as an interpretation, and leads to the client experiencing us as a new object through a corrective emotional experience. Non-verbal interpretations are particularly associated with theoretical models that emphasise deficit as a primary cause of psychological distress. Although they can sometimes be dismissed as 'countertransference enactments', these moments can be pivotal in bringing about change, particularly when clients cannot use verbal transference interpretations. For example, Gerrard (2007) described giving a client a towel to protect herself from an unexpected downpour. As a result the client, who had often believed Gerrard could not stand her, felt warmly mothered and cared for.

Baker (1993) discusses how the act of surviving clients' hostility and anger is in itself a transference communication, since doing so facilitates clients in experiencing their therapist as a new object who can survive. This is not something that is necessarily verbally interpreted, but is to do with the client's ongoing experience of us being there and patiently and consistently continuing the work with him.

Lucas, who was thirty-five, had spent much of his childhood shuttling between residential care and foster parents before he was finally adopted at the age of ten. Although his adoptive parents were very caring, he never felt confident that he was safe and that he would not be sent away again. He came for therapy because he was having difficulty in controlling his anger, particularly in close relationships. Although initially very careful of me, once he settled into therapy Lucas developed a strong negative transference, that was painful for both of us. Anger seeped out of him, and at times he would become overtly angry in the session about some way in which I had failed him. He was convinced that I did not care about him and that I would get away from him as soon as I could. This powerful conviction meant that even the slightest delay in answering the door meant that I had unilaterally terminated therapy. One week I had to change his session time. This was unusual, as I tried hard not to disturb his sessions. It was difficult to find another time and I offered him an evening appointment. Lucas knew this was not a normal part of my working day. When he arrived for his appointment I was slightly delayed coming to the door. Once in the consulting room he said 'You know, for the first time I didn't worry that you weren't coming. I know you are always there. I realise that all this time you have been there and I didn't know it.' Lucas was telling me that I had become not just a transferential object who was not there for him, but a new object who was.

The repeated experience of someone behaving in a way that disconfirms your client's previous experience can, over a period of time, lead to new learning in his procedural memory. It is this that underlies his experience of you as a new object, and the careful work of therapy as a corrective emotional experience.

FURTHER READING

Johnson, S. and Ruszczynski, S. (eds) (1999) *Psychoanalytic Psychotherapy in the Independent Tradition*. London: Karnac.

9

INTERPRETING THE TRANSFERENCE AND COUNTERTRANSFERENCE

The transference interpretation has long been seen as the 'gold standard' of psychodynamic practice and the basis for change; it has become the cornerstone of psychodynamic technique and a central competence for psychodynamic practitioners.

Because the unconscious does not have a sense of time, when we make a transference interpretation we are interpreting the past in the present. We are neither interpreting just the past, nor just the present. The power of the transference interpretation lies in your client seeing how his inner reality is played out in a current relationship as it takes place. This is further strengthened by the fact that, as his therapist, you are an important person in his inner life and therefore interactions with you are associated with heightened affect. If you succeed in facilitating your client in seeing and experiencing himself differently in relation to you, your place in his internal world is changed. In making transference interpretations the overarching aim is to help your client make a link between his internal world and external reality, thus breaching the closed system described by Fairbairn (1958) and by Woods (2003). There are two components of this overarching aim: firstly helping your client to become aware of the difference between how he perceives people and/or events and how they actually are; secondly in helping to modify his internal bad objects, which will help him feel less persecuted by them.

PREPARING YOURSELF TO WORK IN THE TRANSFERENCE

I now want to think in more detail about how to prepare yourself to receive your client's transference communications. This preparation builds on all the other foundations that I have discussed in previous chapters and includes:

- the creation of a setting in which dynamic work can take place;
- the creation of an analytic attitude in yourself which facilitates your client in free associating;

- the creation of a space inside yourself which is receptive to and can process your client's unconscious communications.

To be able to see and work with the transference requires something beyond these skills. It asks for a deep recognition of the power that you have as a therapist and the important place that you have in the inner life of your client. It requires accepting both his loving and hating feelings without an accompanying over-inflated sense of your own importance.

Very often when people write about interpreting the transference they take it for granted that as therapists we both know and are comfortable with how important we are to our clients. I am not convinced this is so. Discussions with colleagues, my own experience as a developing therapist, and supervising and training others have all revealed a struggle within therapists to accept their power and significance in relation to their clients. It is both a great privilege and a huge responsibility that we have in offering ourselves to our clients as transferential objects. It requires a particular form of discipline which is demanding and can challenge the roots of our understanding of ourselves. Although rarely discussed openly it is also something that most therapists have some ambivalence about. This is not surprising, since to be needed in this way imposes a particular discipline; for example, analytic abstinence demands that we do not rebuff our clients' accusations or positioning of us as we would in other relationships. It has a direct impact on our life outside the consulting room, for example holidays and breaks are carefully planned for rather than taken spontaneously. It also means really taking on board how much our clients need us. I strongly suspect that some of our failure to recognise the transference aspect of our clients' communications is a defence against the feelings that can be elicited in us when we truly recognise the extent to which they need or hate us, and the power we can have in relation to them.

During the third break in Tom's therapy Vicky enjoyed both the spontaneity of being on holiday, and not having to be abstinent in her relationships. On returning to work, Vicky did not want to accept that she resented having to be there for Tom each week. She began to dismiss material that could have been understood in the transference, and accused herself of previously over-inflating her importance to him. In supervision, Kate picked up Vicky's lack of attention to transferential material. Initially Vicky held to her position that she did not feel that the material under question was transferential. Then Kate said 'One of the things we haven't discussed is how difficult it can be coming back from a break and picking up the mantle of the transference again. It's to do with more than just coming back to work after a holiday. It's about allowing ourselves to be used by our clients in this special way. Abstinence requires high levels of discipline, and it can be difficult to shoulder it again after a break.'

Kate's normalisation of the process was a relief to Vicky, and it enabled her to openly acknowledge her resentment at starting therapy with Tom again. Having done so, she was able to access how much she enjoyed returning to the work. However, it also raised anxieties for her about how I as her therapist felt after my break. Did I feel a similar resentment? We explored how unbearable it was for her to contemplate that I could have anything other than positive feelings about seeing her. She also thought about how difficult it was for her to recognise herself as someone with power in a relationship, particularly in the therapeutic relationship with her clients.

INTRODUCING WORK WITH THE TRANSFERENCE

One of the major controversies over the years has been to do with when the transference should first be interpreted. Freud recommended interpreting it only once it became a resistance and that, until then, it should be allowed to develop in its own time. He regarded the early transference as delicate, whereas most people today see it as rather more robust. Klein's stance was very different because of her position that phantasy underlies all clients' communications, and modern Kleinians are inclined to take up the transference very early in therapy.

My own position is that I interpret the transference according to my assessment of what would be most useful to my client. If his presentation indicates that his relationships are dominated by his internal world, the transference needs to be attended to early on. I will have become part of that world in a very alive way and not to acknowledge it may leave my client feeling that I have not really heard him. The domination of your client's experience by his internal world may be indicated by early criticisms such as complaining at some length that he had a difficult journey, or had problems finding the house or parking. My approach is to focus first on his anxiety about whether he would be able to 'find' me and whether there was room for him. Depending on how he received my first, anxiety-oriented interpretation, I might then take up his anger or hostility to me if that was in the material. Not to do so might lead to despair about whether I could hear and attend to the angry and complaining part of him.

Coltart (1986) drew attention to the fact that the first phase in therapy is one in which the client asks the therapist for help in dealing with the crisis that brought him to therapy. She likens it to putting out a fire ahead of investigating its cause. If a client presents with an acute crisis in his life, which he is seeking help to make sense of and is therefore externally focussed, I don't feel it is either helpful or respectful to him to interpret the transference at the very beginning of treatment. In a sense I don't feel that he has given me permission to engage with him on this level yet. He may well experience such an interpretation as intrusive and insensitive to his current concerns. This could both delay the establishment of a good working relationship and risk engendering a premature negative transference in the absence of a robust therapeutic alliance. Such clients generally require a period of time in which to begin to value and use me as someone who can help them with their concerns, before they are ready to explore the relationship with me. The same applies to those clients who are more in touch with reality, but may not be in acute crisis. My approach to both groups in making transference interpretations is, generally speaking, quite a gradual one. The literature indicates that too much emphasis on interpreting the transference can both weaken the therapeutic alliance and/or result in a negative transference.

My personal stance is to take an educative approach to clients who have little knowledge of dynamic work, and whose functioning is oriented towards their external worlds rather than dominated by internal reality. I explain how therapy differs from ordinary life experiences, and that important aspects of their relationships with others in their life will become manifest in the relationship between us as we work together. Later, as I begin to draw attention to aspects of the transference relationship, I explain that exploring what happens between us is helpful in understanding in a live way their relationships with others and their own inner world.

As McWilliams (2004) observes, the only experience that most of our clients have of someone who repeatedly draws attention to how they are perceived by the other is with those who are narcissistically preoccupied. This might increase their anxiety that they have sought help from someone who is themselves narcissistically needy. Of course, such a perception is itself grist to the interpretive mill, and says something about how your client perceives the world. But working with it requires both that your client has reached a point in his therapy where he is able to express his anxiety about his therapist's narcissism and that he is oriented towards his relationship with you in such a way that he can use the subsequent interpretation of his anxiety.

MAKING TRANSFERENCE INTERPRETATIONS

In Chapter 1 I discussed the fact that skills in psychodynamic practice cannot be formulaic if they are to be a meaningful response to the client who is in the room with you. This particularly applies to making transference interpretations. The aim of a transference interpretation is to make a link between your client's feelings and/or behaviour and his inner world, and the way in which this link becomes manifest in the therapeutic situation. However, it should always be remembered that an interpretation is no more than a hypothesis – and as such it may be an incorrect hypothesis. I think it is more important to consider how useful an interpretation is at a given moment in time. Whereas a well-timed 'correct' interpretation is often valuable, a 'correct' interpretation that is wrongly timed is not. Paradoxically, an incorrect interpretation may be useful if it opens up a new way of thinking.

I find it helpful to remember Heimann's counsel that we ask ourselves 'who am I at this moment in time for this client?'. Her advice points to the shifts in the transference that can take place over a session as we are assigned different roles in our client's internal drama. Both who we are and how the client responds to us at a given moment in the session will depend on his state of mind.

Vicky had announced an unscheduled break during the previous session. Her mother had had an emergency admission to hospital and Vicky was going home to care for her. Tom had not responded to the news and had denied that the unscheduled break was a problem. Vicky had been surprised by his lack of overt affect, since they had done some important work at the time of her previous cancellations. This was her last session with Tom before she left.

Tom was agitated at the beginning of the session and dismissive of anything that Vicky said. When she tried to take up the forthcoming break he was contemptuous of her for thinking she was important to him. Eventually he said he had had a phone call the previous day from his sister in Canada telling him that she and their mother may cancel their planned trip to the UK. They were due to arrive the following month and were going to spend time with him and his brother in the flat. Tom wanted to see his mother; he felt ready to talk to her about how he felt about her decision to return to Canada just as he started his dental studies. However, when his sister told him that they may cancel the trip, he had found himself unable to say anything. He wanted to beg his sister to ensure they did come. However, he became mute and found himself not even able to ask why the trip might be cancelled.

Vicky began by helping Tom to become aware of his feelings of helplessness and despair about ever having access to his mother. She next made extra-transference interpretations about the repetition for him that his mother may again 'disappear', and his distress that he could do nothing about it. He said 'No-one says anything to her. My sister just stands by and lets it happen.' Vicky made the link between Tom's sister's apparent failure to challenge their mother's wish to cancel and his father's failure to stop his mother from leaving when he was a child. She then said, 'I wonder whether a part of you wishes that I would get on to your mother for you, and tell her that she can't treat you like this.' Her interpretation facilitated Tom in being able to acknowledge just how much he longed for someone to protect him from his mother's neglect, how much he wished that Vicky could change things for him. This led to him being able to feel the hurt that his father failed to protect him from his mother's abandonment and to acknowledge his longing for her not to leave him.

Next Vicky addressed her own 'disappearance' the following week, hypothesising that Tom might feel that, like his mother, she was disappearing without explanation. Tom suddenly became very angry: 'You think you can just go, without any explanation, and I just have to put up with it! Whenever I think I'm safe with you, you disappear. You just go.' He began to weep. Vicky reinforced the importance of him being able to tell her how he felt. She then helped Tom to see that, although it felt to him that she was doing the same as his mother, in that she was going away, she was not doing so without warning or explanation. She went on to say that Tom was dealing with the situation differently in that he was telling her how angry he was with her for going.

This vignette illustrates how Tom's transference to Vicky shifts during the session from experiencing her as an impotent father who cannot stop his mother's neglect of him, to an abandoning mother, who is leaving him without explanation. Quite often the shifts in the transference are more subtle, as our client experiences us as manifesting different aspects of the same object, for example Tom might have experienced Vicky alternately as an abandoning and then a seductive mother.

The vignette also illustrates aspects of technique in making transference interpretations. Lemma (2003) makes a number of recommendations when constructing a transference interpretation, some of which I will use to evaluate the interpretations in the above vignette.

- What is the purpose of the interpretation? How does it fit with the overall aims of treatment? *The purpose of the interpretation was initially to facilitate Tom in moving from a general feeling of agitation to being able to articulate the affects associated with his experience of being abandoned and not protected. Vicky was able to demonstrate the fact that, although she too was leaving him, she was not going without warning or explanation. This fits with the overall aims of treatment since Vicky made a breach in the closed system of his inner world and demonstrated that external reality was different.*

- What is the evidence for making the interpretation? *There was evidence that Tom's anxiety and distress about being abandoned were being experienced in his current life (his mother threatening to cancel her trip); in his inner world (as when he was a child he was unable to articulate his distress); in the transference (he experienced Vicky as an abandoning mother).*

- How useful was the interpretation in relation to its timing? *The timing of this interpretation was appropriate because Vicky's forthcoming absence made the issue of abandonment 'alive'. It was important to take up Tom's distress before she went, so that he had the experience of his protest being heard and acknowledged ahead of the event.*

- Can the client see how the interpretation has been arrived at? *Vicky was able to make a clear link between the past, the current situation outside the consulting room and the transference relationship.*

In linking the present situation, the past, and the transference relationship, Vicky made a full interpretation. However, very often, we are not able to make a full interpretation straight away, and it is not always necessary. Understanding our client's unconscious communication is a painstaking task, which often only becomes clearer over a number of sessions as the situation unfolds. Most of the time we are making partial interpretations of one aspect of the situation. Each interpretation is a small and incremental step towards the creation of a more complete picture of our client's internal world.

Lastly I want to touch on how we gauge the success of our interpretations. A rule of thumb used to be that a successful interpretation was followed by either a complementary emotional reaction from the client (a catharsis) or by further material that was confirmatory of the interpretation. Unfortunately this can become a circular argument since confirmatory material does not necessarily mean that an interpretation was correct – it may be an indication of compliance. More helpfully Klauber (1986) proposed that a successful interpretation brings therapist and client closer together emotionally. Again this is difficult to measure, but the experience is one of feeling connected at a deep level, which happens during right brain to right brain activity and which results in opioid production and a corresponding increase in positive affect.

WORKING WITH THE NEGATIVE TRANSFERENCE

Your client may have difficulty in spontaneously expressing his negative feelings about you. This could be for a number of reasons: the fear that his anger or hostility will drive you away; that his anger will overwhelm and destroy you; that, if he becomes aware of you as flawed in any way, he will become contemptuous of you. In any event, he is likely to fear that he will lose you and be left alone. At some stage you need to help him face, and perhaps even discover, his negative feelings towards you. If he does not he may be stuck in therapy, trapped by a negative transference that cannot be faced. Woods (2003) makes the point that it can be necessary with very damaged clients to wait until therapy has progressed sufficiently that benign objects have been established in the client's mind before it is possible to explore 'the darker side of the transference'. Only when your client feels that the relationship with you is secure, is it sufficiently safe for him to face the negative transference.

When your client does not spontaneously express his negative feelings your task lies in helping him to do so while at the same time holding him safely, so that he is able to face his difficult feelings within the security of the relationship with you. This may involve implicitly or explicitly giving him permission to express his frustration, disappointment, hostility or anger with you. Like Woods, I generally prefer to interpret the negative transference within a positive therapeutic alliance with such clients, so that early interpretations are contextualised within a framework that acknowledges both positive and negative feelings. I also wait until there is an opening where, from experience, I know there is the potential for my client to experience negative feelings.

During her first break in therapy Mary had had a difficult time in my absence. She became depressed and her GP had prescribed anti-depressant medication. At first she did not tell me about her difficulties over the summer, and it came out gradually. I took up her reluctance to tell me by saying that she seemed to want to keep from me how awful the break had been for her. I wondered why this was. She said that she hadn't wanted me to know because she didn't want me to worry about her; she had coped all right in the end. I said that I wondered whether a part of her might have felt that I should have known about how hard the summer break was for her. She reluctantly agreed and said that she had had conversations with me in her head over the summer. I said 'I wonder if you feel that I chose not to hear you, and left you on your own. Perhaps it was then hard to tell me about it when you came back if you already felt I hadn't heard.'

Sometimes, as in the above vignette, such negative feelings are just beneath the surface and are not too difficult to access. But for some, negative feelings towards their therapist have to be buried very deeply, and may not be consciously accessible. Let's imagine an alternative response from Mary to my question about why she hadn't told me how awful the break had been: *'It had never occurred to me that I should tell you.'* I might then say something like: *'It sounds like you are not in touch with a part of you that might really have minded that I went away just when you were beginning to settle in to being here. If you did mind I wonder if you feel that you couldn't tell me.'*

As therapists we tend to vary as to how comfortable we feel with the negative transference, and this is where your own therapy will assist you. If you have been able to express your own feelings of disappointment, anger or hatred with your therapist it will make it easier to tolerate those feelings in your clients. You will know that not only can such feelings be survived, but that the acknowledgement of them also leads to a greater depth of intimacy between you which often heralds therapeutic progress.

Some clients are dominated by their negative transference, and we need to help them to discover their warm feelings towards us. This can feel like an uphill struggle, not least because any indication from us that they might need us or that we are important in their lives can be treated with scorn. Remember that, at some level, your client does need you and that the ongoing expression of his negativity is a way of keeping himself safe. This may be because he fears your contempt if he shows himself as needy or vulnerable, or that you will abandon him. As with interpreting the negative transference, you should look for evidence that there is a nascent positive transference that your client is consciously aware of or that is just below conscious awareness before making interpretations.

Joel was relentless in his criticism of me. He complained about my consulting room being too hot or cold, the timing of his sessions, or the fact that I was 'never there'. He dismissed my attempts to understand or empathise with him. However, he was always on time and never missed a session. I had decided against taking up with him any value he might attach to his sessions with me, since there was evidence from his description of his other relationships that his experience of my uselessness was repeated with other people in his life. I had hypothesised that his sense of self had coalesced around bad objects, and that to challenge that too soon might be unbearable for him.

One day he arrived late for his session; the centre of town was blocked, necessitating a diversion in heavy traffic. He was visibly shaken and described in detail how he had tried to find alternative routes around the congestion. This gave me an opportunity to take up how much he minded being late and missing part of his session. Later, I wondered to him that he might mind me seeing that it mattered to him. Over a number of sessions we began to discuss just how important his sessions were. It took some while for this to be translated into an acknowledgement that I was important to him, but he was eventually able to describe warm feelings for me and how much that scared him.

USING THE COUNTERTRANSFERENCE

Kernberg (2004) reminds us that the more disturbed a client is, the more he will communicate through non-verbal means, which will become manifest in his therapist's countertransference. Although very damaged clients may use this form of communication as their dominant mode, other clients will use it to communicate those parts of themselves that they are cut off from, as well as the more primitive aspects of their functioning.

Countertransference readiness

Countertransference readiness involves making available an internal space in which you can receive your client's transference. You also need to have developed the capacity for honest self-scrutiny, so that you can acknowledge your contribution to his behaviour. Additionally, you need the capacity to observe yourself at the same time as experiencing powerful feelings.

The best preparation for doing this is your own thorough therapy. This is for two reasons. Firstly you will become more aware of your own vulnerabilities, and those areas in which you are prone to distortion; by becoming accustomed to your own emotional responses you will be more aware of when you are in difficulty. Secondly, by strengthening your own ego, you should be better able to become a container for your clients' projections and become more able to observe your own response. While it does not make you immune from making countertransference errors, it does mean that you are more aware of issues you are particularly sensitive to and alert to their possible revival. The countertransference becomes problematic when a client projects aspects of himself that correspond too closely with aspects of his therapist that she has not yet incorporated. This is why it is important to be in therapy during training and to have good supervision once qualified, since it should provide a safe space in which to disentangle what belongs to whom in the therapeutic relationship.

Technique in using the countertransference

Segal (1993) makes the observation that when therapists speak of the transference they recognise that the major part of it is unconscious, but that when they speak about the countertransference they do so in a way that suggests that it is a conscious activity. I think this highlights an important problem in tracking and then using the counter-transference. By definition our unconscious is not available to us; what we become aware of is what Segal calls its conscious derivatives. I think this goes some way to helping us understand why the use of the countertransference remains a contentious issue in psychodynamic practice, and that it is an area that is open to both misunder-standing and abuse. Additionally, there is less guidance about using the countertrans-ference than in other areas, and we rely more on our own capacities than in other aspects of the work. On the one hand there are no formulae for making use of coun-tertransference information; but at the same time we all need to find a way to do so.

Heimann advocated that as well as having freely hovering attention, the thera-pist 'needs a freely aroused emotional sensibility so as to perceive and follow closely his patient's emotional movements and unconscious phantasies' (1960: 10). To do this we use many forms of information generated from within ourselves, including our own intuition, feelings, passing images, physical sensations, memories and fan-tasies. Very often these sensations come without any deliberate attempt to access them, but Cozolino (2004) also recommends 'shuttling down' as a way of accessing one's countertransference. By this he means actively attending to the information in our inner world. He recommends that doing so can be particularly useful when you feel emotionally disconnected from your client; lost or confused by the con-tent of his material; when distracted away from your client or when your interpre-tations are being rejected.

At the same time as being aware of the information from our inner world, we also need to retain a state of uncertainty towards it – we do not know for sure what it relates to. As Bollas observes: 'the most ordinary countertransference state is a not-knowing-yet-experiencing one' (1987: 203). Staying with that experience, without defensively distancing ourselves from it or getting drawn into doing something prematurely (for example making a countertransference-based interpretation with insufficient evidence), is a significant challenge. The first caution is to be patient and to never rush into acting on the basis of your reactions to your client. Segal warns us that countertransference is 'the best of servants and the worst of masters' (1993: 20). This is because we have a tendency to identify with our countertransference and therefore believe that acting on it is legitimate in response to pressure from within. She warns us against 'acting under the pressure of the countertransference, rather than using it as a guide to understanding' (1993: 20). By this she is referring to action through interpretation, rather than acting out, though of course this too is a possibility. The more you feel under pressure to act on your internal feelings, the more likely it is that you would be responding to your countertransference. It is therefore important to stay with the feelings that have been stirred up within you and reflect on them, thereby gaining some distance from them, and with it some perspective. Do not do anything while ever you feel a powerful urge to do so. Only once you no longer feel under pressure to act should you begin to think about making an interpretation.

Tom was buoyant when Vicky returned to work after caring for her mother. She was relieved about this as she had felt guilty about leaving him. However, she was also rather disappointed that he seemed to have managed so well without her. As the end of the session approached she felt herself under significant internal pressure to give him extra time. She rationalised internally that they had reached an important juncture in the session, and that they needed to make up for the missed sessions. This was not something Tom had asked for, but something that emanated from inside her. Although she felt under internal pressure to offer him the extra time, Vicky also felt that it was important to keep to the frame of therapy and maintain the time boundary. Furthermore, she felt uneasy about the pressure she felt under and wanted time to think with Kate about whether she should offer Tom something more.

By the time she arrived at supervision, Vicky had already begun to wonder whether her feelings had been a response to Tom's apparent buoyancy following her absence. Together with Kate, she hypothesised that Tom had been unable to articulate his wish for more of her following her absence, and that he defended himself against his need for her through manic denial. While presenting as buoyant and coping, he had projected the part of him that needed more into Vicky. They wondered if this was how he had reacted when his mother returned after her absences. If this hypothesis was correct, it suggested that Tom had distanced himself from his internal state because it was unbearable to know just how much he had missed her. This meant that it was important to consider the function of the defence and to think about whether Tom needed Vicky to continue to contain and metabolise his feelings, or whether he would be able to hear an interpretation based on Vicky's countertransference.

Vicky also needed to disentangle her own needs, particularly her identification with Tom's longing for an uninterrupted relationship with his therapist. She had found it very difficult that she had missed her own therapy sessions with me, and she wondered if she wanted to give Tom what she was missing out on. She used her therapy sessions to explore this, and her disappointment that I had not offered her extra time to make up for what had been missed. She now felt more confident in taking up Tom's feelings about missing her and his need to distance himself from those feelings.

In the next session Vicky was surprised at the change in Tom's demeanour. He looked sad and defeated. He eventually said that he had felt low since shortly after their last session. Vicky suggested that, in being very upbeat with her, he had distanced himself from the difficulty of coping with the missed sessions. He might have felt that the distressed part of him had not been seen. He agreed that he had found the time she was away difficult, but that he had felt much better by the time of his session. Vicky then asked him if that was how he was when his mother returned after her absences. 'Yes, I was never going to let her see how much I missed her' he said. 'And I think you did not want me to know how much you missed me' she replied. She then wondered if he was concerned that, if she knew how much he wanted to see her, she might feel he wanted too much from her. He said he was afraid she would think he was being needy, and that she would send him away if he couldn't manage without her. This led to them being able to think further about his anxiety that her interest in him was conditional on him not showing her how much he needed her.

In the first part of this vignette Vicky contained Tom's projection of his wish to have more of her, along with his anxiety that to have more would expose his neediness and would lead to his rejection by her. If Vicky had acted on her countertransference impulse to give him extra time there would have been a number of possible outcomes. One is that he would have experienced her as trying to pretend that being away could be made up for as though it had not happened, potentially leading to compliance or rage. Countertransference enactment by therapists can lead to the overwhelming of the client's ego with the fear that his powerful feelings and phantasies are capable of overpowering his therapist. She then ceases to be someone he can feel safe with. If Vicky had made an interpretation based on her countertransference in the first session she may have increased Tom's defensiveness, since it might have been overwhelming for him to have to re-introject the feelings that he was projecting into her.

By containing the feelings for him, Vicky gave Tom the opportunity to have an experience of her as an object who was present for him and could care for him. His sadness in the second session could be understood as him being more in touch with depressive feelings about the break, and missing Vicky. At this point he became more available to hear Vicky making interpretations based on her countertransference. At the same time Vicky had recruited her own observing ego and other resources, in the shape of her supervisor and her therapist to understand and reflect on her response and to disentangle her own feelings from Tom's.

This vignette may give the impression that countertransference is easily understood and resolved, and that interpretations are readily identified. I have done this for the purpose of illustration. Although sometimes the countertransference does present itself in this way, more usually we struggle with trying to understand what is going on. Feelings, images or thoughts are often fleeting or they are not quite possible to make sense of. This can go on for many sessions until they coalesce into something that we can more clearly identify as a feeling or a thought that is recognisable as countertransference in the way I have described above.

FURTHER READING

Alexandris, A. and Vaslamatzis, G. (eds) (1993) *Countertransference: Theory, Technique, Teaching*. London: Karnac.

10

UNDERSTANDING AND WORKING WITH DEFENCES

We need defences to survive. By this I mean that we need ways of protecting ourselves from the psychic pain that is a normal part of the human condition. Indeed, defences have often been likened to a psychic skin, which has similar protective functions to our physical skin by providing a barrier against life's knocks. We tend to take our defences for granted – and indeed are unaware of their operation, since they are almost entirely unconscious. However, although we feel better when our defensive system is working, we can pay a high price if our inner reality becomes too distorted. Defences can be normal and adaptive as well as pathological, so our aim in working with our clients is not to completely divest them of their defences. Rather we aim to enable them to use their defensive system flexibly and to be more in touch with reality.

Our clients often come for help when their defensive system can no longer cope with their level of distress, and they fear being overwhelmed by the resultant anxiety. Defences are most problematic when they are fixed, and therefore overly rigid, and become part of our character structure. Very rigid defensive structures are restrictive in living life and conducting relationships. When defences are used in situations which don't in reality warrant them, their use leads to further distress rather than protecting us from pain.

Delia was twenty-two years old and was unable to go to bed at night without performing a series of rituals. She had been an anxious child, who had responded to the sometimes violent relationship between her parents by going to her room and lining up her dolls in a strict and predetermined order. If prevented from doing so she became very distressed. Her parents separated when Delia was sixteen and she lived with her mother. When her mother began a new relationship Delia became anxious that someone would break into their house at night

(Continued)

(Continued)

and hurt her mother. She needed to check that all the windows and external doors were locked; her mother's reassurance that they were closed was not enough. Her obsession developed gradually, until it took her nearly an hour to go to bed because each ritual had to be performed many times and in a particular sequence. She stopped going out in the evenings, fearing something would happen to her mother in her absence. The idea that her mother could come to harm distressed her. She told her therapist 'I love her very much, I can't bear that anything should happen to her.'

A psychodynamic conceptualisation of Delia's obsessive-compulsive disorder would hypothesise that Delia was actually very angry with her mother for engaging in a new relationship. The conflict between a wish to damage her in order to punish her, and a fear that by doing so she would lose her, was outside Delia's conscious awareness. Because unconsciously she feared her anger was overwhelming and dangerous, she needed to develop a defensive strategy which would keep her fury with her mother from conscious awareness. This defence was to 'undo' the damage she feared she had done her mother through ensuring that her mother was safe from an external and unknown 'other'. In fact, the 'other' represented Delia, and it was herself she was trying to protect her mother from through her rituals. The rituals had become fixed and the defence of undoing a source of distress in its own right. Working with Delia would involve helping her to be able to acknowledge her negative feelings towards her mother in the context of a safe therapeutic relationship. Most probably Delia would find any expression of negative feelings difficult, so considerable work may need to be done in helping her to acknowledge such feelings in safer, extra-transference, relationships. Only then could they be tackled in the transference or in relation to her mother.

The theoretical basis for the concept

The traditional view of defences is that we need them either to manage internal conflict or to manage our relationships with our objects. The former conceptualisation originates from classical theory, the latter from object relations theory. Developmental theorists understand defences as reflecting a developmental arrest before mental structures are in place. Alvarez (1992) proposes that defences have an adaptive function, which enables the child to survive difficult early experiences. Although the approaches originate in different schools of psychodynamic thought, in practice many therapists combine them according to the needs of their client at a particular stage in their work together. It is also important to remember that defences are not in themselves psychic entities, and therefore cannot be understood in isolation from the use we put them to. Thus they can only be understood in terms of the functions they serve.

Stages of development and types of defences

Psychoanalysis has long held that defences originate at different stages of development. There is a distinction between those which originate before oedipal functioning and those that develop afterwards. Thus the defences someone is deploying at any one time are thought to be an indicator of their current level of functioning. It has been demonstrated that people who use more mature defences are more likely to experience successful life adjustments at work, in relationships, and in their medical history (Vaillant, 1977). The excessive use of defences associated with early development is seen as an indication of more severe pathology, with greater accompanying damage to the personality.

Many modern thinkers argue against the practice of labelling defences. They propose that doing so prevents really thinking about our client's defensive solutions to their difficulties. Brenner (1976) observed that, since the whole range of ego functions can be used defensively, no list of defences can ever be exhaustive. Similarly, Steiner (1993) talks about systems of defence rather than individual defences. Lemma argues that 'It is far more useful clinically to describe in plain language what the patient is trying to do and why they need to do it than to use the shorthand of labels' (2003: 210–211).

The features of defences

In healthy functioning, defences are more likely to come into play only when needed. So, for example, a person may use denial to help him cope with anxiety about dying in the face of a potentially terminal illness. However, the same man might be able to face the loss of his home without denial. When defences become entrenched and overused, they also become part of the structure of the personality, or characterological. The person who denies that anything is ever a problem (like Voltaire's hero, Candide, who declared that everything was for the best in the best of all possible worlds) is someone for whom denial has become part of who he is.

While some defences are 'ego-syntonic' (that is there is no conscious conflict about deploying the defence), others are 'ego-dystonic' (the use of the defence causes distress). Someone who manages his social anxiety by avoiding people, but does not regard it as a problem, is demonstrating an ego-syntonic defence. If, by contrast, he is upset about his avoidance and wants to find a way of socialising with others, we would call it an ego-dystonic defence. A defence needs to become ego-dystonic for the client in order to give it up, and it is part of our job to facilitate the process of unhelpful defences becoming ego-dystonic.

One way you can do this is by helping your client to think about his reaction to someone else who uses the same defence. If someone who drinks too much to manage a social phobia talks about an acquaintance who is also drinking too much, you might help him to think about the impact of that person's drinking. It is important not to do so in a way that sounds critical, however. Another way to encourage ego-dystonicity is through your concern for your client. For example, if a man uses alcohol in an

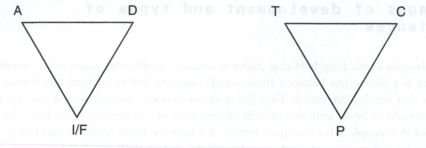

Triangle of Conflict

A = Anxiety
D = Defence
I/F = Impulse/Feeling

Triangle of Person

T = Transference Relationship
C = Current Relationships
P = Past Relationships

Figure 10.1 Triangle of Person and Triangle of Conflict

Adapted from Menninger's (1958) Triangle of Conflict and Malan's (1979) Triangle of Person (Malan, D. (1979) *Individual Psychotherapy and the Science of Psychodynamics.* London: Butterworth)

ego-syntonic way, and tells you about drinking too much to calm his nerves, you might show concern about his need to use alcohol in this way. The experience of a 'concerned other' may begin to facilitate his own concern for himself. It is important to do this in a way that does not patronise him. A third possibility is to suggest to your client that he might already be unhappy with what he is doing. I might say 'The way you are telling me about this sounds as though a bit of you is worried by how much you are drinking.' He may disagree, but the possibility of becoming concerned may begin to take root in his mind.

DEFENCES AGAINST CONFLICT

In working with conflict-driven defences we are pre-supposing the existence of an ego. Menninger's (1958) Triangle of Conflict and Malan's (1979) Triangle of Person are helpful in interpreting conflict. In the triangle of conflict impulses and feelings, defences and anxiety each occupy one of the three points (see Figure 10.1). The triangle of person depicts important relationships in the client's life, thus reminding us that conflict always takes place in an interpersonal context. In the triangle of conflict, the impulse or feeling is at the base of the triangle because this is what drives the intrapsychic system. Anxiety is the reaction to the feeling, and the defence is the mechanism employed to reduce that anxiety.

Davenloo (1980) advocates a robust approach to working with conflict-driven defences in his Intensive Short-Term Dynamic Psychotherapy (ISTDP). He suggests initially identifying the defensive behaviour as it arises, firstly through identifying the defence, and then by clarifying its function – what feeling it is protecting the client from. Next he ensures that the client can distinguish between the defence and the feeling, and if not facilitates this. Lastly, he helps the client identify the anxiety that is elicited as the feeling is uncovered. The vignette below demonstrates how this might unfold (*D* stands for defence, *A* for anxiety, and *F* for feeling).

Vicky's second client, Zoë, is in short-term therapy following the break-up of her relationship with her boyfriend. Zoë is twenty and lives at home with her mother and younger sister, Winnie, whom she talks about in an idealised way. Zoë frequently buys Winnie small gifts or takes her out, while at the same time hinting that Winnie often lets her down, and that she feels outside the relationship between Winnie and their mother. Vicky and Kate hypothesise that Zoë is defending against her negative feelings towards Winnie and that she must be anxious about what would happen should she allow herself to experience them. In this session Zoë describes how Winnie had agreed to accompany her to the tennis club where Zoë and her boyfriend had met. This would be her first visit since the break-up. Winnie let Zoë down at the last moment, saying she needed to study. Zoë had gone into town on the way to her session to buy Winnie a CD 'to compensate for all the hard work she's having to do at the moment.'

Vicky: I have noticed that each time Winnie promises you something and then lets you down, you either tell me what a wonderful person she is or you do something to please her [*D*].

Zoë: [*tearfully*] I know.

Vicky: Do you know why you do that?

Zoë: No. I just can feel this uncomfortable feeling inside me if I don't do something nice for her [*A*]. As soon as I do something nice I feel better again [*D*].

Vicky: Do you think the uncomfortable feeling [*A*] might be to do with being upset [*F*] because she has let you down [*A–F link*]?

Zoë: I don't know. I'm not meant to feel upset. I'm older than her. Mum always said I should look after Winnie.

Vicky: I wonder what you think would happen if you didn't look after her, or you got upset [*A*]?

Zoë: Mum would be cross with me. She'd take Winnie's side. She says I have to understand how difficult life is for Winnie, and that I mustn't be selfish and ask too much of her.

Vicky: It sounds to me as though you're saying that you're frightened of upsetting your Mum [*F*].

Zoë: Yes, when she gets angry with me sometimes she doesn't speak to me for days.

Vicky: It sounds like you get anxious that if you get cross with Winnie your mother won't be there for you [*A*]. So each time Winnie does something to upset you, you have to push down any angry feelings and instead replace them with good feelings about her [*D*]. You prove that by buying her something nice [*D*], because otherwise you become anxious that your Mum will see how angry you really are [*F*] and will leave you on your own.

Zoë experiences a conflict between feelings of anger towards her sister and the fear that if she expresses them she will be punished and lose her mother's approval and support. The defence she uses is a reaction formation and involves being very giving, and forgiving, towards her sister. It was not difficult for Vicky to help Zoë to see this, as it was very near to the surface. It was also not entirely ego-syntonic and therefore more easy to work with.

UNDERSTANDING PRIMITIVE DEFENCES

Klein's contribution has had a profound influence on clinical practice, and I am going to discuss it in some detail. Because Klein believed that babies are born with a partially developed ego, she argued it was possible to identify primitive mechanisms that defend the ego. She consequently proposed that defences are present from the beginning of life. She considered these primitive defences to be aspects of the paranoid-schizoid position and that splitting was one of the most important of these defences.

Splitting

The function of splitting is to protect our objects from our aggression. If we split our object into good and bad we preserve him from being completely destroyed when we attack the 'bad' part of him. Because the 'good' bit of him survives we are protected from being deprived of him. Although some splitting is viewed as a normal part of functioning, it becomes pathological when it becomes a primary way of relating to people. This is because in order to split our objects into good and bad we have to correspondingly split our ego into the parts that relate to the good and bad. A split ego is damaging for a number of reasons. There are distortions in the way we perceive the world; we experience difficulties in making links between things, which interferes with being able to think; we experience our objects as part objects, so they can be terrifying because their 'bad' aspects are not balanced by their 'good' ones.

Mark was referred to therapy for help with anger difficulties. His three year old daughter, Alice, had fallen from a swing in the park. She was briefly unconscious and was kept overnight in hospital. Mark had separated a year previously from Gemma, Alice's mother. Alice lived with Gemma, although Mark had applied for custody. Alice was with Gemma when the accident happened and Mark blamed his ex-wife and accused her of not being sufficiently attentive. He became very vigilant and frequently visited Gemma's home to check up on how she was caring for Alice. This caused increasingly acrimonious rows, but Mark could not stop himself, convinced that only he could properly care for Alice. Gemma threatened legal action if he did not stop coming to the house and following her when she took Alice out.

Mark gradually revealed that, as a child, he had often been left to care for his younger siblings while their parents went out. One day, while looking after his siblings, Mark's younger brother fell from an upstairs window and sustained a severe concussion. A scar on his forehead was a constant reminder of what had happened. Fearful that they would be reported to social services, Mark's parents claimed they were in the house, and he was pressured to lie about what had happened. Mark said that his world fell apart that day as he could no longer trust his parents. He concluded that the only person he could trust was himself, and as soon as he was old enough he had left home and had had little contact with them since.

Mark was cut off from any feelings about his parents other than contempt for them; they were useless and could not be trusted. Similarly Gemma was now the object of his contempt. Gradually he came to see the link between his brother's fall and Alice's accident. However this provided him with only a little relief and he continued to rage against the folly of Alice living with her mother. In his mind he split caring and neglect, lodging the neglect in Gemma and the care and vigilance in himself.

In therapy Mark swung between feeling his therapist was uncaring and that she was too vigilant. Careful work in the transference gradually helped him to experience her as able to look after him, and to see that she could be both caring and at times inattentive to his needs. As the split gradually healed he began to see that he, too, could be inattentive. He was able to face the guilt and distress, that he had long denied, about his inability to care for his younger brother. With that came the realisation of the resentment he felt towards his siblings, and later toward Alice, that he bore the responsibility for their care in the face of not being properly cared for himself.

In this vignette there is a move from paranoid-schizoid functioning, in which splitting of himself and his objects predominated, to a more mature, depressive functioning. Mark was then able to see that his objects, and himself, were both good (caring) and bad (neglectful). This movement both reflects and is a function of a strengthening of the ego.

Klein's other original contribution was to take the concepts of projection and identification and develop a third concept which she called 'projective identification'. Before looking at projective identification, I want to briefly consider projection and identification, since they are both important defensive mechanisms in their own right.

Projection

Projection is the process by which we ascribe our own feelings or characteristics to other people when we cannot 'own' them ourselves. It acts as an unconscious defence because it protects us from having to cope with the distress of the difference between who we are and who we would wish to be. Having projected the unwanted part of ourselves, we can then criticise, punish or even idealise the person who is the recipient of our projection, without having to take any responsibility for our own shortcomings or failures. While we might feel better in the short term from projecting unwanted parts of ourselves, there is a cost. When we project feelings onto someone else, a part of our self or ego gets projected along with the feeling. If this becomes a habitual way of managing our internal discomfort, our sense of self becomes impoverished. There is another problem: if the projection 'boomerangs' back on us, we can feel quite perse-cuted. In our work with clients there will come a time when we need to help them own the projection themselves, a process known as 're-introjection'.

It was some time since Vicky had talked about her work with Tom. This sur-prised me as she had been very anxious about him, and had needed both Kate and me to help contain her anxiety. About a month after she had last spoken about him, she began to talk in quite a distressed way about her conviction that I thought she was unsuitable as a psychodynamic therapist. She could not tell me why she felt this, only that she was sure of it. She was convinced that I was going to contact her training organisation to tell them that she should not progress to the next stage of her training. She protested that she was working hard, that Kate had said she was doing well, and it was important that I realised that. Eventually I said to her 'I think there *is* someone in this room who feels that you're not suitable as a psychotherapist – and it isn't me.' Although startled by this Vicky began to think about her own fears that she did not have the neces-sary personal qualities to become a psychotherapist. In doing so she began the process of re-introjecting her projection.

Identification

Identification refers to the way in which we imitate another person, and as we do so our internal image of ourselves evolves and develops; this happens by virtue of taking aspects of the other person in. Sandler and Perlow (1988) distinguish between primary and secondary identification. In an adult client primary identification leads to an experience in which he regresses and 'de-differentiates'. Consequently the boundaries between himself and other people no longer work and become permeable. At its most extreme it is seen in psychotic states when the person becomes confused between himself and someone else. Secondary identification refers to the more common mean-ing of the term. In this form of identification we retain a sense of ourselves, so we know the other person is not us, but we appropriate his positive attributes for our-selves. In an everyday sense this can be seen in fan clubs, where the fan's self-esteem is enhanced through an association with someone famous.

Identification can be used as a defence in order to manage the anxieties of being separate from our objects, or feelings of low self-esteem. If we are part of another per-son we cannot be abandoned by them, and if we can be associated with someone who has all the qualities we long for we can feel that we, too, are special. However, there is a high price to pay since, as Fairbairn (1952) has observed, identification results in a loss of a sense of 'I' and we become dependent on the person with whom we identify in order to have a sense of self. This leaves us vulnerable if we lose that person.

Lawrence and Sally had been young high fliers in the same bank. Once they married Sally took a back seat professionally to facilitate Lawrence's career. When they had children Sally became a full-time mother and, as Lawrence climbed the corporate ladder, she supported him. She believed Lawrence could get right to the top and she felt that she should be there with him; she talked about 'our career'. Once the children were more independent, Sally put all her energies into excelling as a corporate wife and hostess. However, she began to have anxieties about whether Lawrence would make it to the very top. Although undoubtedly talented, he also had a reputation for upsetting people and, when he went for the next promotion, he failed to get it. Sally was devastated. She knew that, having missed out on this opportunity for promotion, Lawrence was unlikely to reach the top, even if he got promotion in the next round. People younger than he were now at his level or overtaking him.

Sally fell into a deep depression and was referred to therapy. It was clear from early in our work that she lacked a sense of who she was, and that she was almost totally dependent on Lawrence to give her an identity. His lack of success was hers, and with it came a crushing sense of being valueless and empty. Her response to being in therapy was an immediate and powerful identification with her therapist, and initially she contemplated becoming a counsellor. She did not have sufficient sense of herself to be able to consider something that would separate her from her object (in this case her therapist). Therapeutic work involved helping Sally to gradually discover her own thoughts, feelings and desires. She found this terrifying since it threatened her with separateness from her objects and this she could only see as risking total abandonment and rejection.

Projective identification

Klein's original formulation of projective identification was based around the idea that the projection was 'into' the other person, rather than 'onto' them, as it had been conceptualised until then. This implies in some way changing the other person as a result of the projection. Klein thought that projective identification served a number of functions:

- To avoid psychic pain by splitting off and getting rid of parts of oneself that cause it.
- To avoid feelings of separateness by projecting the self or part of the self into an object.
- To invade the object in order to damage or control it.
- To get inside the object and have the good things inside it.

Klein did not just see the negative aspects of projective identification, however. She also felt that by projecting 'good' parts of the self, self-esteem and other good feelings would be enhanced. Klein's ideas have been developed by later writers, and projective identification today is largely understood as having a communicative function. This can be through projecting part of oneself into the other in order that that person will feel or act in accordance with what is being projected into them. This has become the basis for our current thinking about the countertransference.

Projective identification acts as a defence when it gets rid of parts of the self that are unacceptable or unbearable. If successful, it helps the client to maintain his psychological balance or equilibrium. However, once these aspects of the self are located in the other, he or she may actually begin to behave in accordance with what has been projected. So, if hostile feelings are projected, the recipient of the projective identification may actually begin to behave in a persecutory manner.

Tom had made significant progress and Vicky had agreed to his request that they increase their sessions to twice a week. However, soon after doing so, she became increasingly sleepy in his sessions. At first it was imperceptible, but gradually it came to dominate the session. Shortly into the session she felt her eyelids become heavy and she longed to close them. She found it difficult to concentrate on what he was saying as she put most of her energies into staying alert. She could only survive the session, hoping that she would not actually fall asleep. As soon as Tom had gone she was once again alert. She began to feel irritated and undermined by her inability to manage this or connect to him.

Kate suspected that Tom had retreated from the relationship with Vicky following the recent progress they had made. Kate called it a negative therapeutic reaction. Instead of discussing his anxieties about feeling closer to Vicky, he had projected his wish to 'shut down' into her. She had received his projection and was 'shutting down' for him, thus protecting him from the anxiety of being properly connected to her. Vicky tested the hypothesis out by taking up with Tom that he might find their progress difficult, in particular that he was beginning to value what she gave him. He said that he had found it difficult; he did not want to be dependent on her. Vicky hypothesised that he might want to get away from therapy. He agreed: he had been thinking that it might be time to stop. However, he was also aware that he had done that before, and he did want to continue. Throughout the session Vicky was aware that she no longer felt sleepy and was instead connected to Tom.

Tom had used projective identification as a means of defending himself against an unbearable quandary. He wanted to hold on to his object but felt anxious about becoming more intimate with her. In the face of this he shut down and projected his inability to manage the conflict into Vicky who, through the process of projective identification, became disconnected from him. Sandler and Sandler (1978) called this aspect of projective identification 'role responsiveness'. It requires the therapist to respond slightly to the role the client places her in, while at the same time being sufficiently centred on herself and able to retain some objectivity so that she can observe the process as it unfolds. It was only when Vicky was able to articulate the conflict in supervision that she could divest herself of the projective identification and begin to think again.

THE CONCEPT OF DEFICIT IN DEFENCE

Models of the mind which conceptualise deficit as central to psychological distress see defences through a different lens. Winnicott's position is that the quality of his early experience determines how the baby's ego develops. If his mother is 'good-enough' when her baby is at the stage of near absolute dependence, he does not need to organise primitive defences. These only become organised if his mother is unable to be sufficiently responsive to his needs and cannot offer him a 'facilitating environment'. The facilitating environment provides the baby with a protective shield within which he can grow normally. Without this the baby develops his own protective shield, which Winnicott called the False Self. He proposed that the baby's True Self is protected from environmental failure by the defensive False Self which acts to prevent intrusion by a mother who is not sensitive to her baby's needs.

Many psychodynamic practitioners today have incorporated a developmental view into the way in which defensive processes are used and understood. The defensive system is understood to operate in the service of psychological development, not solely in a defensive way. Kohut (1985) argued that many behaviours that were considered defences were in fact filling a genuine developmental need in someone who was insecure because of psychological deficits. Alvarez goes further and proposes that defences can preserve life as well as helping us to avoid pain: 'We should not confuse the building of the house with the building of the defensive fortifications which may eventually surround it. We build houses with walls to keep the weather out, but also to mark, frame and preserve that which may take place within' (1992: 112). She also suggested that a mechanism that is traditionally understood as defensive might signal the beginning of change. Arguing that, at times defensive evasion is necessary because his defences are all that a client has, she noted that such evasion may be the only solution to a situation in which the client has not yet developed sufficiently to manage a more 'mature' modification of his anxieties.

These ideas all understand the client's problem as reflecting developmental arrest before mental structures are in place. As Money-Kyrle (1977) notes, it is important to distinguish between when a client is behaving in a certain way because he is deploying a defence and when he behaves in that way because he is desperate. Sometimes the client does not have the developmental apparatus to enable him to face his losses and fears, and pressurising him to do so involves asking for something he cannot, rather than will not, do. Attempting to force the issue may lead to him breaking down if a direct attempt to interpret his defences undermines his capacity to cope.

In terms of technique this has important implications. If a behaviour is functional, interpreting it as a defence will be experienced as a failure of empathy or, worse, perhaps as an attack. This may interfere with your client's capacity to trust you, and lead him to strengthen his defences – the opposite of what it was meant to achieve. Working with developmental deficit requires a very different approach from working with other forms of defence. It involves staying on your client's side and using the empathic attunement that authors such as Winnicott and Kohut advocate. For clients who have significant difficulties resulting from early damage,

Winnicott proposes the provision of a facilitating environment. This provides the conditions in which he is able to regress to the point where he can allow himself to be dependent on his therapist and find the True Self hidden behind his defensive apparatus. This kind of intervention is more suited to long-term work rather than short-term interventions, and to the greater level of intensity that accompanies more than one session a week.

It can put you under considerable strain if your client's defensive system gets under your skin. If a client forms a strong identification with you, so that you feel as though you are being taken over by him, you might long to directly interpret what he is doing as a way of protecting yourself from his intrusiveness. Taking a deficit approach requires containing and metabolising these feelings, and allowing him the time to develop psychic structures that will enable him to begin to gradually separate from you. This will be based on no longer needing to cope with the anxiety of separation by identifying with you, rather than having a cognitive appreciation of the importance of being separate.

A FRAMEWORK FOR INTERPRETATION

Just as your client's attachment system is activated when he begins therapy, so his defensive system will be activated too. He will need to protect himself from the threat that you inevitably represent to the equilibrium in his inner world. This is nothing to do with his motivation to be in or use therapy, but is a normal response to anxiety about being exposed to another, which is heightened at the beginning of therapy.

> Jeremy was referred by a colleague following a course of CBT, which had not alleviated his depression. I began the first session by asking him to tell me something about his difficulties. He responded by saying adamantly 'I just want you to know that this is nothing to do with my childhood. I had a wonderful childhood. There was no sexual abuse, my parents didn't divorce and I didn't get into any trouble as a teenager.' As he emphatically ticked the items off on his fingers, I was left in no doubt that his relationship with his family of origin was a no-go area.

It is important to be careful in how you respond to a new client's defensive system. You don't know what it is protecting. Until you have got to know him it is better not to challenge his defences, particularly if they are as clearly articulated as Jeremy's were. Your assessment of the level at which he is functioning and what your client might be defending himself against will determine how you work with his defences. This obviously varies, not only between clients, but also within your client at different times in his therapy. It is important to build up a carefully constructed picture of his defences and to be aware of how his ability to think about himself fluctuates within as well as between sessions.

Bearing in mind the caveat that our clients need their defences and that attempting to dismantle a defensive system prematurely can be risky, we need to ask the following questions:

- *Is the defence situational or characterological?* If characterological it will be more threatening to acknowledge and you need to be more gradual in approaching it.
- *Is the defence ego-dystonic or ego-syntonic?* If it is ego-syntonic your client may experience an attempt to work directly with it as an attack on his psychic equilibrium. If it is ego-dystonic, he will be more motivated to ask for help.
- *Is your client aware of the way in which he uses the defence?* If he is, it is much safer to directly interpret it.
- *Is the defence conflict driven or developmental?* If it is developmental, you need to aim your work at repairing developmental deficits. You may not then need to directly interpret the defence.
- *How risky is it to face your client with this defence at this stage of his therapy?* If he is very vulnerable and needs his defences, undermining them might result in a deterioration, or even decompensation.
- *How in touch is your client with the circumstances under which he institutes a particular defence?* He is more likely to be able to use direct interpretation if he is in touch with them.
- *How shamed is your client likely to be by a discussion of his defence?* If he becomes shamed he may become resistant to therapy.
- *Is the defence directed internally, externally or both?* If it is internally directed it tends to exist to ward off unacceptable feelings, thoughts, memories or phantasies. If externally directed, is it being used to manage levels of engagement (or intimacy) with others?

When working with defences you have a number of options. You may elect to work developmentally to repair the deficit underlying the defence, for example by using affective attunement to manage splitting. You may chose to contain the defence, for example by not challenging immediately a projection that your client makes in relation to you, but instead using information from your countertransference to inform your response to him. You may decide to acknowledge the defensive behaviour to your client, but not interpret it. You may, having acknowledged it, elect to interpret it partially or fully. The approach you take needs to be based on a number of factors, which involve deciding whether and how you work with a defence at a particular time will facilitate or hinder therapeutic work. A client who has experienced environmental deficit, and a consequent lack of a sense of himself, is unlikely to find a direct analysis of his defences (as proposed by Davenloo, 1980) helpful. Such an approach is likely to reinforce his defensive system rather than loosen it. The person who has a more integrated ego may value a therapeutic approach that directly addresses some of his defences. By combining heightened affect with cognitive appraisal, he may feel more understood than if you only paid attention to his needs for empathic attunement.

FURTHER READING

Sandler, J. (ed.) (1988) *Projection, Identification, Projective Identification.* London: Karnac.

11

ASSESSMENT AND FORMULATION FROM A PSYCHODYNAMIC PERSPECTIVE

I have put assessment and formulation together in recognition of the fact that, in psychodynamic work, assessment and formulation are intrinsically linked. As we assess a new client we begin to trial hypotheses that we have formulated which then feed into the assessment, which further refines the hypothesis. Although other therapeutic models do this to some extent, assessment and formulation are often more clearly delineated stages of the therapeutic process. In psychodynamic practice they are not only linked but also ongoing throughout the work. This is because we cannot expect to have access to or an understanding of the working of our client's internal world in a few sessions. The nature of dynamic work means that he constantly presents us with new information and understanding which we gradually piece together. This leads to a constant re-working of our hypotheses about our client's ego strength, object relationships and defensive structure. Nevertheless, at the beginning of the therapeutic process most practitioners spend a number of sessions getting to know their clients and actively constructing hypotheses about their difficulties. For the sake of clarity in thinking about the skills required, I am going to separate the two functions.

ASSESSMENT

Why do we need to do an assessment? The main reason is to have enough information to formulate our client's difficulties to determine whether a psychodynamic intervention is one that he wants, can use, can be offered within the time-frame available and at an acceptable level of risk. Implicit in this are questions about how the client's resources, psychological structure, motivation and the amount of time he can give to therapy will impact on his ability to make use of it. There is a second, often overlooked, issue: do you want to work with this client? Most therapists recognise that they work better with, or have a preference for, clients with certain types of difficulty. Usually this is to do with what resources you have in your work. Some clients require a specialist skill set that you may not have, others may make personal demands that you may feel you do not manage well. It is important to acknowledge when you do not wish to work with a particular client or client group, since it is very difficult to do good work with someone you do not wish to work with. Even if you have to work with a client you would prefer not to see, acknowledging how you feel can help the process of doing so.

The aims of assessment

The overarching aim of an assessment is to give you sufficient information to generate a formulation that guides you and your client in deciding whether psychodynamic therapy is the best way of helping him. It is important that we avoid offering a psychodynamic approach to people who we know are unlikely to be able use it, may be damaged by it and who may then feel that they have wasted an opportunity to change. Although none of us is sufficiently omniscient to know for sure how a therapy will turn out, the following are indications for an increased chance of success in short-term interventions (usually less than 20 sessions) and non-intensive psychodynamic work.

- Your client needs to have some capacity for self-reflection. If he cannot do so, it will be difficult for him to use an approach that is exploratory and relies on making links.
- He needs to have some capacity to form and maintain relationships. If he has very little history of doing so he is unlikely to be able to sustain a relationship that requires managing the emotional frustrations of psychodynamic work.
- He needs sufficient ego-strength to manage the primitive needs and longings elicited by the transference relationship. Without it he may not be able to manage the feelings stirred up in him.
- He needs to be motivated to change and be able to take responsibility for his decision to work psychodynamically. Although at some stage in therapy you may need to hold the motivation to continue, motivation needs to be evident at assessment. If it is not, you may become an auxiliary ego maintaining your client in his situation.
- He needs to be realistic about what therapy can and cannot do. Although many clients long for a 'magic wand' he needs to be aware that instant change is a fantasy.
- The risk that he will harm himself, or otherwise act out, needs to be within the limits that can be contained within the therapy and the setting in which therapy takes place. If it can't you need to consider whether other structures can be put in place, or whether your client needs to be seen in another setting.
- He needs to be able to relate a reasonably coherent narrative about his own history. This is known as autobiographical competence. Clients who are very muddled between people, events and times are unlikely to be able to make use of short-term interventions, and may need long-term intensive psychodynamic therapy or alternative therapeutic models such as Mentalization-Based Therapy.
- If you are assessing for short-term therapy, you need to establish that there is an identifiable focus for the work, and that your client is motivated to work within it.

Assessment is a two-way process. Just as you are assessing whether you can work with your client, he is also assessing you. Ideally the decision will be a joint one. However, psychodynamic practice has not relinquished the 'expert' position. If you do not think that your client can be helped by psychodynamic therapy, you need to be clear about it and give him some explanation as to your reasoning. This requires using your authority based on what you know, and the training you have undertaken.

Lemma (2003) advocates a number of things you need to do in the assessment process which will aid you and the client in coming to a decision about whether the psychodynamic approach is going to be useful for him.

- Your client needs to know that he is being listened to, and his difficulties are taken seriously.
- You need to know what has brought him to look for help and how motivated he is to change. You may not find out what your client actually wants help with in the first session, since it is not uncommon for people to quite consciously use a lesser difficulty as a means of accessing therapy. The real reason for coming may only be revealed once he feels he can trust you.
- You need to gain enough information about your client's developmental history and current level of functioning to make a preliminary formulation about the origin and maintenance of his difficulties.
- You need to make a preliminary assessment of the level of risk associated with a psychodynamic intervention. This includes the risk of self-harm or decompensation (breakdown) and the risk of harm to others, including you.
- You need to determine whether the type of help that you can offer would be useful to your client (short-term versus long-term work and frequency of sessions). For instance, you may conclude that a client could use intensive long-term work, but would be traumatised or further damaged by non-intensive or short-term work.
- You need to give your client a sense of how the psychodynamic approach works, so that he can make an informed decision about whether he thinks it is something he can use. This includes maintaining the analytic frame and attitude, as well as offering trial interpretations.
- Lastly, you need to enable your client to feel that you have understood him, and to give him hope – even if you advise against psychodynamic work or feel that you are not suited as a therapeutic couple.

How you conduct the assessment will set the tone for your future work together. Although you need to gather information during the assessment period, if you go through a tick-list of questions you are establishing a mode of working at variance with the exploratory nature of the dynamic approach. You need to ensure that during the assessment phase you attend to both the symmetrical relationship and the asymmetrical relationship. This demonstrates that you are in touch with his adult self as well as his needs and anxieties. Doing so involves asking some direct information-eliciting questions, such as 'Can you tell me about your earliest memory?', as well as using the skills of reflecting, exploration, clarification and linking which will also attend to the needs of the child.

Sources of information

The information gathered during assessment will begin the process of formulation which will guide you in seeking further information, or in clarifying what you have understood so far. There are two primary sources of information you will have access to during the assessment itself, which are information from your client and information from your countertransference. Other sources of information which you may have access to include psychodynamically-based psychometric tests, medical or other notes, and written or verbal information from a referrer.

Structuring assessment

Leiper (2006) identifies four categories or perspectives that we need to take into account when we are assessing, which facilitate us in formulating.

The *dynamic perspective* holds that all behaviour is purposeful and motivated. It focuses on how symptoms can both be a solution to an unbearable conflict and a symbolic communication about the nature of the problem.

> Claire came to see me because she was unhappy at work but did not have the confidence to apply for another job. Half-way through the assessment session, just after I had offered a trial interpretation that she had found helpful, Claire suddenly grabbed hold of her coat which she had placed on the floor and shook it, saying that she was afraid that a spider had got inside. She told me that she was phobic of spiders; she was upset that this limited her life significantly, including avoiding travel to many countries. My hypothesis was that Claire's phobia was a symbolic communication about her fear of being aggressively intruded into, which became projected and actualised into the fear that a spider would get in and damage her. It became manifest in the assessment when I made a helpful intervention, which she experienced as intrusive and therefore frightening. This gave me an indication of the fragility of her sense of self.

The *developmental perspective* holds that our past experience is the key to understanding what is going on in the present because our past experience determines the templates we create as a result of our early experience, which leads to expectations about future relationships.

> Jonathan was sixty-five and described himself as being 'a bit low' following the death of his wife two years earlier. They had been married for forty years and had rarely been apart. During assessment he explained that he had experienced
>
> *(Continued)*

(Continued)

a number of interruptions to his early attachment relationships, particularly in the first year of his life. I began to hypothesise that the early developmental tasks of integration might have been compromised as a result. Jonathan presented as functioning quite well on the surface, but I was alert to the possibility of a greater-than-apparent fragility underneath. I then oriented my assessment towards finding out about other times that he had had difficulty in coping, and what defences he had used to manage. I needed to consider whether he would find non-intensive work sufficiently containing and whether I could offer intensive work should he need it. My ability to provide intensive work if necessary informed my decision about whether to offer him therapy or refer him elsewhere.

Leiper next draws our attention to the *structural perspective*, which is to do with the dominance of our internal mind over the external part of the mind and the balance between internal and external reality. Whereas psychological health is associated with responses to the world that are both more based in reality and more flexible, psychological disturbance is associated with responses that are less in touch with reality and less flexible.

Returning to Claire, her phobia was an indication of the extent to which internal reality dominated her functioning at that moment. From the perspective of external reality, it was extremely unlikely that she would be damaged by a spider in my consulting room. It was the wrong time of year for spiders, it was unlikely that one would get inside her coat, and there are no poisonous spiders in the UK. The existence of a phobia is a signal of powerful projective mechanisms that are not tempered by reality. Claire located the intrusive object outside herself, which gave me an early indication of the difficulty for her in experiencing me as a benign rather than an intrusive object.

Leiper's last perspective is the *adaptive perspective*, which includes an assessment of the way in which a client's current life reflects the key developmental and dynamic themes at issue. He reminds us to spend time in assessment in looking at the successful compromises the client has made, and the way in which he has managed developmental traumas. Often clients come for help when the dynamic 'compromise' that helps them cope with internal conflict and psychic pain no longer works, because something happens which overwhelms their normal coping mechanisms.

Jonathan's close relationship with his wife had acted as a significant protective factor throughout the years of their marriage. She had contained his anxiety about the loss of other important people which had enabled him to survive earlier separations, such as when their children left home. However, her loss had robbed him of the protective shield that had enabled him to cope, and he was no longer able to manage his terror of being alone.

RISK ASSESSMENT

Although the assessment of risk is an integral part of any assessment, and an ongoing consideration throughout therapy, I feel it needs separate consideration. There are two risks for your client. The first is that his defensive structure collapses, so that he decompensates. In this case the assessment of risk is one of determining the strength of his ego and the friability and rigidity of his defensive structure. The second is that he harms himself, or that he will harm you or someone else.

Sometimes clients will speak openly about wanting to die. However, even if it is not explicitly discussed, I am always mindful that a new client might be sufficiently distressed to want to harm himself. If it is in the material of the session, or I have countertransference concerns, I will ask more explicit questions. I will actively pursue the issue of risk if a client tells me he is depressed, or he talks in a general way about feeling overwhelmed or that everything feels pointless. In response I will say something like 'I wonder whether things might feel so bad that you have had thoughts about harming yourself, or even about ending it all?'. Likewise, if he tells me stories of his life and/or about dreams whose latent content indicates suicidal ideation, I will probe further to assess risk. I might phrase it in the following way: 'You have told me a story/dream that seems to be about things coming to a end, about dying. I wonder whether in some way you might wish that you could come to an end, that you didn't have to go on.' Other times I might feel myself anxious for a client's safety in the absence of any material in the session; in that case I usually ask about self-harm as if it were a routine part of my assessment. Dependent on how the client replies, there is an incremental cause for concern:

- *Stage One:* this involves the client talking about feeling helpless and hopeless or indicating that life is not worth living. You need to establish whether he has had thoughts of harming himself. It is not unusual for clients in distress to talk about 'not wanting to go on'. Provided he is not someone who you have assessed as having poor impulse control, on their own these feelings should not cause too much alarm and should be explored with your client in the same way as other painful feelings. Indeed, it might be important to your client that he can tell you about such frightening states of mind and feel you can contain them. Being able to discuss suicidal ideation can be an important part of therapy where the actual risk of harm is relatively low, and it is one of the uncertainties that psychodynamic practitioners routinely manage. However, you should also be alert to the possibility that his feelings could escalate to the next stage.
- *Stage Two:* if during assessment your client says he has felt he no longer wants to live you need to ask if he has thought he might act on his feelings. If he says 'yes' the situation is more serious and you need to establish whether he has made any plans to harm or kill himself. If he has not made any specific plans you may choose to make a contract with him that he will let you know if the feelings get worse, or if he begins to

make specific plans. You will also need to consider whether he has sufficient impulse control to manage an escalating wish to harm himself. You may decide to work more supportively using extra-transference interpretations until you establish a strong therapeutic alliance and can assess how he manages the vicissitudes of being in therapy. Transference work or even the setting in psychodynamic therapy might put further pressure on a weakened ego and increase the chances of decompensation or acting out.

- *Stage Three:* if your client reveals during assessment that he is making specific plans to harm himself you need to take this very seriously. This is almost certainly a contraindication for psychodynamic work at this time. You need to be very experienced and have the appropriate back-up to consider work with someone at this level of risk. Such a client is certainly not someone to see if you are inexperienced or as a sole practitioner in private practice and should only be seen within a clinic context.

Suicidal ideation can become manifest at any stage in therapy, and a client who had not presented with obvious risk issues at assessment may become a suicide risk later in treatment. This is why it is important to think of risk assessment as an ongoing activity.

The staged approach described above can also be applied to risk regarding harm to other people. However, if a client talks early in therapy about fantasies of harming his therapist, I would see that as a serious matter and most probably a contraindication for therapy, unless the referral had very specifically been for help with anger or violence. It is not unusual that, as therapy progresses, clients can experience quite aggressive and violent fantasies towards their therapist. Such revelations in the context of a strong therapeutic relationship and a knowledge of the client's impulsivity are part of the stuff of psychodynamic work. There is a proviso, however. The aggression should not be enacted, rather it should be expressed verbally. When aggressive fantasies are expressed early in the relationship, it suggests the client has a significant difficulty in managing the boundary between phantasy and reality. Sometimes such information comes indirectly, as the following vignette illustrates. It describes an experience of mine that occurred very early on in my career. I should perhaps add the caveat that this experience is memorable and noteworthy in part because it is so unusual.

Mr Lane, a single man in his mid forties, was referred by his GP for private therapy for depression. At the time my consulting room was a downstairs room in my home, and I often worked when no-one else was in the house. During the initial assessment session Mr Lane told me about his depression and the difficulties and sadness in his life. Normally I would have felt empathy and concern for his predicament, but instead I became increasingly focussed on the fact that his chair was between me and the door and there was no-one at home. Being relatively inexperienced, I was not as quick then as I hope I would be now to recognise that I clearly perceived danger.

I dreaded the thought of seeing him again. Indeed when I thought of him I was aware of a blackness, of something very unpleasant. During the second session Mr Lane told me that he had specifically asked for a female therapist because he felt he could be best helped by a woman. He then described in detail the violent fantasies he had about harming women. His relationships with women were sado-masochistic and he was rejected as soon as he told them about his fantasies. He then told me of the sadistic fantasies he had had about me after the first session. He wanted the experience of being with a woman who would accept his fantasies, and that was his aim in seeking therapy. In the first session my countertransference had alerted me to his dangerousness, but I had not realised the significance of my response. Had I done so I would have understood that such a powerful countertransference was a contraindication to working with this man in the setting in which I practised.

It is important to spend a little time thinking about how to manage your own safety, particularly if you are a lone practitioner, or are at a physical distance from help. Although the vast majority of clients are safe to work with, we do take a risk in working with our clients' unconscious disturbance. Almost always the risk is at an acceptable level, but nevertheless it is important to properly acknowledge that we are working with the unknown, and to take some sensible and fairly straightforward steps to maximise our safety.

- Ensure that your chair is nearest the door so that if necessary you can get out of the room first.
- Get a panic alarm fitted that you can easily access from where you are sitting.
- See new clients when there is someone else on the premises, particularly if they have not been previously screened.
- Take note of your countertransference. You may be unconsciously aware of danger before either you or your client is consciously aware of it.

FORMULATION

A formulation is a hypothesis that links the origins and maintenance of a person's difficulties with a body of theory that accounts for it, which is then used to inform a therapeutic intervention. As Aveline points out, a formulation provides an overall view of the work, and 'serves both as a map for therapy and a guide to which map to choose' (1999: 202).

Formulating serves a number of purposes, in particular how to select and guide interventions:

- It discourages 'wild' speculation which is not founded in theory; others may not agree with your formulation, but they should be able to see how you have reached it.
- It facilitates decisions about how to proceed therapeutically. For example, your formulation will determine whether you take a more interpretive or more developmental stance with a client.
- It helps us in predicting the likely efficacy of our intervention and in managing setbacks, since they can be understood through reformulation.
- It helps us decide what the criteria are for a successful therapeutic outcome.

Constructing a psychodynamic formulation

Lemma (2003) summarises the components of a psychodynamic formulation as follows.

Firstly it describes the problem as seen by the client; secondly it places the problem in a developmental framework taking into account: temperamental disposition, physical givens, traumatic experiences, life events, past and present relationships and socio-cultural factors; thirdly it identifies recurring themes or conflicts in the client's relationships to himself, to others, to his body and to work.

Lemma (2003: 169–171) also sets out a six-step guide to formulation, which is a helpful way of ensuring that you have covered all the aspects you need to when you begin to formulate.

- *Step One* requires you to describe the problem from your client's perspective and to establish the nature of his 'core pain': what he is most afraid of or trying to avoid.
- *Step Two* involves describing the psychic cost of the problem. This includes how it effects your client's ability to function and how his perceptions of himself and others are distorted.
- *Step Three* involves placing the problem in an historical and environmental context through identifying factors such as whether there is a history of trauma; the developmental factors that influence how trauma is processed; your client's family constellation and his place in it and other relevant life events. It also involves identifying biological givens that might impact on his problem such as illness or disability.
- *Step Four* requires you to describe your client's most dominant and recurring object relationships. By asking how your client experiences himself in relation to others, you will be able to determine which object relationships dominate his internal world; who does what to whom in your client's world, and the associated affects that he experiences; how those internal object relationships are manifest in your client's current life; and how they manifest themselves in the transference relationship.
- *Step Five* involves identifying how your client protects himself from psychic pain. This includes his habitual ways of managing psychic pain and whether he primarily uses pre-oedipal or oedipal defences.
- *Step Six* involves identifying the aims of treatment: this includes identifying both the kind of help the client wants and/or needs and the possible consequences of change. You also need to be able to indicate your reasons for recommending a psychodynamic approach or for not doing so.

Formulating Tom's difficulties

The problem from Tom's perspective: Tom experienced such high levels of anxiety that he was unable to participate in social relationships, for example he had difficulty on his course as a result of anxiety about relating to his dental patients and sitting in lectures with other students. He was unhappy about the social isolation that he was experiencing.

The psychic cost of the problem: Tom was feeling alienated from people, which led to feelings of being alone and unwanted. He also felt depressed and attempted to self-medicate through drinking too much. This created conflict as he struggled with the difference between how he was actually behaving and his ego ideal.

The context of Tom's problems: Tom experienced significant levels of anxiety related to the unpredictability of his mother's availability when he was young. His first memory is of calling for her and her not being there. When he was older, she often left home following rows with his father. He was left in a state of confusion and anxiety, not understanding why she had gone, and fearing that she would not return. He felt he had no-one to turn to in her absence, since his father withdrew into himself. Tom eventually learned to shut down his feelings, which left him feeling very alone.

Tom's feelings of abandonment were re-evoked when he was attacked in South America. He had rowed with his travelling companion, so was alone when he was attacked. Tom feared that he would die in the attack, which undermined his confidence in his capacity to take care of himself, and was a blow to his sense of invulnerability. Tom experienced a further blow when his parents returned to Canada as he was about to start his studies; he again felt abandoned by them and unsafe.

Tom's dominant and recurring object relationships: Tom's overriding experience with his objects was that they were unreliable and could not be trusted to be available. His internal object relations were with an object who did not take seriously his need for security and protection. There was some evidence that Tom experienced invitations to intimacy in a sexualised way, so that he felt seduced by his objects. This may have left him caught between fearing abandonment or being seduced and overwhelmed. Glasser (1979) calls this the 'core complex'. It could also be hypothesised that Tom defensively identified with his absent and abandoning mother by himself withholding from or leaving his objects.

How Tom protects himself: Tom had developed a number of ways of managing his internal distress and his object relationships. He coped with regulating the distance between himself and his objects by trying to control them. This was indicated by his lateness early in therapy when he tried to impose his timing on the sessions, thereby regulating the amount of time he spent with Vicky. He also regulated distance by withdrawing altogether from relationships and/or devaluing them, as he did with previous therapists. Tom did not look to his objects to help contain his distress, instead he self-medicated using alcohol, which gave him a sense of a secure base, but one which was pathological (Holmes, 2001). At an intrapsychic level Tom managed his distress by mechanisms such as splitting, which he used to separate painful feelings from his memory of events. He also used denial, for example by telling Vicky that he didn't mind having to tell his story again to another therapist. He also used projection, in that he located his anxiety about being able to care for himself in the external world which he then experienced as threatening.

The aims of treatment: one treatment aim would be to help Tom develop a benign protective shield through the internalisation of Vicky as an object who can hold him and contain his distress. Another aim would be to help him work through and integrate the traumatic experiences of being abandoned and of being attacked. Since there was evidence that Tom used a number of primitive mechanisms in protecting himself from distress, therapy would initially be more oriented towards the maternal (developmental) rather than the paternal (interpretive) functioning of his therapist. For the same reason Tom would need to have an opportunity to work longer-term, rather than in focussed short-term work.

FURTHER READING

Doctor, R. (ed.) (2003) *Dangerous Patients: A Psychodynamic Approach to Risk Assessment and Management.* London: Karnac.

12

MANAGING THE THERAPEUTIC PROCESS

STRUCTURING THE SESSION

Many therapeutic couples will establish an identifiable rhythm to how sessions are structured; at the same time that structure will mutate over the course of a therapy as the client comes to use his therapist differently and the manner in which the therapist makes herself available to her client similarly develops.

The beginning of the session

Quite often the beginning of the session is characterised by a period of 'catching up' on what has happened, or been thought about, since the last session. Most clients arrive with what Sandler called an 'analytic crust', which has grown over the previous session's work. They need time to ease themselves into using the analytic space again. It can be particularly difficult if the previous session has been very important and a strong positive or negative transference has been expressed. It is not uncommon for clients to experience frustration with themselves and you that they can't get back to the previous session immediately. They need help with their feelings of loss for an intimacy they feel they had with their therapist and have since lost.

Sometimes the 'beginning' can take up a large part of the session. Winnicott described one client who always did the work of the session just before it ended. Other times clients will have started the session with the 'therapist in my head' ahead of their actual arrival. They may launch straight into the session, having got the preliminaries out of the way en route, and/or have to adjust to the person of their corporeal therapist once they are in the room with her. It is particularly important at the beginning of a session to attend to those skills you use in establishing the frame, particularly neutrality and abstinence, to help your client get back into using the analytic space. However, you should not treat the beginning of the session as inconsequential and solely as a 'warming up' period. Not infrequently the important issue that needs addressing is either directly mentioned or alluded to at the beginning of the session – sometimes as you are escorting your client to the room.

The middle of the session

This is the time when your client settles into the work for the day. Clients who are deeply engaged in the work of the session may enter a state that Jungians call 'child time' when time expands and he loses the sense that the session will end. The skills you need in this part of the session are those associated with containment and interpretation and in maintaining a space in which your client can do the work.

An important aspect of our work lies in fostering emotional disclosure – it is a key function of the work we do and we need to ensure that the movement in the session is in the direction of that disclosure. The timing of such disclosure is important, in that it is the moment in time when the client is ready to know a truth about himself, or his relationships with others, that he could not previously allow himself. Part of your skill lies in detecting when that moment has arrived through your interaction with your client. This comes through listening with an analytic ear and allowing your own unconscious to be attuned to that of your client.

I now want to look at what we mean by and how we conceptualise depth in a session. Cox (1978) identifies three stages of disclosure of material: unconscious, conscious-withheld and conscious disclosed. The process of working at depth involves providing the conditions under which your client can allow material from his unconscious to emerge into consciousness and be shared with you. In doing so you facilitate the client to do for himself what he cannot do on his own.

It is not the content of what he talks about so much as the way in which he discusses something that distinguishes the depth at which your client is working. His affective experience is the marker of depth and will be indicated by such things as his body-language, his ability to maintain eye-contact, and the extent to which his narrative becomes hesitant. For example, one client may reveal sexual fantasies about his sister-in-law and think of it as a joke. Another may think of it as a relief that he has begun to fantasise at all. But a third may feel deeply shamed by having such fantasies. Each example indicates one of Cox's three levels of disclosure. These are: trivial (everyday comments such as 'it's cold this morning'); neutral-personal (factual comments, such as 'I was born in Berlin'); or emotional-personal (comments about oneself that are emotionally relevant and not easy to make, such as 'my mother left when I was five').

We need to become sensitive to when an apparent level one or two disclosure is actually a level three disclosure. So 'I was born in Berlin' may become a powerfully significant disclosure if your client is Jewish and born prior to the Second World War. Or 'It's cold this morning' may have a real significance from a client who has never previously allowed himself to have any bodily needs. By definition a third-level disclosure is not easy to make, so it is important we identify 'pseudo–disclosures' of apparently level three material. For example 'My mother left when I was five' might be said in a highly emotional, perhaps over-dramatic way, but one which is cut off from real affect, in order to rivet you. In such cases it can be the acknowledgement of the need to be noticed that involves your client in making a level three disclosure, and it is that which he needs help with.

Some therapists conceptualise depth as gradations of consciousness, meaning that some parts of our unconscious mind are more readily accessible than others. Generally speaking, in trying to access the unconscious, we are usually working with the preconscious, that part of the unconscious that is most close to consciousness: Bollas's 'unthought known' (1987). It is important that you try to confine your observations about unconscious material to this level. If you try to interpret material that is much deeper your client will not be able to make sense of it at an emotional and perhaps even an intellectual level. At best this can lead to confusion, since it does not connect with anything meaningful for him. At worst you risk alienating him, or inducing compliance, as he reacts either with complete rejection or goes along with you 'because you know best'.

The end of the session

The end of the session can be experienced as a cold reality as your client has to give up the illusion that that he is the only preoccupation in your life. Coping with the separation that inevitably follows can be very painful. One of the reasons for meticulous attention to the time boundary at the end of sessions is that your client needs to know when the end is coming. Your knowledge that the session is due to finish in a few minutes will convey itself subtly to him, as will any lack of clarity about when to end. I am aware both from my experience in my own analysis, and from the feedback that clients give me, that subtle changes take place as the session draws to an end. Observing myself at the end of sessions, I have noticed that my voice changes slightly, pauses lengthen and I am less likely to make an interpretation that will heighten affect appreciably. This is my own idiosyncratic response to the knowledge that the ending is near, and I am not advocating this as an approach to be learned or adopted by others.

If your client does not know when the end is, he cannot begin to prepare himself for the separation from you. Reaching the end of the session suddenly is not necessarily problematic; like everything else it will vary not only from client to client but also from session to session. But reaching the end of the session when he is unprepared for it can leave your client feeling suddenly dropped, which can be distressing and humiliating. Some clients need to know where they are in the session, so I place a clock where they can see it if they so wish. If someone is very disturbed or distressed I may indicate that the session has nearly ended, to give him due warning of the forthcoming rupture in our relationship. This is not something I do routinely, but for some clients it is part of providing a protective shield at a particular time in our work together.

How you manage the end of the session is always significant to your client. While I by no means advocate cutting someone off in mid-sentence because the end of the session has arrived, I do feel that a lack of meticulousness to the time boundary can ultimately undermine his sense of safety. This was brought home to me early in my career. I had been occasionally allowing my sessions with one client to over-run by up to five minutes. I was very aware of how precious to her my client's time with me was, and I found it hard to stop her if she was in the middle of something. One day, after finishing on time the previous session, she complained that she did not know where she stood with me. As we deconstructed what this was about, she revealed how difficult she found it that sometimes I gave her extra time and others I did not. She concluded that there was a link between being given extra time and whether I liked her that day. She could not work out why I should like her more one day than on another. This led to confusion about what she needed to do to be liked by me and thus to 'earn' extra time with me. She did not have a sufficiently robust theory of mind to contemplate that my motivation was internally determined rather than organised by her behaviour. By breaking the time boundary I had introduced another layer into the process of ending the session. Fortunately my client was sufficiently brave to discuss it, and it resulted in some very productive work. However, another client may not have told me, and my action could have contributed to a therapeutic impasse.

Some clients cannot bear the separation and need to feel in control of the ending. Sensing it is near, they may suddenly become distressed, or talk about something very disturbing so that it feels cruel to finish. It is important to end the session, but to do it in a way that doesn't leave your client feeling dropped. I usually say something like 'I'm sorry to have to interrupt you when you are upset, but we do need to stop now. Perhaps we can come back to this next time.' I might then suggest that he might like a minute to gather himself before leaving. If your client repeatedly brings up very painful material or tells you things that are highly disturbing as the session ends, you need to be proactive in taking this up. This could be at the beginning of the next session, or you could look for something in the material that would give you an opportunity to raise the matter with him.

Another frequently encountered problem is when clients delay leaving after the session has finished. This may be by continuing the session at the consulting room door, by bringing up an 'administration' issue such as needing to cancel a session or announcing a holiday, or by writing out a cheque in a way that takes a lot of time. This can result in powerful feelings in therapists, especially if you need to attend to something between sessions. Handling such situations gracefully can be a significant challenge. It is important to get these 'extra-session' issues back into the session because, by treating them as though they are separate, your client is denying an important aspect of the therapeutic frame. I generally say that we need to return to the issue the next time we meet, when we can give it proper attention. If a client repeatedly delays leaving I will comment on it at the time and say that we need to discuss it next session. It is important to set the limit as well as interpreting it. If you only interpret it, and don't demonstrate that you will maintain the boundary, you give your client a mixed message, which is confusing.

While some psychodynamic practitioners see their clients off the premises, I say goodbye in the consulting room. This can make it more difficult when clients have problems leaving, but it signals that the relationship with you is boundaried by the setting in which the work takes place. Seeing your client to the front door can be experienced as an implicit invitation to continue the session outside of the consulting room or to engage in a more social relationship with him.

PHASES OF THERAPY

Each client's therapy involves a period of engagement, a period when much of the work is done (whether or not it is time-limited), and the period during which client and therapist know they are working towards an ending. Each phase has distinctive characteristics.

The first phase

In most therapies the first stage has a limited duration; it starts with the first session, and progresses until the tasks of the first stage have been completed. During this time you and your client begin the process of finding a common language. At the same time each of you articulates your expectations of the other and adjusts to being with them. I find attachment theory particularly helpful in thinking about the first phase. It conceptualises the beginning of therapy as a time of attachment crisis, in which the client's attachment system is activated in the face of being vulnerable in the presence of someone he perceives as being more powerful. Your task is to provide a secure base (Bowlby, 1988) through making yourself emotionally available to your client, which in turn facilitates him in beginning to explore his inner world.

The first stage can be characterised by much ambivalence about whether the therapist is the right one and other resistances. The early transference is inherently unstable and not fixed. Glover (1955) put it elegantly when he compared the transference at the beginning of therapy to placing a compass on a table. At first the needle oscillates a lot, then less, then it fixes itself on north, which is the therapist. He called the early transference a 'floating transference'. For those clients who are in touch with external reality the first stage of the work is usually characterised by the conventional rules that govern social intercourse. He is generally polite, keeping his thoughts about his therapist to himself, particularly the more disturbing or powerful ones.

The middle phase

Most writers agree that the first stage comes to an end when the therapeutic alliance is established and the transference is 'gathered up'. By this they mean that once Glover's compass is fixed, the floating transference coalesces to reflect the client's core disturbance as it is played out in relation to his therapist. It may be an indication that the second stage has commenced when your client says something normally considered as socially inappropriate, and knows you will understand it as a free association rather than rudeness. One client announced the end of the first phase by complaining that she could not comprehend how I could have chosen the colour of my newly-painted front door.

The middle phase is the time when the bulk of the therapeutic work is done. It can last from a few weeks or months to many years, depending on the needs of your client and the framework within which you work. During that time your client's aims in therapy will develop and change as he becomes increasingly aware of the nature of his difficulties and the changes he needs to make. Together you will weather the vicissitudes of your relationship as you manage the ups and downs of therapeutic work.

The middle stage in long-term therapy is the one that really tests your abilities as a therapist and sometimes your endurance. Sustaining an analytic attitude in the face of powerful transference and countertransference experiences is a significant challenge, and especially so with clients who are very damaged. One of the fundamental tasks in this stage is to contain your client's anxieties and difficulties in bearing the frustrations of the therapeutic relationship, and the sometimes painful slowness of progress. Another is interpretation, which can be either deficit or conflict oriented according to the needs of your client at any one time.

The ending phase

Firstly I want to make a distinction between stopping and ending. Stopping therapy involves no longer attending sessions. But there is a question about when, or indeed whether, the therapeutic process, once begun, actually ends. One of the criteria for ending therapy is that your client has sufficiently internalised your functions, or discovered you as a new object, so that he can continue the process of ongoing psychological exploration and growth without you. There is evidence that change continues following the end of therapy and that the end of therapy results in an increase in psychological growth.

So how do we know when it is time to stop? Much has been written about this, and I want to start by looking at the three factors identified by Etchegoyen (1999) as being pertinent to ending.

- *What are the criteria for cure?* This is going to vary according to whether the work is short or long term. The aims in the former are circumscribed, specified at the outset of therapy, and more easily evaluated than in longer-term work when the aims will be more global, less easily specified, and more likely to develop over time. Most definitions of cure in longer-term work involve signs of increased ego integration and strength. They are further elaborated and framed according to the theoretical model in which one is working. A Kleinian might consider a favourable outcome to be when the paranoid and depressive anxieties of the first year have been worked through. Someone using Winnicott's model might consider the development of the True Self to be the sign that the main objective of therapy had been achieved.
- *What are the indicators that the client is ready to finish?* Again these will be partly determined by your theoretical understanding of what constitutes mental health. One indicator is that your client's symptoms are no longer as problematic. However, symptom relief neither constitutes a sufficient reason for ending, nor does the continuing existence of some residual symptomotology indicate therapeutic failure. Other indicators include improvements in family and social relationships, and in the client's relationship with himself. Emotions such as anxiety, guilt and shame should be less problematic and there should also be evidence that your client has internalised you as a benign object. Your client should be able to face the truth about himself and his situation without the over-deployment of defences. He should be more in touch with reality, including the transference relationship. Linguistic indicators, including an ability to narrate his story in a way that is coherent and properly elaborated, should be in evidence.

- *What technical factors need to be taken into account in order to finish?* This is the how and when of finishing. It requires that both you and your client recognise that he is ready to work towards the ending. The length of time needed to work through the tasks of termination will vary according to the depth and length of therapy. In once a week therapy of a year's duration you would need at least a month, preferably two. If you have been seeing your client for more intensive work over a longer period, you might need a year or even more. Preparing for termination and setting the date to end are two different things in long-term work. Although a long period might be needed to undertake the work of termination, it is important to set a date that the client can imagine. Setting a date too far ahead can be impossible to envisage, and consequently becomes meaningless; however, neither should it be too soon. Clients can often want to bring a sudden end to long-term work to avoid the distress involved in the process of leaving. It is important not to go along with his urge to get the whole thing over with, and collude with him in avoiding the pain of a proper ending.

Planning to end therapy is inevitably accompanied by anxieties about whether your client has had or done enough to cope with his ongoing life without you. Such anxiety can be positive since it also brings a sense of urgency, which often creates significant therapeutic opportunities. The work of the ending involves mourning the loss of a unique relationship which can never be replaced, even if your client goes elsewhere for further therapy at a later date. Clients can sometimes find it difficult to imagine that the end of therapy is a loss for us too, especially after a long therapy. Therapeutic work involves the development of deep attachments in both directions, and one of the emotional strains for therapists is the breaking of affectional bonds with clients we have become attached to.

The termination phase involves re-working the conflicts and deficits that originally brought your client into treatment; this time in the context of saying goodbye. This can be challenging for both parties, particularly if your client deteriorates and attacks you for your perceived or real therapeutic failures. Even without actual deterioration, both of you may become anxious that the decision to terminate was premature. Sometimes it is necessary to review the timing of the ending, especially since some clients do not bring central issues to be worked with until they are faced with the loss of their therapist. If you do decide to postpone the end date, it is important to make it clear that you are still in the termination phase in order to maintain the sense of urgency and focus. You need to have a very good reason (such as the death of a parent) for changing the end date more than once. Your client needs to know that his relationship with you is not ever-lasting. Indeed one function of therapeutic ending in long-term work is to help your client face his own ending – that his life, like his relationship with you, is finite.

You have a number of tasks in the termination phase of therapy with regard to your client:

- To facilitate and cope with your client's sadness, grief at the loss of his relationship with you, and the mourning that accompanies it. This requires that he accepts the reality of his separateness from you.
- To help him acknowledge what he has achieved and to mourn what he has not. You will need to hear and facilitate his disappointment with you for what you were unable to achieve with or for him, even following a successful therapy.
- To help your client to re-introject or own the projections you have contained for him, since you will no longer be there. He has to learn to bear and process these himself.

- To help your client to recognise his own uniqueness, that he cannot be replaced by someone else – the next client. If he cannot do so he will be unable to manage feelings of envy or jealousy of the client who 'replaces' him, which could undermine the progress he has made.
- You need to be able to properly accept your client's gratitude for what you have given him. Being grateful signals a significant psychological achievement, since it indicates that he is able to acknowledge that you have the capacity to give. Doing so helps internalise you as a good object.

You also have a number of tasks with regard to yourself, which will facilitate you in helping your client to leave:

- Dealing with your own sense of loss, particularly if you are attached to your client and he is someone who, under different circumstances, you may have enjoyed a social relationship with. It is important to properly recognise the impact of saying goodbye to your clients.
- Managing your sense of failure if your client has not made the progress you had both hoped for. When a client does not make progress we can experience it as a narcissistic injury, and it is necessary to recognise the omnipotent fantasy that underlies the belief that you should have been able to help him, no matter how great the damage. This can also result in guilt which, paradoxically, together with omnipotence, can lead to lengthy therapy if we cannot give up the fantasy that we could and should heal him.
- Helping your client to relinquish any ongoing idealisation of you and the therapeutic process and to replace it with a realistic appraisal of what has and hasn't been achieved. This could entail giving up your own idealisation of the therapeutic process, which may be an unresolved remnant of your own therapy.
- Deciding whether you are going to make any changes to the way you and your client relate. Some therapists, and I include myself, argue that a marginally increased level of self-disclosure during the termination phase can facilitate both the real relationship and the dissolution of the transference.

Derman (2008) makes the point that you cannot end therapy unless you have begun it in the first place. By this she means that if your client has never properly engaged in the work of therapy, he can never properly complete it. He can stop, but that is very different from ending. Never having begun underlies some premature terminations of therapy, when clients stop before the work has properly started.

The literature tends to suggest that most therapies are worked through to a mutually agreed termination. However, premature terminations happen frequently, and for a variety of reasons. Sometimes, as Derman describes, the therapy has never really got past the first stage, with its resistances and ambivalence, even though it may have been going through the motions for some time. More frequently, clients undergo a change in their lives that necessitates a move away, or a change of job can mean that it is no longer possible to get to therapy. At other times, although the client has reached the middle stage of therapy, something happens which undermines the work. This might be from within the client, for example he is unable to manage the frustrations that are an inevitable part of therapy. Or it might come from within the therapist, perhaps because she can no longer contain her clients. Many years ago a colleague described how a number of well-established clients left therapy when his marriage broke down. He recognised that he no longer had the capacity to contain them in the face of his own emotional turmoil.

After three years of therapy Vicky felt Tom had made significant progress in his ability to use her as a facilitating and containing object. Despite struggling with his dental studies, he had passed his final examinations and was applying for jobs in the locality. He was more active socially and no longer drank to manage his anxiety. The gap between his ego and his ego-ideal had narrowed, and he was more able to realistically appreciate what he was, and wasn't, capable of. Areas needing further work included his relationship with his parents, and he still found it difficult to manage his distress when his mother failed to notice his needs. Also, he had not had a relationship with a partner that lasted more than a few dates. Each time he met a new person in whom he was interested, he found that his contempt, which had begun to diminish in relation to Vicky, was re-evoked.

Tom returned to Canada to attend a family wedding during the summer and was away for six weeks. About a week before his return he wrote to Vicky, saying he had 'met the person with whom I want to spend the rest of my life'. He was returning to England to pack up his things before going back to Canada to live. He would be in the UK for about a month, partly because he wanted the time to say goodbye to Vicky. 'I hope that's alright with you' he wrote. Vicky was stunned by the news. She reflected that her experience of the shock of suddenly being left might be similar to Tom's own shock, when his mother suddenly disappeared. After three years of therapy, a month was very little time in which to attend to all the tasks of ending.

Tom was buoyant when he arrived for his first session after the break, and Vicky felt he had projected all his anxiety and doubts about ending into her. She was anxious that he would experience any discussion of her concerns as disapproval of his happiness. Eventually, however, she said to him 'I feel that I've got the task of being the one who is concerned about how short a time we have to end. I know you have a month to say goodbye, but you need to know I am worried that this may not be long enough. There is quite a lot to do when we say goodbye and I'm concerned that we may not have enough time to do it properly.' Tom registered Vicky's concern, but he had already arranged his return flight as he had commitments in Canada. However, he was planning to return for graduation in a few months' time, and they discussed having some sessions then if they were unable to complete the work of ending in the timeframe. Also, because he was not working, Tom had spare time and he and Vicky decided to meet more often during the month he was in the UK.

The decision to intensify therapy in the end-phase might seem counterintuitive since your client is needing help to manage without you. Indeed many people consider that as they work towards the ending therapy should become less intensive, and contact diminished, in order to facilitate this. In my opinion, working towards an ending should not automatically imply a reduction in session frequency. I think that reducing the intensity of the work denies the client the opportunity to engage properly with tasks that can only be undertaken during the ending phase. Similarly I think that there are some occasions when there are good reasons for increasing contact and thus intensity, even when there is no time restriction as there was for Tom. My reasoning is to do with the fact that clients' defensive structure is likely to be reinstated as they approach the loss of their therapist. Those who have had difficulties associated with separation and loss, or who have struggled to let their therapist into their inner world, may withdraw in the face of the ending. It is much more difficult to avoid dealing with important aspects of the ending if therapeutic intensity is maintained or increased.

POST-THERAPY CONTACT

Many clients wish to continue the relationship with their therapist after therapy has ended. Some overtly ask for a friendship or occasional social contact. Others ask for ongoing contact that continues at a professional level. This is a vexed issue, and one that therapists often have strong feelings about. At the heart of it there is a double message. Post-therapy contact for most of our clients consists of Christmas cards, or occasional letters, if at all. However, when we become therapists, we join the same world our own therapists inhabit. Thus the separation for us is never as complete, even if only in phantasy. At the very least, as we work with our clients, we are reminded of our own therapy, particularly in the early years, and the relationship with our therapist consequently stays very alive. Or we may attend the same conferences, or belong to the same therapeutic organisation. Some therapists have ongoing contact with their own therapist in order to manage professional relationships after therapy, or hear about them on the social grapevine of the therapy world.

The implications of post-therapy contact need to be thought through. For some it is important to stay in contact with a person who has occupied a very important place in their lives. I think it is particularly the case for those clients who experienced a major environmental deficit in their early development. These are people for whom their therapist may have become not just a new object, but perhaps their first constant object. Post-therapy contact may well help continued progress, and is a recognition that, for very damaged clients, ongoing contact may be needed to maintain the progress made thus far. This contact may be in the form of letters, or it might involve occasional formal sessions. Such contact does not preclude seeing the client for further therapy if the need arises.

Social contact is a different matter. Sometimes we work with people who, in different circumstances, would have become friends and it can be tempting to attempt the bridge into friendship. I cannot think of an occasion that I am aware of when this has worked. The relationship is inevitably contaminated by unanalysed or unresolved transferences in both directions, and, importantly, it means that the client cannot return for therapeutic help if the need arises. You cannot be your client's therapist again if you have once been his friend. In that respect I think the client loses out twice. You can neither be a real friend because of your past relationship, nor can you offer further therapeutic help if he needs it.

If a client invites me to engage in a social relationship after therapy I usually respond in the following way. 'My first duty to you is as your therapist. This means I would not want to do anything that would compromise you coming back to see me in the future, should you need to do so. If I became your friend that would not be possible, and being your therapist is, in my mind, the most valuable thing I can offer you.' This is not a contrived or rehearsed response, and almost always when I have to say it I am aware of the regret that this is how it is.

FURTHER READING

Novick, J. and Novick, K. K. (2006) *Good Goodbyes: Knowing How to End in Psychotherapy and Psychoanalysis.* New York: Jason Aronson.

13

THE REAL RELATIONSHIP AND OTHER DILEMMAS

The challenge of being a skilled practitioner lies in having a relationship to technique whereby it is our servant rather than our master. This requires us to be able to recognise its limitations and to evaluate how we use it. Over the years psychodynamic practitioners have become anxious about flexibility in technique, feeling punished by their own superego, or that of their professional organisation, when they are more flexible. I think this is because therapeutic work always creates a potential for acting out, due to the strength of the phantasies and longings that we and our clients work with. According to Tonnesmann (2005), some of Freud's anxiety about changes in technique was to do with the potential for therapists to enact their erotic countertransference. However, abuse of clients can be much more subtle, and a therapist's attitude towards deviations from technique or boundaries can be an indicator of unethical practice. Deviations from standard practice continue to tap into this anxiety, not least because occasionally scandals about abuse of clients come to light. This serves as an ongoing reminder that we need to maintain our vigilance about what deviations from standard practice might signify, while still engaging with technique in a way that enables us to respond to our clients and develop our skills.

Our anxiety about deviations from standard practice can lead to becoming too rigid in the application of theory, which in turn leads to a less humane interaction in the therapeutic relationship. As Safran and Muran (2000) argue, if theory is used with a light touch, it can guide and point us towards exploring aspects of the relationship that might otherwise be missed. Many of the dilemmas that we confront, that challenge our relationship to technique, are to do with how we manage the boundaries around therapy. I have included the real relationship in this chapter because it falls within how we manage the boundaries that frame our work. Especially during the early years of one's career, it can be a significant challenge to stay in touch with ourselves as people in the therapeutic relationship, at the same time as coping with dilemmas and difficulties as they come up.

THE REAL RELATIONSHIP

The concept of a real relationship allows that our clients have the capacity to see and engage with us in a way that is based in reality, that they can see us as another human being with whom it is possible to have a connection that is relatively free of transference dynamics. The different psychodynamic schools vary in the value they ascribe to this concept. Many Kleinians have less use for it because they hold that there is an isomorphism between the internal and external world. Consequently, they hold that all aspects of the therapeutic relationship are experienced through the distorting lens of the transference. They are also concerned that paying attention to the real relationship will dilute the strength of the transference.

However, other authors take the view that the transference is a more robust phenomenon. Indeed Lipton (1977) argued that a more real experience of his therapist facilitates the client in developing a strong transference. Both King (1977) and Gill (1979) argue that there are factors in the therapeutic relationship that are to do with the reality of what happens between the two people involved, and are not just a manifestation of the client's distortion. Consequently, not everything that is communicated is directly related to the transference. Indeed, some therapist reactions are those of one human being who works with another. This adds another layer to the relationship, and can contribute to rooting therapy in the real world. The following vignette demonstrates how the interplay between reality and the transferential aspects of the therapeutic relationship can become manifest.

Shortly before Tom's session Vicky received a phone-call from her friend Patrick, informing her that he had just had confirmation of a diagnosis of cancer. Vicky was very upset for him, and was still in the middle of the phone-call when Tom arrived several minutes early. She felt irritated with him for interrupting. She let him in, settled him in the waiting area, and went back to finish her conversation. She began the session on time, but was aware that she was distracted. She could not put the phone-call out of her mind and found it difficult to pay attention to Tom. Part way through the session Tom complained that he felt Vicky didn't really want him there any more. The material of the session had been about Tom not feeling wanted by his brother, with whom he was having a difficult relationship at present. In an attempt to be more social, he had agreed to accompany his brother to a party, but his brother had gone without him. Since Tom had also been talking about his difficulties regarding a forthcoming break in recent sessions, Vicky took up the transference aspects of what he was saying by making links to the break, and that he might fear that she would be glad to 'go off and party' without him.

Kate felt that Tom had been responding to something about the real relationship. In arriving early he had interrupted the phone-call with Patrick, and, given how distressed Vicky was feeling, he would no doubt have seen it on her face as she answered the door. His perception of not being wanted at that moment

(Continued)

(Continued)

was accurate. Vicky acknowledged that she resented him being there because she had wanted to carry on talking to Patrick. Kate pointed to the fact that, while the transference relationship no doubt coloured his experience of her unavailability, nevertheless it would have been helpful to acknowledge the reality of his perception that something had distracted her. She suggested that Vicky could have done it without impinging on Tom with information from her private life if she had said that she was aware she was distracted that day.

It is important to help your client to differentiate between his accurate perceptions and the distortions that are the result of his internal object relationships. It is part of our objective to help our clients be more in touch with reality, and in my opinion not acknowledging events in the real relationship further distorts their perception of that reality. In this instance Vicky treated Tom as though his communications to her were based on his inner world, rather than on his ability to perceive her actual state of distress. If she did this on a regular basis it might contribute to reducing Tom's confidence in his own accurate perceptions, and therefore his capacity to differentiate inner and outer reality. This would ultimately be unhelpful to his development.

Kate's opinion that Vicky should have acknowledged Tom's accurate perception of her distraction was not an invitation to violate the frame. Vicky could have acknowledged that she was distracted without telling him why. This would have served the dual purpose of acknowledging his realistic perception of her state of mind, without burdening or over-exciting him with information about her personal life.

SOME COMMON DIFFICULTIES WITH BOUNDARIES

During the course of your work you will meet situations which challenge the frame of therapy, resulting in dilemmas about how to react. When these things happen we can't always wait for supervision to discuss how to handle them, and at times you have to make a decision in the moment. The main things we call on at those times are our internal frame, as discussed in Chapter 4, and the supervisory functions we have internalised from our therapy and supervision. I have already discussed some of these challenges as they have arisen in other chapters, but I want to pay attention to some that I have not addressed so far.

Setting limits

A number of clients who come for therapy have not had a good enough experience of parents who can set limits in a way that is both containing, and that takes their needs into account. Inconsistent or over-harsh limit-setting in childhood can lead to later difficulties in managing relationships with people in authority. These clients are more likely to push the limits in therapy.

If others' rules are always seen as the senseless exercise of power, your client is going to resent the boundaries around therapy. Clients who push the limits for this reason quite often demand a more quid pro quo relationship, in which confidences are shared; they resent the asymmetrical aspect of the relationship. Their resentment might be about having a specific time when they can see you, the length of sessions, or in private practice, the fact that they have to pay for missed sessions. Early in therapy it is hard for such clients to see any benefit to themselves of the boundaries that are part of the analytic frame, and asking them to take this on trust is likely only to arouse their suspicion further.

McWilliams (2004) advocates emphasising the therapist's needs for the boundary. She proposes that framing the need as being in the client's best interest can be experienced as like the child who is told 'this is for your own good.' She argues that since the boundaries do, in part, act to protect the therapist, with such clients one might as well make it clear. For example, in response to a client who wanted between-session contact at the time of his choosing, she pointed out that doing so would leave her feeling over-burdened and resentful. Having done something similar myself on occasions, I can testify to the relief with which clients later come to realise that I will not put them in a position where I resent what I give them. This can be particularly important for people whose parents have combined an authoritarian attitude with grudging giving. They begin to have confidence that what I give them is freely given, not dragged from me, which ultimately constitutes a new experience.

Client acting out

Acting out is when your client communicates something of importance to you through action, rather than through talking about it. Freud made the observation many years ago that, when something is being acted out, it isn't analysable. Acting out may therefore have to be worked with directly, through the use of the symmetrical relationship, if it involves a threat to the viability of the therapy. The aim of working with acting out is to help your client to the position where he can engage in a reflective conversation about his inner world rather than communicating through action. It is always important to hold in mind that clients can be shamed when faced with their acting out, and it is important to maintain empathy for the predicament they are in. This can be a significant challenge, particularly if their behaviour touches something in you that has not been fully worked through. Occasionally acting out has to be contained through you doing something that creates a boundary around it. At other times it can be contained through normal therapeutic work, since as a healthy ego develops, your client will be increasingly able to think rather than act. Tyndale (2002) described someone who acted out by using a baby voice in her sessions. Eventually therapist and client were able to reflect on, and later understand, what the acting out was communicating. This kind of acting out is usually managed routinely in therapy, and therapist countertransference reactions processed with the help of supervision. However, there are other types of acting out within the session that are less easy to cope with.

Presents

I have put presents in this section as giving gifts can constitute a form of acting out, as well as presenting us with an ethical dilemma. It is not unusual for clients to want to give us presents. Those that are given at Christmas, after a holiday or before a break are different from the ones that are given at the end of therapy. The latter can signify real gratitude for the work done, which itself is an important development for some clients. Of course there is also the concretisation of the message that says 'don't forget me'. One client gave me a door-stop as a parting gift, and we reflected on her hope that I would keep the door open for her to return if she needed to. However, gifts given during therapy can have defensive underpinnings. A Christmas gift might signify difficulty in recognising the professional nature of the relationship, instead treating you like a friend. A gift just before or after a break may be a reaction formation against your client's anger that you are about to leave, or have left him.

There is considerable variability in how therapists deal with gifts. Some accept no presents and will insist their client takes them away, others interpret the meaning of the present as it is given, and others don't interpret, seeing the giving of gifts as a form of acting out which will cease when the client can verbalise his feelings. My own stance is generally to accept the gift, unless it is expensive. Whether I interpret the giving of the gift in the session or not will depend on whether I think that the interpretation can be received without humiliating my client. If my client's ego is sufficiently strong to be able to think about the meaning of the gift, an exploration of his underlying motivation is always useful. If, however, my client has significant deficit problems, I do not interpret unless I am given a specific invitation to do so. This is because an uninvited interpretation in such circumstances can be experienced as an attack, and will disturb trust.

Non-payment of fees

If you are in private practice, and your client regularly postpones payment by forgetting his chequebook or paying very late, there are two factors you need to attend to. One is that you have a contract which is the basis on which you and your client meet. The other is the exploration of the meaning of the late or non-payment. At a practical level your client needs to be reminded of the reality of the contract and, in the event of non-payment, you have to decide whether you are going to continue seeing him. This is never an easy decision, but it is important that you have a guide in your mind as to how much leeway you feel comfortable with. This internal boundary is transmitted unconsciously to clients, through an attitude regarding the value you put on your work. It is not uncommon for psychodynamic practitioners to privilege an understanding of the dynamic roots of a client's non-payment and lose sight of the fact that, unless the fee is paid, the contract has been violated. I think part of the reason for this lies in the extent to which we have resolved our own feelings about being paid for the work we do. Both our clients, and those who write about money, draw our attention to the parallel between therapy and prostitution (Taylor, 2002). This can be an uncomfortable dynamic for therapists to adjust to. Also, the depressive dynamics that take us into therapeutic work can make it difficult for us to ensure that our own needs are as important as those of our client.

Very often a partial resolution is forthcoming if you and your client are able to understand something of his difficulty in paying you, in the context of a clear message that there is a financial contract that he has to honour. While taking up the meaning for him, it is also important to reflect on your own relationship to being paid. The client, in withholding payment, may not only be communicating something about his early difficulties. He may also be communicating his feelings about how the fee was set, the amount he is being charged, or an unconscious awareness of your attitude towards being paid.

Contact outside the session

Therapists occasionally describe being overwhelmed by a client whose needs for additional contact lead to a deluge of letters, phone-calls, faxes or emails. As with much in therapy, there is no formula setting out a specific course of action. How you manage the situation will depend on your client, the specifics of what is happening, your formulation as to why he is behaving in this way, and the setting in which you work. Your formulation about the underlying dynamics will help guide you as to how to proceed. If the predominant dynamic is sado-masochistic and involves punishing you, it is more important to put a firm boundary around the behaviour. This serves to protect both you and your client from the cruelty of what he is doing. However, it is important that you set the boundary in a way that acknowledges his humanity, so that you do not enact the sadistic position, which would only serve to perpetuate the sado-masochistic cycle. The invitation to engage in a sado-masochistic relationship is a very powerful one and, if you find yourself in this situation, it is important to take it to supervision in order to avoid a relationship dominated by punishing your client or being punished by him. Managing this kind of dynamic can be particularly challenging if elements in your own experience have involved cruelty by your objects.

A formulation indicating that your client is unable to contain massive anxiety, that has been stirred up as a result of his therapy, requires a different response. If you deny him all additional contact you may repeat an early environmental failure, which could reinforce rather than ameliorate his difficulties. You may first consider whether you can, or whether it would be helpful, to increase the number of sessions he has in a week either temporarily or permanently. If this is not possible or appropriate, it may be important to establish a contract with your client that allows a limited amount of additional contact for a specific length of time, which can be re-negotiated if necessary. This is one of those occasions where it is important to communicate through the symmetrical, rather than the asymmetrical, relationship in order to re-negotiate the boundary. Doing so will help prevent further infantilisation, and reduce his humiliation. It also is important not to get drawn into punishing your client for his neediness by using interpretations that emanate from your superego. Quite often such clients elicit powerful negative transferences from the people who work with them. This is particularly the case when working in a team, where they can be labelled as 'manipulative'. It is often the job of the psychodynamic therapist to help other team members to see the client's behaviour as an expression of a request for help and to think about the realistic steps that can be taken to meet his needs.

Aggression within the session

Verbal hostility and aggression are part of therapy, although it is important not to allow yourself to be verbally bullied, and for your client to be aware of the impact of his verbal aggression on his objects. However, it is a different matter if your client threatens to enact his hostility. Powerful transferences can lead to this kind of acting out, which can occur in both intensive and less intensive therapy. It often happens when psychotic functioning threatens to overwhelm a client's capacity to stay in touch with reality. At such times your first duty is to keep both your client and yourself safe. Very often this is achieved through attending to the reality aspects of what is happening before thinking with your client about the meaning of his actions.

Many years ago one of my weekly clients, whose functioning was dominated by her internal world, brought a knife to therapy and began to play with it in front of me in a way that frightened me considerably. I was unclear whom she might harm and she was unable to tell me. What was clear, however, was that work could not proceed until she surrendered the knife and I had put it out of sight. Only once the knife was safe did I begin to look at what bringing it had meant to her. In this instance I returned the knife at the end of the session, but with the clear injunction that if she brought it again I would not be able to continue therapy. Putting a firm boundary around the acting out, both by taking the knife, and saying that I could not continue seeing her if she brought it again, enabled her to feel safer. She later said that she had been relieved that I had not allowed her to keep the knife during the session, and had taken from her the responsibility of managing the violent fantasies that had overwhelmed her.

THERAPIST ACTING OUT

None of us is immune to acting out under the pressure of the countertransference, or when unanalysed parts of us are triggered by powerful dynamics in therapy. Furthermore, we are all capable of using the frame defensively as a way of protecting ourselves. In itself this is not necessarily problematic, unless we rationalise it rather than recognising that we have done so for self-protection. Sometimes we only become aware of how we are enacting something that can't be thought about when we present our work in supervision; other times we are aware that we feel uneasy about a course of action, but manage to rationalise it. The full range of therapist acting out would take a book in itself since, like defences, this can become manifest in any area of practice. However, I have outlined some of the more common ways in which it happens.

At one end of the scale I include not starting on time or finishing the session early; not giving adequate warning of breaks; cancelling sessions at short notice because we want a day off; answering the phone or the door; giving interpretations that meet our need for self-protection rather than the client's need to be understood; not properly addressing it when your client acts out, for example by missing sessions. In the mid-range I would include dressing in a sexualised way that over-stimulates your client; raising fee levels to the point that your client can no longer afford to pay them; using your client's ambivalence as a pretext for ending therapy prematurely; giving your client personal information that he does not need and which will over-stimulate him; touching him because of your own need or because you have rationalised it would be good for him; keeping him dependent when his developmental trajectory propels him towards increasing independence. At the top end of the scale there is the kind of emotional, physical or sexual abuse that is under-reported, but which is massively damaging to clients and leads to therapists being struck off or in some cases prosecuted when it is.

Tom had been in therapy for about two years and was making steady progress. Vicky began to think that Tom no longer needed to come twice a week. So when he began to wonder about reducing his sessions, in preparation for his final year of studies, she accepted his proposal without an exploration of what lay behind it. She took it very much as a symmetrical issue and was practical about thinking with him which session to drop. It was only when she was challenged by Kate, about not taking up Tom's underlying reasons for wanting to reduce his sessions, that she came to question why she had not done so. The realisation that she would be happy for Tom to reduce his sessions because it now suited her was very uncomfortable. Vicky had just completed her training and was building up her private practice. Tom's sessions were in the evening and these were times that other people wanted, and for which Tom paid a reduced fee. Vicky needed the money from clients who paid full fees, but had not considered or processed her resentment towards Tom that he prevented her from offering these times. Vicky was grateful to him for enabling her to complete her training, and found it difficult to see herself as someone who would resent his continued use of these session times. This led to her enacting her resentment by encouraging him to reduce his sessions because she could not process her feelings through thinking.

REFERRING ON

Knowing the limits to your skill and experience is an important competency. It is a particular challenge in psychodynamic work because the reasons for feeling incompetent, or believing that someone else would do a better job, can be understood concretely, as a fact, or can be viewed as part of the transference–countertransference matrix of therapy. If it is clear from the outset that your client needs to see someone else, the issue is straightforward in that you need to determine whether you can refer and to whom.

However, because clients also project their feelings of incompetence into us, we need to unpick what has been projected and what actually belongs to us. You need to keep an open mind about whether you have the competences to work with him safely until you have considered whether you are reacting to projective mechanisms. As is often the case with projected material, the reason it 'hooks' is because it touches on something that we actually feel or fear. This is especially so if you are relatively inexperienced, since you will not have developed a reliable sense of your own limits as part of your professional identity. The only way to deal with these projections properly is to reflect on them both internally and in supervision. Only once you have done so will you be able to determine what, if anything, to do next.

The question of referring on is complicated by a number of factors. One is interprofessional rivalry. Many years ago Freud set the seeds when he made the distinction between the 'pure gold' of psychoanalysis and psychotherapy, which he regarded as a lesser intervention. At the time psychoanalysis was one of the few psychological treatments, and neither psychotherapy or counselling were professions in their own right. However, there is still a sense of a hierarchy in which psychoanalysts are seen to occupy the top echelons, with everyone else in descending order. This tends to be reinforced in the UK public health sector, where often psychoanalysts occupy the senior posts.

The way practitioners deal with this will depend on their own relationship to hierarchy. Unfortunately, a number of therapists from all sections of the wider profession do not manage it well. At its worst some psychoanalysts can be patronising towards those who have undergone a less intensive training. It is as though having a more intensive training automatically makes them better therapists. This fails to appreciate the quality of the training other practitioners have had or their personal capacity for being therapeutic. At the same time some therapists and counsellors can become envious of the psychoanalysts' higher status and take the view that 'I'm just as good as her' in a way that denies the difference in length and depth of training. This attitude is untherapeutic, especially if clients are treated for a long time in non-intensive therapy when they need the kind of developmental work that could only be undertaken by someone who has been trained to work intensively.

Sometimes we will continue work with clients who we know we should refer on for more intensive work because we identify strongly with what it would mean to them to lose us. At other times this is out of ignorance of what someone's needs and underlying difficulties are, and how they can be helped by more intensive work. Occasionally I fear that it is about a difficulty in acknowledging that someone else has skills that are beyond those of the less intensively trained therapist. This refusal to see the value of what other practitioners can offer can go both ways. It is rare for someone who has been trained to deliver three, four or five times a week therapy to suggest that someone trained to do once a week work would be more suitable for clients who want weekly therapy. This kind of therapeutic arrogance, that the skills one learns doing intensive therapy can be easily translated into doing less intensive work, helps to feed resentment and envy. In turn this makes it more difficult to value the skills that each section of the profession has, which is ultimately to the detriment of our clients.

Another issue is to do with our own internal world. Feelings of omnipotence, that we can take on anyone's difficulties, or a belief that we have to struggle on with clients who stretch us beyond what we feel we can manage, are equally unhelpful. In both cases our inability to recognise the implications of the limits of our competence can mean continuing with clients who might be made worse because we do not recognise they need to see someone else. One of the areas that is particularly difficult for mental health practitioners to identify is when we are not fit to practise. Sometimes this can lead to taking on clients whom we should not see because their developmental needs are congruent with our own. Good supervision often helps us avoid these difficulties, but we also need to be prepared to be honest with our supervisors about the kinds of difficulties we are in or might encounter.

Once the decision to refer on has been made, you need to be able to help your client to deal with the sequelae. Sometimes this is a decision that is reached mutually, but even so, your client will have some ambivalence about leaving you. It is much more difficult if you feel that he needs to see someone else, and he doesn't want to change therapists. In referring on, you need to give your client the time to undertake the tasks of mourning and leaving as in the ending of any therapy. Often the ending takes place over a shorter period of time than it would if it was a planned ending of a complete therapy. And, in circumstances where both of you are feeling sad that the referral on has to be made, it is more tempting than usual to truncate the ending as a way of defending against the sadness of loss. However, for the referral to have the best chance of success you and your client need to properly address issues such as your client's anger with you for not being able to undertake the work yourself; his distress about having to see someone else, who he will inevitably regard as a 'stepmother'; a proper acknowledgement of what you have accomplished together; a decision about whether you will have any future contact.

With regard to the last issue, I have very occasionally maintained contact with a client who I have referred on, usually for developmental reasons. However, it has been with the explicit agreement of the therapist to whom I have referred, and also with the explicit understanding that my client and I will not be a therapeutic couple in the future. However, this is not my normal practice and, if done, needs to be carefully thought about both in supervision and with the therapist receiving the referral, to ensure that such contact does not compromise the client's future therapy.

FURTHER READING

Alfille, H. and Cooper, J. (eds) (2002) *Dilemmas in the Consulting Room*. London: Karnac.

14

SKILLS IN USING SUPERVISION

I have included a chapter on supervision for three major reasons. Firstly, being able to use supervision is a necessary competency for psychodynamic practitioners. Secondly, the quality of our therapeutic work is related to the quality of the supervision we engage in. Lastly, good supervision after qualification acts as a protection against becoming burnt out.

There are two other reasons for including a chapter on supervision. The first is that supervision is not an optional extra. Ongoing supervision of our work is both a requirement for registration with professional bodies, and a part of clinical governance within the organisations in which we work. Being able to use supervision well is important to our professional lives, since much of our ongoing professional development as psychodynamic practitioners is transmitted through it. The other reason is that, although supervision helps us cope with the work, it also ranks as one of the top five stressors for trainee therapists (Cushway, 1992). When therapists are given the opportunity to discuss their experiences of psychodynamic supervision, there are always a significant number who describe difficult or painful supervisory relationships (Johnson, 2007). These can remain unmetabolised years later. The reasons for this no doubt include supervisor attributes, but there is also a powerful regressive pull during training, when the issues being dealt with in therapy can spill over into supervision, resulting in powerful transferences.

Scaife has defined supervision as 'what happens when people who work in the helping professions make a formal arrangement to think with another or others about their work with a view to providing the best possible service to clients and enhancing their own personal and professional development' (2001: 4). The skills of supervising and being supervised are complementary. Hawkins and Shohet observed that 'The first prerequisite for being a good supervisor is being able actively to arrange good supervision for yourself' (2001: 41).

THE TASKS AND FUNCTIONS OF SUPERVISION

Understanding the tasks and functions of supervision can help you feel less at sea at the beginning of a supervisory relationship. Sometimes supervision is set up without much formal discussion of the task, which can put those new to being supervised at a disadvantage in understanding what is required of them. In any new supervisory relationship this can lead to confusion about what the expectations of supervision are. Paradoxically, although supervision is now ubiquitous, at times people embark on the relationship without a discussion of aims, or without being explicit about the contract they are implicitly agreeing to.

The tasks of supervision

The overarching task of supervision is to ensure the care of your client. This task is achieved through a number of sub-tasks, which together facilitate you in being more effective in helping people.

The supervisory alliance

The first and most important task of any supervisory relationship is to create a supervisory alliance. In the same way that the therapeutic alliance is the most important factor in client work, the supervisory alliance is the primary factor determining the effectiveness of supervision. Cushway and Knibbs (2004) found that trainee therapists who had a poor supervisory alliance did not disclose important aspects of their work in supervision, which had implications for their clinical practice. If you are unable to establish a good supervisory alliance your learning will be inhibited. Indeed, Webb and Wheeler (1998) found that the quality of the supervisory alliance predicted the outcome of counselling.

Having a good supervisory alliance involves establishing a relationship of trust with your supervisor, in which potentially difficult or painful issues can be explored. This is not a given, and reports of unsatisfactory supervisory relationships are common. Good supervisors have been described as supportive, respectful and non-critical. Crucially, they do not attempt to turn the supervisory experience into psychotherapy. Such supervisors demonstrate high levels of empathy, respect, genuineness, flexibility, concern, investment and openness. One way of enabling the supervisory alliance is to share information about yourselves, which can help reduce some of the transferential aspects of the relationship.

In their first supervisory session Kate discussed the supervisory alliance with Vicky. She suggested that they get to know a bit about each other and discuss

(Continued)

(Continued)

what their expectations of supervision were. They exchanged information about their professional careers to date, and discussed the expectations each had of the other in supervision, including the therapy/supervision boundary. Kate also asked Vicky if she had any anxieties about being supervised, and whether there was anything she might find difficult to hear from her. Vicky replied that she knew that she was a perfectionist and would find it difficult if Kate was very critical of her when she made mistakes. Then Kate asked Vicky if there was anything personal that it would be helpful for her to know that would facilitate their working relationship. Vicky said that she tended to take too much responsibility for other people, which she was aware might impact on her therapeutic work. Kate said it was very helpful to know this, and that she would hold it in mind. Kate then said she felt it would be helpful for Vicky to know that she, too, had needed to work on knowing the limits of her responsibility for others, and that it was something she was still mindful of. The conversation ended with each of them discussing what had drawn them to the psychodynamic model. Vicky had chosen a supervisor who had the same theoretical orientation as her therapist. This was helpful in both building identifications between them as well as understanding the ways in which they were different.

This type of conversation immediately sets up a relationship between two colleagues, one of whom is senior to the other, but both of whom contribute to the success of the supervisory alliance. You will see that Kate took the lead in the discussion. It is important that your supervisor does this, but if this does not happen you may need to become proactive.

The supervisory contract

Most who write about supervision advocate having an explicit supervisory contract to facilitate the establishment of the supervisory alliance. One of the reasons for doing this is that your supervisor has a position of power vis-à-vis you. Effective contracts can guard against the abuse of power in supervision, since they reduce hidden agendas. Unfortunately, the majority of supervisory contracts have a minimal level of explicit contracting, which just includes the frequency and timing of sessions and, if appropriate, fees. The majority of the contract remains implicit, leaving scope for misunderstanding. This increases the likelihood of the supervisory contract becoming more like a therapeutic one, with attendant opportunities for transference issues to disturb the alliance.

Hawkins and Shohet (2006) suggest that in contracting five key areas should be covered:

- *Practicalities*, such as frequency, place, fees.
- *Boundaries,* particularly between therapy and supervision, and including confidentiality.
- *The working alliance*, particularly the style of supervision each prefers, expectations of supervision and hopes and fears for the work ahead.

- *The session format*, for example what is discussed, and how material should be presented, for example whether verbatim notes are expected.
- *The organisational and professional context*, particularly ethical and professional codes, and any responsibility a supervisor has to an employing organisation.

There is also a psychological contract, which is almost never explicit, and has both conscious and unconscious elements. This is to do with the psychological transaction that takes place between you and your supervisor; what each of you wants from the other. Supervision can elicit powerful needs in supervisees and you will bring your template of relationships into supervision, as you do into other situations. At the same time supervisors' unconscious attitudes towards supervising can be complex, and result in a set of expectations about their supervisees which is not articulated. This may involve wanting to be experienced as a wise and caring elder, or the supervisor may emphasise her gatekeeper-to-the-profession role. It can be helpful to remember that your supervisor also has needs, anxieties and blind-spots, and that she too will struggle with aspects of her work.

Supervision as a safe space

The second task of supervision is to provide a regular space for you to discuss your work. This space needs to be one in which you feel safe and contained, and where you can share any personal distress as well as the transference and countertransference issues that emerge in your work. It is important that you are not unnecessarily left to carry difficulties, problems and projections alone.

Skills development

Hawkins and Shohet (2006) identified a number of avenues through which supervision develops skills: helping you to acquire information-based skills; facilitating the development of your therapeutic skills; helping you to make theory-practice links; offering you another perspective on your work; helping you to use professional and personal resources effectively; encouraging you to be proactive rather than reactive where appropriate.

Responsibility

The supervisor is tasked to ensure that you are both clear about who is responsible for your work. She also has responsibility for addressing any ethical concerns she may have about your work. She may be tasked to ensure that you work within the constraints set down by an employing organisation, training organisation and/or relevant professional bodies. Together, you and your supervisor are also tasked to ensure that you can openly discuss how well supervision is going.

The functions of supervision

A number of authors have detailed the functions that supervision has, that is, what we expect it to achieve. Hawkins and Shohet amalgamated the findings of a number of authors (2001: 50–51).

- *The educative or formative function*: This is to do with developing your skills, understanding and abilities, and is done through reflection on and exploration of your client work.

- *The supportive or restorative function*: During the intimate work of therapy you need to allow yourself to be affected by the distress, pain and fragmentation of your clients. The restorative function allows you time and space in which to become aware of how the work has affected you, and to deal with any consequent reactions. Some writers have referred to this aspect of supervision as 'pit head' time, alluding to the time set aside at the end of a coal-miner's shift to clean the grime of the mine off before returning home. It is intended to help you process any emotions stimulated from your own past, and to deal with your clients' projections. This militates against both over-identification with and cutting off from clients. It is ultimately aimed at preventing therapist and/or client acting out, as well as therapist burn-out. The focus of the restorative function can be wide-ranging, including relationships with colleagues, the organisation and clients, or the impact of life events. This is the area where therapy and supervision can overlap, and it is important for you and your supervisor to negotiate what is and isn't open for discussion within your relationship, and where the boundaries lie.

- *The managerial or normative function*: This aspect of supervision provides the 'quality control' function of your work. It can involve: identifying your training needs; identifying your 'blind-spots'; identifying where your personal vulnerabilities or prejudices interfere with your work; ensuring that ethical standards are maintained; ensuring the standards set by the organisation you are responsible to are maintained. If you and your supervisor are employed by the same organisation, or she is your training supervisor, she will have obligations to both you and the organisation. If this is the case, it is important to be clear about the contractual duties she has to each of you. Your supervisor might be caught between pressures to meet the needs of the organisation and the conflicting need to nurture and develop you.

THE MODELS SUPERVISORS USE IN SUPERVISING

Until recently it has been assumed within the psychodynamic community that seniority and competency as a therapist confer the qualities necessary to supervise. Consequently we have often been slow to use those models of supervision which describe and account for how we supervise (Howard, 2007). Even so, although we may be unaware of what it is, we all have an implicit or explicit model of how to supervise and what we expect from supervision, including what we consider should be focussed on during supervision. In psychodynamic practice the focus is usually on the unconscious dynamics within your client, between you and him, and the way in which this is played out in supervision. In order to achieve this, you and your supervisor need to create a space in which it is possible to both think about your client and explore the affective aspects of the therapy session. This fits with the educational goals of supervision, which are to help you to apply and interpret psychodynamic theory within the clinical situation.

Therapy models of supervision

Models of supervision that are isomorphic with a therapeutic approach are known as therapy-based models. These were the first of the supervision models and remain the most influential within psychodynamic practice. How supervisors supervise within these models reflects the nuances of their therapeutic approach. It is important to ensure that the model your supervisor uses is explicit and that you understand how that model impacts on how she supervises, particularly if you receive supervision from someone who comes from a different psychodynamic tradition from your own. In most instances the mechanics of supervision are the same: material is presented and reflected on in a way that parallels therapy.

Therapy models in psychodynamic supervision have followed the development of psychodynamic theory and practice. Thus, in the first half of the last century, when psychodynamic thinking was dominated by the one-person model developed by Freud, supervision emphasised the workings of the client's mind. Both therapist and supervisor were seen as relatively uninvolved experts, and not as contributors to the process. The second half of the twentieth century was dominated by two-person models of therapy, which emphasised the early mother-infant dyad, and the importance of the counter-transference as a source of information. This development was paralleled in supervision, with a corresponding emphasis on the necessity of understanding the influence that therapist and client have on each other's minds. If you are working with a supervisor who uses this model she will understand you and your client as a dyad, in which the internal world of each of you contributes to what happens in the session and therapy.

The second half of the twentieth century also saw the beginnings of supervision theory within the psychodynamic tradition. Searles (1955) was the first to describe the 'reflection process' – what we now often think of as 'parallel processing'. He noticed how the transference-countertransference dynamic between client and therapist could impact on how supervisor and supervisee interacted, so that the same dynamic might get evoked in the supervisory relationship. Thus the role of the supervisor came to include comments on the supervisory process, and how that reflected or paralleled the therapeutic process. This has been formalised in Hawkins and Shohet's (2001, 2006) supervisory model. You will find that many supervisors working within a psychodynamic framework today use these ideas in their supervision with you, which is why it is helpful to have discussed this when establishing your contract.

Although many supervisors now explore parallel processes in supervision, the model used is still essentially dyadic. Thus the emphasis is on the client's mind, and that of the supervisee. However, a number of writers in the relational tradition of psychotherapy, such as Frawley-O'Dea and Sarnat (2001), have begun to explore more overtly relational models of supervision. This approach recognises that the minds of client, therapist, and supervisor all have an impact on what happens in both supervision and therapy. If you are working with a supervisor using this model, she will reflect on and process what happens between herself and you, as well as what happens between you and your client. Unconsciously motivated material such as dreams, feelings and enactments become part of what is discussed in relational supervision. Such a mutual interaction can be difficult if you are inexperienced, since you may well want more direction than is implicit in this model. If your supervisor uses this model, it is important that you discuss how it will impact on the supervisory relationship when you set up the contract.

Developmental models of supervision

As supervisory theory developed, models were created that dealt specifically with the process of supervision without allegiance to a specific model of therapy. Of these I think that developmental models are amongst the most helpful in thinking about psychodynamic supervision, since they are implicit in our model. They attempt to explain how the supervisee makes the transition from being a novice therapist to an experienced clinician. Stoltenberg and his colleagues (1998) identified four stages of supervisee development: dependency; dependency-autonomous; conditional dependency and master professional. You might like to consider which of these most closely describes your own stage of development.

- *The dependency stage*: If you are functioning at the first stage you are likely to experience high levels of anxiety and insecurity. This can make it hard for you to attend fully to your client and process material as it comes up in the session. You might find that you are focussed on just surviving the session; you look forward to getting back to supervision to be told what to do next. Your supervisor's role is to provide structure, safety and containment. She should take the major responsibility for the supervisory session, and encourage your development by giving you positive feedback and listening attentively. It can be helpful at this stage to see your supervisor struggling so that she models a 'coping' rather than an 'expert' model of her own practice.
- *The dependency-autonomous stage*: If you are functioning at stage two, you will probably swing between feeling over-confident and overwhelmed. You will have developed a range of intervention skills, but might feel that your understanding of theory exceeds your skills level. Although now confident that you can survive the session, you may find it difficult to participate in the session while simultaneously monitoring process issues and your countertransference. It is not unusual to easily feel discouraged about the work and your own capacities at this stage, and these feelings can be directed at your supervisor. Stoltenberg and his colleagues recommend that supervisors use a persuasive rather than an authoritarian supervisory stance if you function at this stage, which encourages your autonomy.
- *The conditional dependency stage*: By the third stage you will feel your skills are more consistent, and you will have more confidence in your work. You will be able to focus on process issues and your own countertransference within the session. You will have become more spontaneous and creative in your work, and more able to acknowledge both your strengths and weaknesses as a therapist. Generally speaking you will be less dependent on your supervisor, unless there is a clearly identified issue where you have developmental needs. Supervision at this stage will rarely focus on strategies for surviving a session, rather you will concentrate on the thinking and feeling that informs your work. Your supervisor should balance being supportive with challenging you. It is suggested that supervisors use joint exploration as the preferred method for conducting supervision at this stage.

- *The master professional stage*: If you have reached stage four, your work will be characterised by your autonomy and your ability to confront personal and professional issues. The relationship between you and your supervisor will have become much more collegial and consultative. There is a shared responsibility for the structure and process of supervision, and, since you are probably supervising yourself by now, you may also discuss issues to do with your own supervision practice.

Stoltenberg et al. (1998) argue that few, if any, therapists reach stage four in all domains of clinical practice, so there is never a time when the task of development is complete. Indeed as we move jobs, develop new skills through further training or face crises in our lives, even someone who is working mostly in stage four will find that they have needs that are more in keeping with earlier, more dependent, stages. And, since we can never know the contents of our own unconscious, we will still need a space in which we can reflect on our blind-spots, the impact of the work on us and our countertransference, regardless of how senior we are.

Developmental models can also be applied to becoming a supervisor. If you are interested in finding out more, Stoltenberg and his colleagues propose a complementary model for supervisors.

It is important that your supervisor structures supervision according to your developmental level. It is also helpful to know how experienced your supervisor is, as her own stage of development may have a significant impact on how she copes with supervising you. Watkins (1995) suggests avoiding some pairings of supervisor and supervisee. It is generally advisable for beginning supervisors to work with beginning supervisees. Beginning supervisors can find stage two supervisees problematic because they are generally considered the most difficult to supervise. If, as a beginning supervisor, she is grappling with her own lack of confidence or feelings of being overwhelmed, your supervisor is not going to be able to offer you the level of stability stage two supervisees need. Similarly stage three or four supervisees can completely overwhelm a supervisor who lacks confidence or experience. She can find herself feeling anxious or redundant with supervisees at this stage, since they are autonomous, and may also be better therapists than she is.

Developmental theory maps on well to psychodynamic therapy models. There is an acceptance that you will initially be heavily reliant on your supervisor. Gradually, through the process of introjecting your supervisor, you will begin to emulate her. As you progress you will develop the capacity to use your own internal supervisor (Casement, 1985).

DYNAMICS IN SUPERVISION

Just as we bring ourselves into our work with clients, both we and our supervisors bring ourselves into the supervisory relationship. Attitudes towards authority, diversity, different groups of clients and other closely held beliefs are laid bare in the supervisory relationship. Our defensive structure is also exposed. As Twyman (2007) notes, these factors can have a profound impact on how supervision is conducted and what is discussed. Additionally both supervisor and supervisee bring into the supervisory relationship their transferential reactions to the process of supervision, the organisation involved (whether training, professional body or employing) and the other person in the supervisory dyad. Johnson (2007), drawing on her experiences as a supervisee, describes 'The Eye-Opener', 'The Humiliator', 'The Know-it-all', 'The Facilitator', 'The By-passer', 'The Colleague' and 'The Restorer'. The story behind each pseudonym unfolds to illustrate how the interlocking personalities and transferences of supervisor and supervisee impacted on Johnson as a developing therapist.

Transference and countertransference in supervision

Like all teachers, supervisors are often the focus of major transference feelings. In many cases there is a degree of regression in the supervisory relationship, particularly if your developmental needs reflect those of a particular client. Sometimes the supervisory relationship can be adversely affected by trainees' negative transference to the training organisation. Trainees can either become suspicious of a supervisor who is endorsed by the organisation, or will idealise her if she becomes a bulwark against it. Neither is conducive to a solid supervisory relationship. Supervisors also have an evaluative and gate-keeping role alongside their educative role. The gate-keeping role can evoke (sometimes powerful) persecutory feelings in the supervisee. Together these factors can make you more vulnerable to powerful transference reactions to a supervisor, and less able to function as an adult in the relationship.

Because the supervisory relationship is between colleagues (however great the difference in status and experience), rather than client and therapist, transference and countertransference feelings can be much more difficult to handle. But they need to be handled, and the person primarily responsible for doing so is the supervisor, particularly if you are at the beginning of your career and diffident about approaching the subject. The supervisory transference relationship is rarely discussed in supervision, so there are limited opportunities to normalise it. This prevents an exploration of how the supervisory transference impacts on the supervisee's development or work with her client. Weiner (2007) proposes that there is always some auxiliary analysis in supervision, so it is essential to handle the supervisory transference well. In doing so, however, it is important that your supervisor treats you as a colleague, not as a client.

As in the therapeutic relationship, the supervisory transference and countertransference can begin before the first session, as the vignette below illustrates.

> Richard had nearly completed his training, and was anxious about financing the last year. He had sacrificed a lot to train, including selling his house and buying a flat so that he could work part-time. When his supervisor, Graham, unexpectedly retired, Richard urgently needed a new supervisor. Graham suggested that he contact Murray, an experienced supervisor, who had spaces because he had only recently moved into the area. Graham added that he had recently talked to Murray, who was worried about finding enough patients and supervisees to

maintain his income. When Richard rang Murray he explained his situation. On asking about the fee Murray named an amount much higher than Richard was expecting, or could really afford. Feeling he had no choice, Richard accepted it, but underneath felt rather used. This stirred up powerful transference feelings about his father's contempt for his needs when Richard was a child. He tried to deal with these by defensively identifying with Murray and imagining that, like him, he lived a frugal life trying to make ends meet, so needed to charge a high fee. However, when Richard arrived at Murray's house for his first supervision session, he experienced almost uncontrollable anger. Not only did Murray live in a large house, but he had two luxury cars sitting on the drive.

Supervisors can also experience strong feelings in relation to their supervisees. Sometimes this is a countertransference to the material or the client. Parallel processing (Searles, 1955) is potentially the source of useful information about what is going on in the therapeutic relationship. At other times, however, complex identificatory and defensive mechanisms in relation to the supervisee and/or client can negatively impact on the quality of both supervision and therapy. Jacobs (1993) makes the point that, whereas in the clinical situation we are always sensitive to the countertransference, it is often avoided in the supervisory relationship. Because of his identification with a supervisee, he uncritically went along with unconventional treatment approaches that he would normally have questioned. This had a negative impact on the client's progress in therapy. Reflecting on this experience, Jacobs argued it can be particularly difficult for supervisors to sort out what they are responding to because a number of diverse phenomena impact on them. These include the supervisor's unconscious responses to the client, to the supervisee, to the supervisee's therapist, and to the supervisor's own former therapist and training supervisors as well as the organisation that the supervisee is training with or working for.

How the transference/countertransference matrix unfolds between supervisor and supervisee will impact on the therapeutic work, just as the therapeutic transference/countertransference matrix impacts on the work of supervision. It also impacts on the capacity of the supervisee to learn, as Dewald (1987) observed. The successful handling of the supervisory matrix can deepen and enrich both supervision and therapy, but sometimes an acute negative transference can undermine the viability of supervision. This can go in either direction, and sometimes is mutual. If this occurs it requires effort and input, from both you and your supervisor, to try to overcome it through an honest and non-blaming discussion of what is happening between you. If this is not possible the only option may be to change supervisors.

Shame in the supervisory relationship

Ours is a profession 'where the main tool used is the person of the individual, rather then simply the skills that he/she has, and where the focus of the training is to enable the beginner to practice in his/her own way' (Carroll, 1996: 26). In supervision we expose our own unconscious functioning and distorted view of the world as well as that of our client. This presents a challenge to both supervisor and supervisee. As supervisees it can be painful to confront the difference between how we want to function as therapists and how we actually do, particularly when we participate in the playing out of the dynamics between us and our clients. As supervisors it can be difficult to hold on to benevolent ego and superego activity in the face of a supervisee's distortions or acting out (Driver, 2008).

Taylor further proposes that the involvement of a supervisor in the work re-creates the oedipal triangle, this time of client, therapist and supervisor. She notes that 'supervision adds a further dimension to psychotherapy, another layer of complexity, where the supervisor appears as the third other person in the therapist-patient dyad' (2007: 125). The supervisor can be experienced as 'a chaperone on a honeymoon', who comes between the intimate relationship of the therapeutic couple (Berman, 2000: 276). As in the classical story of Oedipus, the third other, in seeing what is going on in the dyad, gives the couple knowledge about the true nature of their relationship. Whilst the accompanying insight can be valued and worked with, such knowledge can also elicit shame.

Shame is also potentiated by the inherent power imbalance in supervision, which can induce a regressive element in the relationship, with accompanying fear and longing in the supervisee. Associated idealisation of a supervisor's expertise can further potentiate shame as the idealised supervisor becomes incorporated into the supervisee's ego ideal. This is why the personal characteristics of the supervisor and the establishment of a good supervisory alliance are so important. Where there is a strong supervisory alliance shame-inducing experiences can be managed or diffused much more easily.

People vary in the extent to which they are prone to experiencing shame. If you are 'shame-prone' you might struggle with being in supervision at all because your limitations are seen by the third other. If you have a harsh superego and an idealised notion of the therapeutic relationship, you will be particularly vulnerable to feeling shamed when aspects of your therapeutic work reveal your vulnerability. This might be through having negative or sexual reactions to a client, participating in an enactment in therapy, or facing a situation of failure or impasse. Alternately, you may fear being disliked or negatively evaluated by your supervisor. All these are normal anxieties in supervision, but exacerbated if you are shame-prone.

Experiencing shame can lead to behaviours that can militate against good therapeutic practice. You may hide aspects of your work from your supervisor, in order to protect the intimate relationship between you and your client. You may consciously rationalise that your supervisor doesn't understand, or need to know, as a way of justifying keeping aspects of the relationship secret. However, this kind of non-disclosure of your relationship with your client can lead to acting out and, sometimes, even unethical behaviour. Certainly it will result in a reduction in your curiosity and therefore learning. Over the years I have come to suspect that I am hiding from something if I always find a reason not to take a particular client, or an aspect of the material, to supervision. Inevitably, when I have discussed my client, I become aware that there was something I had not previously wanted to see, and was not ready for my supervisor to illuminate for me. Interestingly, once I do take my client or material, I have learned things that both facilitate the therapeutic work and act as a stimulus to my own development.

Being in supervision can also stir up uncomfortable feelings of competition with, or envy of, your supervisor and the knowledge and power that she has. This can lead to difficulties in the relationship if you cannot bear her to have, or demonstrate, greater knowledge than you. You may defend yourself against this by becoming contemptuous of her, or by trying to prove that you know just as much, and not allowing her to give you anything. Again this is often linked to shame about being in a less powerful position where your work is open to scrutiny.

We all employ our defensive structure to protect ourselves from shame. However, the need to constantly defend against it can have a negative impact on our capacity to be available to our clients and maintain empathy with them. It is therefore important to take steps as a supervisee to ensure that the shame dynamic is acknowledged and worked with in your own supervision as it arises. If you know you are shame-prone you should, if possible, find a supervisor who is able to give you sensitive help with managing the situations that can induce it.

USING SUPERVISION EFFECTIVELY

If you are in a position to choose your supervisor, you would be well-advised to find someone whose theoretical orientation is the same as your own therapist's. It can be confusing to experience two very different viewpoints about technique or theory early in your career. As a trainee, your supervisor and therapist in effect constitute a parental couple. If they advocate different approaches, it can feel as though one is a child in a family where the parents disagree about what constitutes 'correct' behaviour. This has the potential both to infantilise you and delay your development.

Being supervised is not a passive process and there are a number of things you can do to use supervision more effectively. Hawkins and Shohet (2006) make some useful suggestions about how you can become a more effective supervisee, including thinking clearly about your supervisory needs and setting up a supervisory contract. This stance requires that you take some responsibility for the relationship with your supervisor, and the quality of the supervision you are receiving. In psychodynamic supervision doing so can be a significant challenge. The inherently hierarchical apprentice model, combined with the regressive pull in dynamic supervision, militate against a more assertive approach. Not all psychodynamic supervisors will have undertaken a formal supervisor training and therefore may not have been exposed to models of good practice. However, it is important to get the best out of your supervision in order to facilitate your own growth. Doing so may necessitate you confronting some of these inherent difficulties.

FURTHER READING

Hawkins, P. and Shohet, R. (2006) *Supervision in the Helping Professions* (3rd edition). Buckingham: Open University Press.

REFERENCES

Alexandris, A. and Vaslamatzis, G. (eds) (1993) *Countertransference: Theory, Technique, Teaching*. London: Karnac.

Alfille, H. and Cooper, J. (eds) (2002) *Dilemmas in the Consulting Room*. London: Karnac.

Alvarez, A. (1992) *Live Company: Psychoanalytic Psychotherapy with Autistic, Borderline, Deprived and Abused Children*. London: Routledge.

Aveline, M. (1999) 'The advantages of formulation over categorical diagnosis in explorative psychotherapy and psychodynamic management', *European Journal of Psychotherapy, Counselling and Health*, 2 (2): 199–216.

Baker, R. (1993) 'The patient's discovery of the analyst as a new object', *International Journal of Psychoanalysis*, 74: 429–434.

Balint, M. (1968) *The Basic Fault: Therapeutic Aspects of Regression*. London: Tavistock.

Bateman, A. and Fonagy, P. (2004) *Psychotherapy for Borderline Personality Disorder: Mentalization-Based Treatment*. Oxford: Oxford University Press.

Berman, E. (2000) 'Psychoanalytic supervision: the intersubjective development', *International Journal of Psychoanalysis*, 81 (2): 273–290.

Bion, W. R. (1962) *Learning from Experience*. London: Heinemann.

Bion, W. R. (1963) *Elements of Psychoanalysis*. London: Heinemann.

Bion, W. R. (1970) *Cogitations*. London: Karnac.

Bollas, C. (1987) *The Shadow of the Object: Psychoanalysis of the Unthought Known*. London: Free Association.

Bolton, G., Howlett, S., Lago, C. and Wright, J. (eds) (2004) *Writing Cures: An Introductory Handbook of Writing in Counselling and Psychotherapy*. London: Brunner-Routledge.

Bowlby, J. (1988) *A Secure Base: Clinical Applications of Attachment Theory*. London: Routledge.

Brafman, A. H. (2006) 'Touching and affective closeness'. In G. Galton (ed.), *Touch Papers: Dialogues on Touch in the Psychoanalytic Space*. London: Karnac.

Breckenridge, K. (2000) 'Physical touch in psychoanalysis: a closet phenomenon?', *Psychoanalytic Inquiry*, 20: 2–20.

Brenner, C. (1976) *Psychoanalytic Technique and Psychoanalytic Conflict*. New York: International Universities Press.

Carroll, M. (1996) *Counselling Supervision: Theory, Skills and Practice*. London: Cassell.

Casement, A. (2001) *Jung and Analytical Psychology*. London: SAGE.

Casement, P. (1985) *On Learning from the Patient*. London: Tavistock.

Casement, P. (2000) 'The issue of touch: a retrospective overview', *Psychoanalytic Inquiry*, 20: 160–184.

Clarke, G. S. (2006) *Personal Relations Theory: Fairbairn, MacMurray and Suttie*. London: Routledge.

Coltart, N. E. C. (1986) '"Slouching towards Bethlehem" … Or thinking the unthinkable in psychoanalysis'. In G. Kohon (ed.), *The British School of Psychoanalysis: The Independent Tradition*. London: Free Association.

Coltart, N. E. C. (1993) *How to Survive as a Psychotherapist*. London: Sheldon.

Cooper, J. (2002) '"I treat her like a human being": the role of naturalness in a boundaried relationship'. In H. Alfille and J. Cooper (eds), *Dilemmas in the Consulting Room*. London: Karnac.

Cooper, M. (2008) *Essential Research Findings in Counselling and Psychotherapy: The Facts are Friendly*. London: SAGE.

Cox, M. (1978) *Structuring the Therapeutic Process: Compromise with Chaos*. Oxford: Pergamon.

Cozolino, L. (2002) *The Neuroscience of Psychotherapy: Building and Rebuilding the Human Brain*. New York: Norton.

Cozolino, L. (2004) *The Making of a Therapist: A Practical Guide for the Inner Journey*. New York: Norton.

Crits-Christoph, P. and Connolly Gibbons, M. B. (2003) 'Research developments on the therapeutic alliance in psychodynamic psychotherapy', *Psychoanalytic Inquiry*, 23 (2): 332–349.

Cushway, D. (1992) 'Stress in trainee clinical psychologists', *British Journal of Clinical Psychology*, 31: 169–179.

Cushway, D. and Knibbs, J. (2004) 'Trainees' and supervisors' perceptions of supervision'. In I. Fleming and L. Steen (eds), *Supervision and Clinical Psychology: Theory, Practice and Perspectives*. Hove: Brunner-Routledge.

Davenloo, H. (1980) *Short-term Dynamic Psychotherapy*. New York: Aronson.

Derman, S. (2008) 'Endings and beginnings'. Paper presented to the Institute of Psychoanalysis English Speaking Conference, London, October 10–12.

Dewald, D. A. (1987) *Learning Processes in Psychoanalytic Supervision: Complexities and Challenges*. Madison, CT: International Universities Press.

Doctor, R. (ed.) (2003) *Dangerous Patients: A Psychodynamic Approach to Risk Assessment and Management*. London: Karnac.

Driver, C. (2008) 'Assessment in supervision', *British Journal of Psychotherapy*, 24 (3): 328–342.

Etchegoyen, R. H. (1999) *The Fundamentals of Psychoanalytic Technique* (2nd edition). London: Karnac.

Fairbairn, W. R. D. (1952) *Psychoanalytic Studies of the Personality*. London: Routledge.

Fairbairn, W. R. D. (1958) 'On the nature and aims of psychoanalytical treatment', *International Journal of Psychoanalysis*, 39: 374–385.

Fonagy, P. and Target, M. (2003) *Psychoanalytic Theories: Perspectives from Developmental Psychopathology*. London: Whurr.

Forrester, J. (1997) *Truth Games: Lies, Money and Psychoanalysis*. Cambridge, MA: Harvard University Press.

Fosshage, J. L. (2000) 'The meaning of touch in psychoanalysis: a time for reassessment', *Psychoanalytic Inquiry*, 20: 21–43.

Frawley-O'Dea, M. G. and Sarnat, J. E. (2001) *The Supervisory Relationship: A Contemporary Psychoanalytic Approach*. New York: Guilford.

Freud, S. (1923) *Two Encyclopaedia Articles*. Standard Edition 18.

Gerhardt, S. (2004) *Why Love Matters: How Affection Shapes a Baby's Brain*. Hove: Brunner-Routledge.

Gerrard, J. (2007) 'Enactments in the countertransference: with special reference to rescue fantasies with hysterical patients', *British Journal of Psychotherapy*, 23 (2): 217–230.

Gill, M. (1979) 'The analysis of the transference', *Journal of the American Psychoanalytic Association*, 27 (Supplement): 263–288.

Glasser, M. (1979) 'Some aspects of the role of aggression in the perversions'. In I. Rosen (ed.), *Sexual Deviation* (2nd edition). Oxford: Oxford University Press.

Glover, E. (1955) *The Technique of Psychoanalysis*. New York: International Universities Press.

Greenson, R. (1967) *The Technique and Practice of Psychoanalysis*. London: Karnac.

Hart, S. (2008) *Brain, Attachment, Personality: An Introduction to Neuroaffective Development*. London: Karnac.

Hawkins, P. and Shohet, R. (2001) *Supervision in the Helping Professions* (2nd edition). Buckingham: Open University Press.

Hawkins, P. and Shohet, R. (2006) *Supervision in the Helping Professions* (3rd edition). Buckingham: Open University Press.

Haynal, A. (1993) 'Ferenzi and the origins of psychoanalytic technique'. In L. Aron and A. Harris (eds), *The Legacy of Sandor Ferenzi*. Hillsdale, NJ: Analytic.

Hebb, D. O. (1949) *The Organization of Behavior: A Neuropsychological Theory*. New York: Wiley.

Hedges, L. E. (2000) *Facing the Challenge of Liability in Psychotherapy: Practicing Defensively*. Northvale, NJ: Aronson.

Heimann, P. (1950) 'On countertransference', *International Journal of Psychoanalysis*, 31: 81–84.

Heimann, P. (1956) 'Dynamics of transference interpretations', *International Journal of Psychoanalysis*, 37: 303–310.

Heimann, P. (1960) 'Countertransference', *British Journal of Medical Psychology*, 33: 9–15.

Holmes, J. (2001) *The Search for the Secure Base: Attachment Theory and Psychotherapy*. Hove: Brunner-Routledge.

Holmes, J. (2006) 'Mentalizing from a psychoanalytic perspective: what's new?'. In J. G. Allen and P. Fonagy (eds), *Handbook of Mentalization-Based Treatment*. Chichester: Wiley.

Howard, S. (2006) *Psychodynamic Counselling in a Nutshell*. London: SAGE.

Howard, S. (2007) 'Models of supervision'. In A. Petts and B. Shapley (eds), *On Supervision: Psychoanalytic and Jungian Analytic Perspectives*. London: Karnac.

Hurry, A. (1998) 'Psychoanalysis and developmental therapy'. In A. Hurry (ed.), *Psychoanalytic Monographs No 3: Psychoanalysis and Developmental Therapy*. London: Karnac.

Jacobs, M. (2004) *Psychodynamic Counselling in Action* (3rd edition). London: SAGE.

Jacobs, T. (1993) 'Transference-countertransference interactions in the supervisory situation: some observations'. In A. Alexandris and G. Vaslamatzis (eds), *Countertransference: Theory, Technique, Teaching*. London: Karnac.

Johnson, S. (2007) 'Some personal experiences of supervision'. In A. Petts and B. Shapley (eds), *On Supervision: Psychoanalytic and Jungian Analytic Perspectives*. London: Karnac.

Johnson, S. and Ruszczynski, S. (eds) (1999) *Psychoanalytic Psychotherapy in the Independent Tradition*. London: Karnac.

Kernberg, O. F. (2004) *Contemporary Controversies in Psychoanalytic Theory, Techniques and their Applications*. New Haven: Yale University Press.

King, P. (1977) 'Affective responses of the therapist to the patient's communication', *International Journal of Psychoanalysis*, 61 (4): 451–573.

Klauber, J. (1986) *Difficulties in the Analytic Encounter*. London: Free Association Books/ Maresfield Library.

Kohut, H. (1985) *The Analysis of the Self*. New York: International Universities Press.

Kumin, I. (1996) *Pre-Object Relatedness: Early Attachment and the Psychoanalytic Situation*. New York: Guilford.

Leiper, R. (2006) 'Psychodynamic formulation: a prince betrayed and disinherited'. In L. Johnson and R. Dallos (eds), *Formulation in Psychology and Psychotherapy: Making Sense of People's Problems*. London: Routledge.

Leiper, R. with Kent, R. (2001) *Working Through Setbacks in Psychotherapy: Crisis, Impasse and Relapse*. London: SAGE.

Lemma, A. (2003) *Introduction to the Practice of Psychoanalytic Psychotherapy*. Chichester: Wiley.

Lemma, A., Roth, A. and Pilling, S. (2008) *The Competencies Required to Deliver Effective Psychoanalytic/Psychodynamic Therapy*. Research Department of Clinical, Educational and Health Psychology, UCL. Available at www.ucl.ac.uk/clinical-psychology/CORE/psychodynamic_framework.htm

Leuzinger-Bohleber, M. and Target, M. (2002) *Outcomes of Psychoanalytic Treatment: Perspectives for Therapists and Researchers*. London: Whurr.

Lipton, S. (1977) 'The advantages of Freud's technique as shown in his psychoanalysis of the Ratman', *International Journal of Psychoanalysis*, 60: 255–273.

Little, M. (1986) *Transference Neurosis and Transference Psychosis: Towards Basic Unity*. London: Free Association Books/Maresfield Library.

Luborsky, L. and Crits-Cristoph, P. (1998) *Understanding Transference: The Core Conflictual Relationship Theme Method* (2nd edition). Washington, DC: American Psychological Association.

Luepnitz, D. A. (2002) *Schopenhauer's Porcupines: Intimacy and its Dilemmas: Five Stories of Psychotherapy*. New York: Basic.

Malan, D. H. (1979) *Individual Psychotherapy and the Science of Psychodynamics*. London: Butterworth.

Mander, G. (2007) *Diversity, Discipline and Devotion in Psychoanalytic Psychotherapy: Clinical and Training Perspectives*. London: Karnac.

McLaughlin, J. L. (1995) 'Touching limits in the psychoanalytic dyad', *Psychoanalytic Quarterly*, 64: 433–465.

McLeod, J. (2004) *The Counsellor's Workbook: Developing a Personal Approach*. Maidenhead: Open University Press.

McWilliams, N. (1999) *Psychoanalytic Case Formulation*. New York: Guilford.

McWilliams, N. (2004) *Psychoanalytic Therapy: A Practitioner's Guide*. New York: Guilford.

Meltzer, D. (1967) *The Psychoanalytic Process*. London: Heinemann.

Menninger, K. (1958) *Theory of Psychoanalytic Technique*. New York: Basic.

Mollon, P. (2000) *Ideas in Psychoanalysis: The Unconscious*. Cambridge: Icon.

Mollon, P. (2001) *Releasing the Self: The Healing Legacy of Heinz Kohut*. London: Whurr.

Money-Kyrle, R. (1977) 'On being a psychoanalyst'. In D. Meltzer and E. O'Shaughnessy (eds), *The Collected Papers of Roger Money-Kyrle*. Strath Tay: Clunie.

Montagu, A. (1986) *Touching: The Human Significance of the Skin*. New York: Harper Row.

Novick, J. and Novick, K. K. (2006) *Good Goodbyes: Knowing How to End in Psychotherapy and Psychoanalysis*. New York: Aronson.

Parsons, M. (2007) 'Raiding the inarticulate: the internal analytic setting and listening beyond countertransference', *International Journal of Psychoanalysis*, 88: 1441–1456.

Rippere, V. and Williams, S. (eds) (1985) *Wounded Healers: Mental Health Workers' Experiences of Depression*. Chichester: Wiley.

Roth, A. and Fonagy, P. (2005) *What Works for Whom?: A Critical Review of Psychotherapy Research* (2nd edition). London: Guilford.

Safran, J. D. and Muran, J. C. (2000) *Negotiating the Therapeutic Alliance: A Relational Treatment Guide*. New York: Guilford.

Sandler, J. (ed.) (1988) *Projection, Identification, Projective Identification*. London: Karnac.

Sandler, J. and Perlow, M. (1988) 'Internalization and externalization'. In J. Sandler (ed.), *Projection, Identification, Projective Identification*. London: Karnac.

Sandler, J. and Sandler, A. M. (1978) 'On the development of object relationships and affects', *International Journal of Psychoanalysis*, 59: 285–296.

Sandler, J. and Sandler, A. M. (1997) 'A psychoanalytic theory of repression and the unconscious'. In J. Sandler and P. Fonagy (eds), *Recovered Memories of Abuse: True or False?* London: Karnac.

Sandler, J., Dare, C. and Holder, A. (1973) *The Patient and the Analyst*. London: Maresfield Library.

Scaife, J. (2001) *Supervision in the Mental Health Professions: A Practitioner's Guide*. Hove: Brunner-Routledge.

Schore, A. N. (1994) *Affect Regulation and the Origin of the Self: The Neurobiology of Emotional Development*. Hillsdale, NJ: Erlbaum.

Schore, A. N. (2003) *Affect Regulation and the Repair of the Self*. New York: Norton.

Searles, H. F. (1955) 'The informational value of the supervisor's emotional experience'. In H. F. Searles (ed.), *Collected Papers in Schizophrenia and Related Subjects*. London: Hogarth.

Segal, H. (1993) 'Countertransference'. In A. Alexandris and G. Vaslamatzis (eds), *Countertransference: Theory, Technique, Teaching*. London: Karnac.

Shriver, L. (2005) *We Need to Talk about Kevin*. London: Serpent's Tail.

Siegel, D. J. (1999) *The Developing Mind: Towards a Neurobiology of Interpersonal Experience*. New York: Guilford.

Steiner, J. (1993) *Psychic Retreats: Pathological Organizations in Psychotic, Neurotic and Borderline Patients*. London: Routledge.

Steiner, J. (2008) 'Transference to the analyst as an excluded observer', *International Journal of Psychoanalysis*, 89 (1): 39–54.

Sternberg, J. (2005) *Infant Observation at the Heart of Training*. London: Karnac.

Stewart, H. (1992) *Psychic Experience and Problems of Technique*. London: Tavistock/ Routledge.

Stoltenberg, C. D., McNeil, B. and Delworth, U. (1998) *IDM Supervision: An Integrated Developmental Model for Supervising Counsellors and Therapists*. San Francisco, CA: Jossey-Bass.

Symington, N. (1986) *The Analytic Experience: Lectures from the Tavistock*. London: Free Association.

Symington, N. (2008) 'Generosity of heart: source of sanity', *British Journal of Psychotherapy*, 24(4): 488–500.

Taylor, D. (2002) 'Money – symbol and reality'. In H. Alfille and J. Cooper (eds), *Dilemmas in the Consulting Room*. London: Karnac.

Taylor, D. (2007) 'The supervision triangle'. In A. Petts and B. Shapley (eds), *On Supervision: Psychoanalytic and Jungian Analytic Perspectives*. London: Karnac.

Tonnesmann, M. (2005) 'Transference and countertransference: an historical approach'. In S. Budd and R. Rusbridger (eds), *Introducing Psychoanalysis: Essential Themes and Topics*. London: Routledge.

Twyman, M. (2007) 'Some dynamics in supervision'. In A. Petts and B. Shapley (eds), *On Supervision: Psychoanalytic and Jungian Analytic Perspectives*. London: Karnac.

Tyndale, A. (1999) 'How far is transference interpretation essential for psychic change?'. In S. Johnson and S. Ruszczynski (eds), *Psychoanalytic Psychotherapy in the Independent Tradition*. London: Karnac.

Tyndale, A. (2002) 'The patient's narrative: the therapist's response'. In H. Alfille and J. Cooper (eds), *Dilemmas in the Consulting Room*. London: Karnac.

Vaillant, G. E. (1977) *Adaptation to Life*. Boston: Little & Brown.

Vanheule, S. (2009) 'Psychotherapy and research: a relation that needs to be rein-vented' *British Journal of Psychotherapy*, 25 (1): 91–109.

Wallerstein, R. (ed.) (1992) *The Common Ground of Psychoanalysis*. New Jersey: Aronson.

Watkins, C. E. (1995) 'Psychotherapy supervisor and supervisee: developmental models and research nine years on', *Clinical Psychology Review*, 15 (7): 647–680.

Webb, A. and Wheeler, S. (1998) 'How honest do counsellors dare to be in the super-visory relationship? An exploratory study', *British Journal of Guidance and Counselling*, 26 (4): 509–524.

Weiner, J. (2007) 'The analyst's countertransference when supervising: friend or foe?'. In A. Petts and B. Shapley (eds), *On Supervision: Psychoanalytic and Jungian Analytic Perspectives*. London: Karnac.

Winnicott, D. W. (1965a) 'Ego distortions in terms of true and false self'. In D. W. Winnicott (ed.), *The Maturational Process and the Facilitating Environment*. London: Hogarth.

Winnicott, D. W. (1965b) 'The aims of psycho-analytical treatment'. In D. W. Winnicott (ed.), *The Maturational Process and the Facilitating Environment*. London: Hogarth.

Winnicott, D. W. (1975) 'Hate in the countertransference'. In D. W. Winnicott (ed.), *Through Paediatrics to Psychoanalysis: Collected Papers*. London: Karnac.

Woods, M. Z. (2003) 'Developmental considerations in an adult psychoanalysis'. In V. Greene (ed.), *Emotional Development in Psychoanalysis, Attachment Theory and Neuroscience*. Hove: Brunner–Routledge.

INDEX